ALBERT AXELL has interviewed more than 30 of Stalin's generals over the past 25 years. In Moscow he also met Russian women pilots who flew a thousand missions at night over German-Nazi lines. During the late Brezhnev and early Gorbachev years he covered the Cold War from Moscow. The author of books on Russia, Japan, China and Mongolia, he makes his home in London.

Praise for *Russia's Heroes*

"The author of this valuable book belongs to a new generation of experts making use of previously inaccessible archives and the last surviving participants in the Nazi-Soviet War. This original and highly recommended book gives a wholly accurate picture of the great events of 1941–45 on the Eastern Front, while underlining the decisive role of heroes and heroism in the struggle against the Nazi hordes'.
Oleg A. Rzheshevsky, President, Russian Association of WWII Historians

"Evidence is culled from legions of Soviet memoirs, but above all from interviews he conducted with veterans over the past 25 years. The result is a haunting and evocative portrait of life and death on the Eastern Front."
Rirchard Overy, *Daily Telegraph*

"A cracking read . . . it gave me a great deal of pleasure."
Robert Service, Professor of Russian Studies, University of Oxford

"While there are books that say something about individual heroic exploits with a section of the war . . . none so thoroughly examines the subject over the whole canvas of the Soviet-German war."
Robert Johnston, *Library Journal*

"Engrossing . . ."   Robin Buss, *Financial Times*

"A unique achievement . . . authoritative . . . indispensable reading."
Martin McCauley, Russian expert and author

RUSSIA'S HEROES

Albert Axell

CARROLL & GRAF PUBLISHERS
New York

Carroll & Graf Publishers
An imprint of Avalon Publishing Group, Inc.
161 William Street
New York
NY 10038 2607
www.carrollandgraf.com

First published in the UK by Constable,
an imprint of Constable & Robinson Ltd, 2001

This edition first published in paperback in the UK by Robinson,
an imprint of Constable & Robinson Ltd, 2002

First Carroll & Graf edition 2002

ISBN 0–7867–1011–X

Printed and bound in the EU

Library of Congress Cataloging-in-Publication Data is available on file.

Dedicated with gratitude to
Jane Cunningham, V.V. MacArrow, Janet Q. Treloar,
Anne Baring, James Wickam, Martin Blakeway,
Eliecer Romo, and of course Jay and Dominique.

Contents

Contents

List of Maps and Illustrations

List of Maps

List of Illustrations

List of Maps and Illustrations

Acknowledgments

This book could not have been written without the help of many people, from academics to librarians, but most particularly it could not have been undertaken without the willingness of veterans of "The Great Patriotic War," from marshals to ordinary soldiers, to talk of their experiences. I am particularly grateful to: Nadezhda Popova (pilot-commander); Polina Gelman (pilot); Alexei Maresyev (pilot); Sergei Rudenko (Air Marshal); Sergei Gorshkov (Admiral of the Fleet); Afanasy Beloborodov (General of the Army); Dmitri Volkogonov (General, military historian); Evgeni Djugashvili (Stalin's grandson); David Dragunsky (Colonel-General); Alexei Zheltov (Colonel-General); Semyon Krivoshein (Lieutenant-General); Vasily Morozov (Colonel, military historian); I.G. Pavlovsky (General of the Army); Ivan Shavrov (General of the Army); Yuri Levitan (Stalin's chief radio announcer); Mikhail Sholokhov (novelist and war correspondent – Nobel Prize for Literature, 1965); Lev Skvirsky (Colonel-General).

Three British veterans of the Anglo-American convoys that ferried supplies to wartime Russia kindly gave me firsthand information about the hazards of sailing in the icy Barents Sea, especially when enemy dive-bombers hovered overhead and U-boats lurked below. They are Eddie Grenfell, Neil Hulse and Ronald James Wren.

I would also like to thank the staff of Russian State Military Archive, the Central Archive of the Ministry of Defence, the Museum of the Brest Fortress, the Museum of the Battle of Stalingrad, the Museum of the Defence of Leningrad and the Central Museum of the Armed Forces, Moscow for their help. Closer to home, I wish to thank the staff of the British Library, Imperial War Museum and the Society for Cooperation in Russian and Soviet Studies.

Some of the recollections in this book, including remarks by General Eisenhower and Marshal Zhukov, and the story of the Brest Fortress, the ace snipers and Georgi Gubkin's infantry company, are taken from published memoirs and other sources listed in the Notes and Sources.

I am grateful to the following historians and experts on Russian and military history for reading the manuscript and offering their comments. John Erickson, Richard Overy, Martin McCauley, Robert Service, Evan Mawdsley, B.P. Pockney, Geoffrey Roberts and Dennis Ogden.

Finally I would like to thank Nick Robinson and the entire staff of Constable for their generous assistance and affability.

Note to Readers

Some important name changes occurred after the demise of the USSR in 1991. For instance, the city of Leningrad resumed its pre-revolutionary name, St Petersburg, and the Byelorussian Republic became the Republic of Belarus. To simplify matters, contemporary names are mainly used in this book. Also, the more familiar spelling is often used, for instance, for the northern city, Archangel (instead of, as the word is pronounced in Russian, Arkhangelsk). The name "Russia" is used throughout except where it makes more sense to use Soviet or USSR. During the war, Allied leaders such as Churchill and Roosevelt spoke of "Russia" and "the Russian army". Stalin himslf often said "we Russians" when speaking or writing to his Anglo-American allies.

Preface

A black-and-white photo taken in 1939 has frozen for eternity an incident in Poland involving two generals, a Russian and a German. The latter, grim-visaged and ruggedly handsome, is the Panzer General Heinz Guderian, a god of tank warfare and a favourite of Adolf Hitler. The trim Russian, sporting a clipped black mustache, is Semyon Krivoshein, who has seen action as a tank commander in the Spanish Civil War and also against a Japanese incursion into Mongolia in the summer of 1939. In the photo he has his arms akimbo. As the caption informs, the two generals are verbally sparring over a demarcation line between the two converging armies. Precipitate action by the Russian has effectively blocked the advance of a Nazi train carrying Guderian's tanks east; that is, closer to the Soviet state border. To accomplish this, Krivoshein had placed his tanks athwart the tracks, thereby enraging the panzer leader.

I first saw this photo while turning the pages of my father's pictorial album of the Second World War, and it made an indelible impression on my youthful mind. Forty years passed and one day in Moscow I met the Russian general whose strutting image in the Polish photo had stayed with me.

When I mentioned the photograph, Krivoshein smiled and helpfully filled in a few details. To a demand by Guderian that Russian tanks be speedily removed from the rail tracks, he had replied with a straight face: "Sorry, General, but our tanks are out of fuel."

Incidentally, in a postwar memoir, entitled *Panzer Leader*, Guderian gives a terse account of this 1939 open-air confrontation in Poland with Krivoshein. He makes no mention of their heated dialogue, saying only that the demarcation line (at the frontier River Bug) that was finally agreed upon was "disadvantageous" to Nazi Germany.

A driving force behind my interest in events in Russia and the Second World War were a number of epic film documentaries produced by my father, Herman Axelbank. These historic films include: *From Tsar to Lenin, Stalin the Horrible*, and *The German-Soviet War*. They are now a part of my father's film archive at the Hoover Institution at Stanford University in Palo Alto, California.

My interest in Russian affairs soared when I visited Moscow for the first time in the mid-1960s and found myself following a fellow American, Richard Nixon, around town, including a quick tour of Lenin's Mausoleum. This was a few years before the Nixon presidency.

A few years passed and one day a Wall Street newspaper asked me to represent them in Moscow, then considered a "hardship post". I readily accepted the offer. Working as a journalist allowed me to meet distinguished Russians such as Dr Andrei Sakharov and other intellectuals. But at the same time I became possessed by the desire to meet as many surviving World War Two generals and marshals as possible. As a graduate student in America, I had had a continuing interest in war and politics and had spent a year or two researching the lives of Lincoln's generals, obtaining interviews with the last three surviving Civil War veterans.

As the years went by my desire almost became an obsession. Over twenty years I met many of the men and women who appear in this book, mainly in Moscow and its suburbs: a few were alive and well at the beginning of the new millenium. Meeting them over such a long period I became aware that although many Russians knew of the deeds performed by these men and women, they were practically unknown in the West. Yet it was their wartime feats, multiplied many times over by others, that caused a dramatic turn of the tide in the Second World War.

Preface

The Eastern Front – in the number of troops and weapons involved and the frontage of the attack – was the main theatre of operations in the World War II. There were some fifty major battles fought on the Eastern Front. The most important of these were the battles of Moscow (1941–42), Stalingrad (1942–43), Kursk (1943), Operation Bagration (1944), the Yassy-Kishinev Campaign (1944), the Vistula–Oder Operation (1945) and Berlin (1945). At different stages of the war the two sides had from 8 to 12.8 million troops, from 5,700 to 20,000 tanks and assault guns, from 6,500 to 18,000 aircraft and from 84,000 to 163,000 artillery pieces and mortars.

Until the Allied landings in France in June 1944 the number of Axis divisions operating against Russia was fifteen to twenty times greater than that of the divisions fighting against the Allies.

In terms of sheer courage, stamina and endurance, I do not see how anyone could fail to be in awe of the Russian women who each logged up to 1,000 bombing missions. As I write these lines I can see in my mind's eye one of these intrepid girls (the majority were in their late teens or early twenties) leaning out of an open cockpit under a black sky, the temperature well below freezing, trying with half-frozen fingers to dislodge a bomb that had become stuck under the wings.

Nevertheless, they and their war have remained a largely unknown quantity for many in the West. For obvious reasons during the Cold War the British and American peoples tended to focus their attention on their own efforts and achievements in the Second World War and this tendency has resulted in the scale of the conflict on the Eastern Front being overshadowed in the popular imagination. As the stories in this book show the scale of fighting during The Great Patriotic War dwarfed by comparison the fighting in the West. This book is a modest attempt to restore a few missing pages to the history books.

Albert Axell
London, February 2001

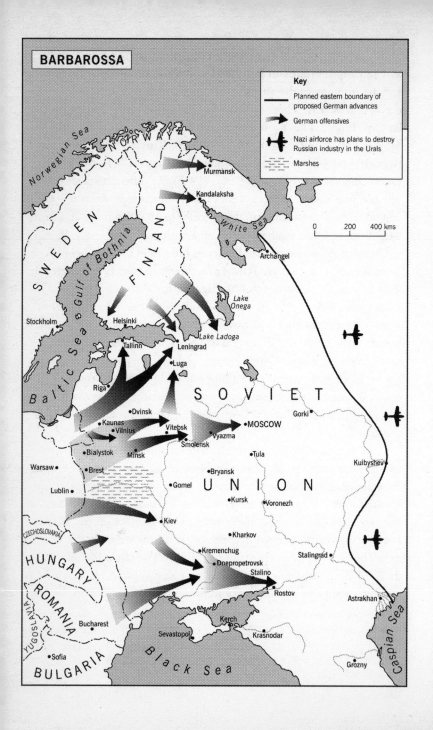

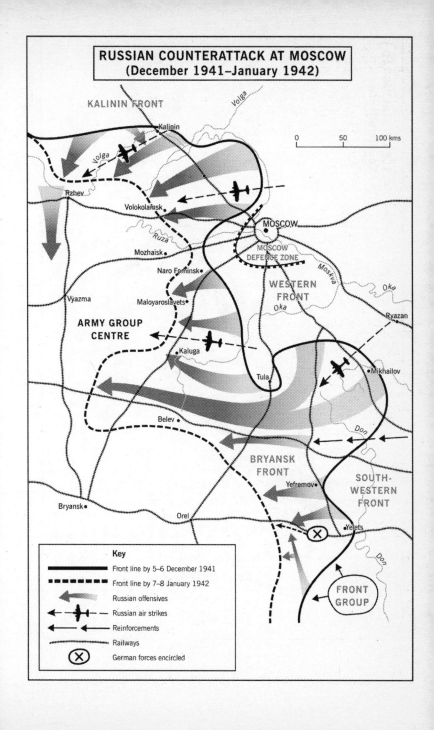

RUSSIAN COUNTERATTACK AT MOSCOW
(December 1941–January 1942)

KALININ FRONT

Volga

Kalinin

0   50   100 kms

Volga

Rzhev

Volokolamsk

MOSCOW

Ruza

MOSCOW
DEFENCE ZONE

Moskva

Mozhaisk

Oka

Naro Fominsk

WESTERN
FRONT

Vyazma

Maloyaroslavets

Oka

Ryazan

ARMY GROUP
CENTRE

Kaluga

Tula

Mikhailov

Belev

Don

BRYANSK
FRONT

SOUTH-
WESTERN
FRONT

Yefremov

Bryansk

Orel

Yelets

Don

FRONT
GROUP

Key

━━━ Front line by 5–6 December 1941

┅┅┅ Front line by 7–8 January 1942

Russian offensives

Russian air strikes

Reinforcements

Railways

Ⓧ German forces encircled

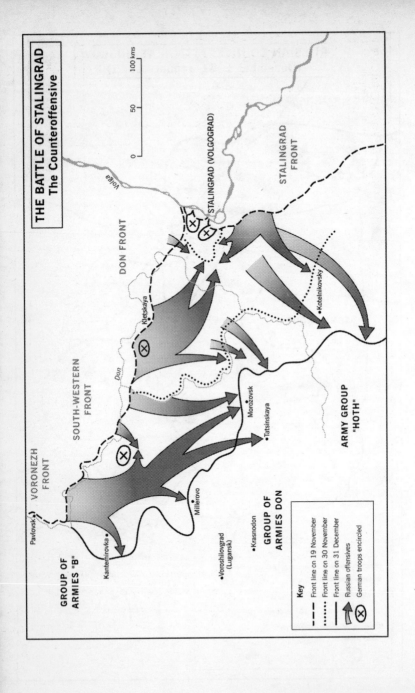

THE BATTLE OF STALINGRAD
The Counteroffensive

GROUP OF ARMIES "B"

Pavlovsk

VORONEZH FRONT

Kantemirovka

SOUTH-WESTERN FRONT

Don

Volga

DON FRONT

STALINGRAD (VOLGOGRAD)

STALINGRAD FRONT

Kletskaya

Kotelnikovsky

Millerovo

Morozovsk

Tatsinskaya

Voroshilovgrad (Lugansk)

Krasnodon

GROUP OF ARMIES DON

ARMY GROUP "HOTH"

Key
- - - Front line on 19 November
· · · Front line on 30 November
······ Front line on 31 December
➤ Russian offensives
⊗ German troops encircled

0   50   100 kms

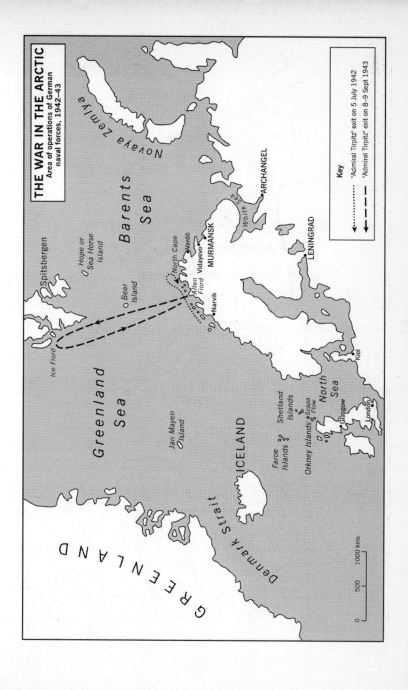

THE WAR IN THE ARCTIC
Area of operations of German
naval forces, 1942–43

Novaya Zemlya

Barents Sea

Spitsbergen

o *Hope or
Sea Horse
Island*

o *Bear
Island*

North Cape
Vardø
Vidayevo MURMANSK
Alten
Fiord
Narvik

Ice Fiord

White Sea

ARCHANGEL

LENINGRAD

Kiel

*Greenland
Sea*

*Jan Mayen
Island*

ICELAND

*North
Sea*

Shetland
Islands

Faroe
Islands   Scapa
Flow
Orkney Islands   Glasgow

London

Denmark Strait

GREENLAND

Key

......▶ 'Admiral Tirpitz' exit on 5 July 1942
– – –▶ 'Admiral Tirpitz' exit on 8–9 Sept 1943

0   500   1000 kms

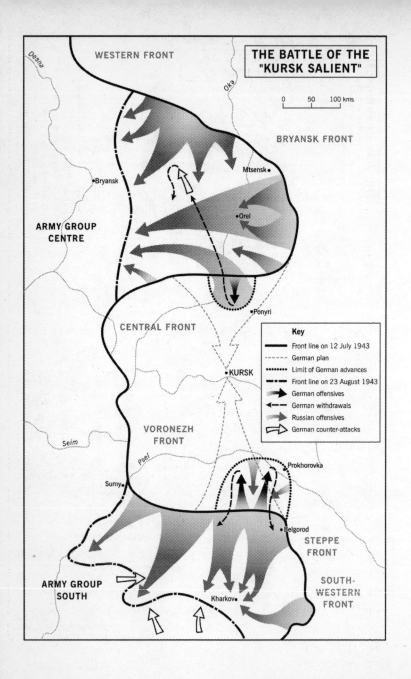

THE BATTLE OF THE "KURSK SALIENT"

0   50   100 kms

WESTERN FRONT

BRYANSK FRONT

•Bryansk

Mtsensk •

•Orel

ARMY GROUP CENTRE

Ponyri •

CENTRAL FRONT

KURSK

VORONEZH FRONT

Prokhorovka •

Seim

Psel

Sumy •

Belgorod •

STEPPE FRONT

ARMY GROUP SOUTH

Kharkov •

SOUTH-WESTERN FRONT

Desna

Oka

Key

Front line on 12 July 1943
German plan
Limit of German advances
Front line on 23 August 1943
German offensives
German withdrawals
Russian offensives
German counter-attacks

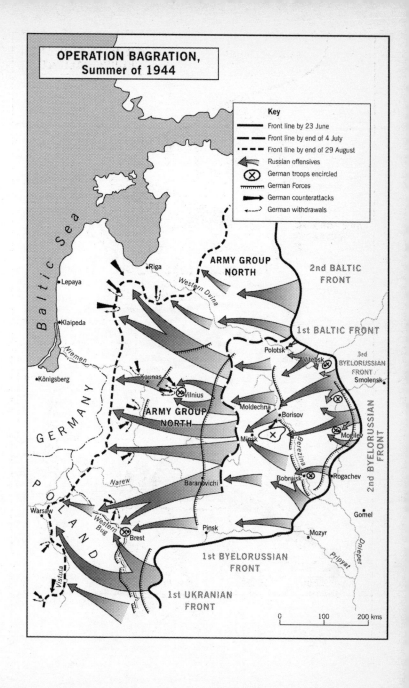

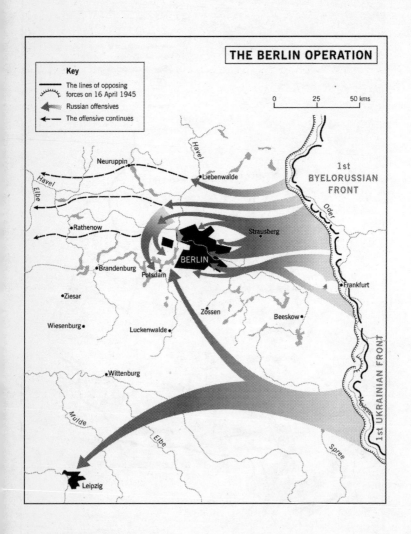

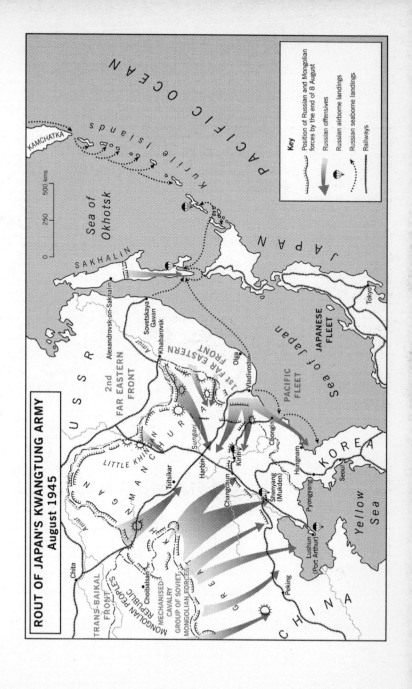

Prologue: The Russians

When news of Hitler's invasion flashed across the world in June 1941, masses of Russian emigrés, crossing political and religious lines, from members of the royal family and Russian Orthodox clergymen to taxicab drivers and intellectuals (including those who most violently hated the Bolsheviks) suddenly sympathized with Russia in her time of peril; and they were uplifted by the dogged resistance to the invader. Three days after the invasion *The* (London) *Times* of 25 June 1941 published a letter from Prince Vsevolode, nephew of Nicholas II, the tsar executed by the Bolsheviks. "We are fighting," wrote the prince, "a common foe and whatever our differences in the past have been I feel that all Slav races should now unite to rid the world of Nazism."

I have been told stories (by their descendants) of emigrés as far away as Australia who, at that time of crisis, dropped everything and returned to Russia to help in her defence. Patriotism and love for *Rodina* (the Russian birth-land) – which in extremity means readiness to die when the Motherland is in danger – are durable features of the Russian character.

Indeed, it is possible to say that the best features of the Russian character – those which are revealed in times of national crisis – include loyalty, self-sacrifice, patriotism (but not the jingoist variety), and capacity for endurance. Siberian General Afanasy Beloborodov, one of the heroes of the Battle of Moscow in the autumn of 1941, has himself spoken of "the best traits" of the Russian soldier. These, he told me in an interview (on his 81st birthday), were "coolness and selfless bravery". A much-decorated officer, he also extolled the "inexhaustible optimism" of his soldiers. Looking back on the ordeal of war and at the individual heroism of the men under his command, Beloborodov mentioned the difficulty or inability of Hitler and his retinue to understand, in the general's words, "the mysterious Russian soul". His face betrayed a hint of a smile as he uttered these words. After the Wehrmacht's "collision with Russian tenacity", Beloborodov added, the invader lost all hope of ever conquering Russia.

Loyalty and self-sacrifice are deeply rooted in Russia's past. After the Nazi invasion, slogans, placards and newspapers cited utterances by prominent personalities of old, beginning with the distant past, such as that by Russian Prince Svyatoslav, who said in the tenth century: "Let us not shame the Russian land. We shall rather lay down our lives, for the dead know not shame." There is the famous maxim of Field Marshal Alexander Suvorov, an eighteenth century military wizard who remains a Russian icon: "Save your comrade even if you die." A longer paraphrase of this maxim appeared in the Field Manual of the Red Army during the Second World War: "Every serviceman must aim at mutual aid and at all times help his comrades with fire, bayonet, grenade, spade and personal assistance."

The best generals of Russia's past had set great store by the moral factor in achieving victory over the enemy and used every means at their disposal to boost the morale of their troops. To mention a few, there were Alexander Nevsky (thirteenth century), Dimitri Donskoi (fourteenth century), Alexander Suvorov (eighteenth century) and Mikhail Kutuzov (eighteenth-nineteenth centuries). They and other celebrated generals made a point of addressing their troops, appealing to patriotism and love of country, knowing that their men had imbibed stories of the exploits of their fathers and grandfathers before them who had stood fast on "the sacred soil of Russia" to protect it from the onslaught of enemies.

Hundreds of thousands of books and articles have been written about the Second World War. Some authors prefer to stress the presence of punitive squads behind Russian troops at the frontlines with the implication, or suggestion, that deeds of heroism were far from being voluntary. The late American military historian Hanson Baldwin has claimed that the Russian *muzhik* (peasant) fought well only because of the iron discipline fostered by commissars coupled with the fear of punishment. His argument doesn't stand up. Fear alone does not make men heroes. Readers of the novelist Leo Tolstoy's sketches of Sevastopol (about the Crimean War in the 1850s in which Tolstoy was a front-line officer) will be aware of the legacy of heroism in Russian history. So too, during the war with Hitler, legions of Russian men and women volunteered for battlefield assignments from which the chances of survival were slim.

In Antony Beevor's acclaimed book, *Stalingrad*, he mentions Stalin's Directive 227 which ordered: "Not one step backwards!" (Anyone caught retreating against orders was almost certain to receive a bullet from his own side.) The historic links of this Directive (down the ages the motto of Russian patriots was: "Give up your life but do not yield an inch of territory!") can't be ignored. But perhaps the most significant thing about Directive 227 is that due to the patriotism and impatience of Stalingrad's defenders, the great majority of generals, junior officers and ordinary soldiers applauded it. The Russian wartime generals I have met who fought at Stalingrad, and the generals who allude to Directive 227 in their postwar and post-Stalin memoirs, give it unqualified approval.

A factor that can't be overestimated is the very real danger that loomed over Stalingard. Military historian Lev Bezymensky, who fought at Stalingrad, has described to me in six words how grave the situation was for the Russians: "Further retreat would have spelled disaseter."

Shortly after Hitler's armies stormed across the Soviet border, there emerged a pantheon of new national heroes. Only four days after the invasion, Captain Nikolai Gastello, whose aircraft had been hit and was aflame, dived his blazing bomber into a column of German tanks and cars, destroying many of them. Another early hero was Private Alexander Matrosov who was nineteen years old when he performed a feat that became an enduring symbol of courage. When his unit attacked the enemy at the village of Chernushki in the Pskov Region of western Russia, Matrosov flung himself on the gun-port of a German pillbox, shutting out the murderous fire with his own body, giving his unit the opportunity to advance. Posthumously he was awarded his country's highest combat medal. But these exploits were not isolated cases. The Defence Ministry archives reveal up to 200 cases of pilots and soldiers who performed similar deeds during the war.

To better understand what has been called "the absolute order of heroism" on the Eastern Front, it may be helpful to turn to Russian war poetry – there were hundreds of poems published in frontline newspapers during 1941–5. ("Love of poetry is our national feature," Russian poet Bella Akhmadulina has explained, adding: "Only in Russia can thousands of people listen to poetry recitals for three hours running.") Virtually all of the best-known Russian writers published poems during the war, including Boris Pasternak, Anna Akhmatova, Konstantin Simonov, Ilya Ehrenburg, Alexander Tvardovski and Olga Bergholtz. Many of the poems glorify death for the sake of the Motherland. Some of the poems even have a religious aura: the dead machine-gunner who hangs on and, resurrected, keeps firing his gun; or the mortally wounded Russian who is buried by the enemy but rises up and kills his grave-diggers. A constant theme is the sacredness of the Motherland – or of the Russian soil. One poet (August Prokofyev) extols the vastness and eternal nature of Russia and the immortality of the people. Another poet (Alexei Surkov) has a stanza written in 1941 that may be likened to an early endorsement of the Stalingrad Directive. It says: "Not one step backwards because Moscow is behind us!" One poem (author unknown) says that the Motherland "demands" that the enemy be stopped; the enemy's hands are "wet with Russian blood." On 24 June 1941 (two days after the invasion) the government newspaper *Izvestia* printed a poem called "The Holy War" which enjoined every adult to rise up to "fight to the death." The poem was immediately set to music and became popular overnight.

A prose poem called "The Russian Character" written in 1944 by Alexei Tolstoy (a distant relative of the author of *War and Peace*), about the reluctant homecoming to his beloved of a wounded soldier whose tank had been ripped apart and set afire by an enemy shell, also became instantly popular. It has these closing lines about the disfigured hero, Yegor Gromov: "A man may seem ordinary enough but, when trouble comes, he is endowed with great strength – the beauty of the human heart."

Almost all Russians felt a personal loss from the invasion. I have come across an obscure Gallup-type poll taken among Russian soldiers of the 2nd Guards Tank Corps during a lull in the fighting towards the end of the war. To my knowledge this poll has not been published outside Russia. Out of the relatives of the 5,848 servicemen polled, the Nazis had killed 4,447, maimed 1,169 and forcibly deported to Germany 908. They had also burnt down 2,430 villages, towns, cities and settlements where the servicemen had lived before the war. In London in November 2000, the toll on the Eastern Front was made starkly real when a Russian colonel, an army attaché of Cossack origin, told me that five of his great-uncles fell on that Front.

During his only visit to Moscow at the end of the war, America's General Eisenhower said that he was astonished by the number of Russian heroes in the war. His host, Marshal Zhukov, who spent almost the entire war on one gigantic battlefield after another, told his American guest that Russia had "many battalions" of heroes. At the same time, Eisenhower was introduced to many of the Red Army's top commanders who were responsible for major victories against Hitler's forces. The future US President did not mention the oft-repeated claim by some critics that what actually ruined Hitler's chances on the battlefield were other "unbeatable Generals": Winter, Mud, Colossus and Populus. But this was not out of politeness on Eisenhower's part. The Cold War had not yet hardened East-West attitudes and so Eisenhower was able to speak frankly. He was, he said, a great admirer of the victories that had turned the tide on the Eastern Front. Speaking to the Soviet leaders at the Kremlin, he said that in future all cadets at the United States Military Academy at West Point would study the battles at Moscow, Stalingrad, Kursk and

Berlin as assiduously as they had once studied the ancient Battle of Cannae.

In a second meeting with Zhukov after the war, this time in Berlin, Eisenhower was lectured by the Marshal on the basics of patriotism. "You [in America] tell a person he can do as he pleases, he can act as he pleases, he can do anything. But we Russians tell him that he must sacrifice for the State." (In Russia the state is often a synonym for "country" or "Motherland.") Eisenhower records that he had difficulty in replying. Incidentally, a gentler, but similar, form of patriotism was formulated by US President John F. Kennedy in the 1960s when he rallied Americans with the cry: "Ask not what your country can do for you but what you can do for your country." And during the Battle of Britain in 1940 a young airman wrote a letter to his mother containing a similar high order of patriotism: "Those who serve England must expect nothing from her. We debase ourselves if we regard our country as merely a place to eat and sleep." The letter was published posthumously in *The Times* on 18 June 1940.

The tragedy of the *Kursk* submarine in Russia's Arctic waters in August 2000 gave rise to Western criticism of the Russian Motherland; of perceived Russian clumsiness, disorderliness and secrecy. Some Western commentators interpreted Russian respect for the Motherland to mean condoning every dark spot in Russia's past. During the days following the *Kursk* incident a five-column headline appeared in a leading British newspaper (*The Independent*): "The curse of Russia has always been its pride in the Motherland." A US paper (*The New York Times*) spoke of Russia's alleged "indifference to human suffering". The criticism was as difficult to substantiate as it was stinging. No mention was made that from this pride flowed Russian wartime sacrifices and achievements that, some of our eminent historians tell us, helped reduce the casualties of the Western democracies.*

---

* And not only historians. A group of distinguished American authors and journalists who reported the war from Russia, including John Hersey (author of *Hiroshima*), Edgar Snow and Richard Lauterbach, issued a joint statement in 1946 informing Americans that Russian sacrifices in the late war "had saved us incalculable bloodshed and suffering".

CHAPTER I

Barbarossa to Berlin

Hitler had a fistful of cynical war plans, but the one with the biggest risk was Operation *Barbarossa*: the invasion of Russia and the annihilation of its people. His other plans included *Orient* – the capture of Iran, Iraq, Syria and Afghanistan, and the invasion of India; *Tannenbaum* – the capture of Switzerland; *Silberfuchs* – the capture of Sweden; *Felix-Isabella* – the annexation of Spain and Portugal; *Ikarus* – the capture of Iceland. There was also *Sea Lion* – the invasion of Great Britain; and an ambitious scenario awaiting the American continent. But that plan, like the others, depended first of all on the defeat of Russia, a colossus comprising one-sixth of the earth's land surface. And to achieve this Hitler would have to subdue not only a huge army but scores of millions of men and women who had a powerful, even mystical love for their Motherland.

But the Fuhrer was ecstatic about his Russian plan: "When Barbarossa commences the world will hold its breath and make no comment."

The world had for twenty years been sliding towards another World War. An arms race had grown in intensity and militarism had asserted itself. In his vitriolic book *Mein Kampf*, which was published in the 1920s, Hitler formulated a programme for the future destruction of Soviet Russia. The year 1939 was fateful. In the summer of that year military talks between Britain, France and Russia to form an anti-Hitler alliance failed and Hitler signed a non-aggression pact with Stalin. Even after he seized Poland in 1939, setting off the Second World War, Hitler did not risk attacking the Soviet Union. Rather, he decided to wait until after the Anglo-French bloc was defeated. But on 23 November 1939 Hitler told a military conference: "I was in doubt for a long time whether or not to start with an attack in the East [i.e., against Russia] and then to switch to the West . . . Circumstances have compelled us to leave the East for the immediate future . . ." Hitler then went on to say: "We have a treaty with Russia. However, treaties are observed only while they offer advantages."

In December 1940 Hitler signed a Directive containing instructions for the invasion of Russia. Prior to this in September an Axis partnership had been signed between Germany, Italy and Japan.

In advance of the invasion it was necessary to engage in legerdemain, something in which the Axis powers excelled. A cover-up for the invasion was needed. Operation *Barbarossa*★ stressed the need for strictest secrecy, with the words, "If information about our preparations leaks out . . . this may entail the gravest political and military disadvantages." Still, the instructions that were issued to commanders to camouflage the transfer of troops from Western Europe to the Soviet border were inadequate because a multi-million-man army with thousands of aircraft, tanks, guns and motor vehicles was being readied for action. All this could not be done in secret.

A solution was put forward: to deceive public opinion in Germany and abroad.

On 15 February 1941, in accordance with Hitler's orders, the General Staff of the Armed Forces issued the *Directive on Misleading Information* which stated that deception must be used to hide preparations for *Barbarossa*. The misinformation measures had two stages. First (up to about 14 April) the deployment of troops was to be explained as the transfer of units from the western to the eastern parts of Germany; and also for assembling troops for Operation *Marita* (the invasion of Yugoslavia). For the second stage (from April up to the actual invasion of Russia) the deployment was to be explained as a

★ Barbarossa, or Redbeard, was the surname of Frederick I, the Holy Roman Emperor (*circa* 1123–90). His campaigns of conquest culminated in a series of defeats. Yet many chauvinists glorified his name, creating legends about him. One of these legends says that Barbarossa was "installed" alive in a mountain retreat in Thuringia; that he would one day leave his retreat to lead Germany once more in an Eastern campaign.

huge hoax carried out for the purpose of diverting attention from preparations for the invasion of Britain.

The Directive noted that, "although there has been a considerable slackening of preparations for Operation *Sea Lion*, all measures must be taken to create the impression among the troops that preparations for a landing in Britain, even if in a totally different manner, are still being conducted despite the fact that the forces trained for this operation are being dispatched to the rear for a definite period. It is necessary to keep even those troops which will take a direct part in operations in the East misinformed about the real plans for as long as possible."

Admiral Wilhelm Canaris, head of the Intelligence and Counter-Intelligence Division of the General Staff of the Armed Forces, supervised the fabrication and dispatch of misinformation to his attachés in neutral countries and their attachés in Berlin. The Directive emphasized that "misleading information should resemble a mosaic picture which is determined by a common tendency." False information was spread through the press and radio as well as diplomatic channels. General Alfred Jodl, Hitler's Chief of Operations, shed some light on the propaganda activity of the German General Staff that was aimed directly at Russia when he said: "The use of all means of active propaganda against the Red Army promises greater success than in the struggle against all the former enemies of the German Armed Forces. Therefore it is intended that it be used on a great scale."

On the Russian side, the military historian, General Pavel Zhilin, says the ruse was at least partially effective. Zhilin has written: "There is no denying the fact that extensive dissemination of false reports coupled with the secrecy with which troops were shifted and concentrated in the East enabled the German Command to achieve positive results in its preparations for a surprise invasion of the USSR."

On Sunday, 22 June 1941 Nazi Germany threw men and equipment against Russia in unprecedented numbers: 190 divisions, over 4,000 tanks, almost 5,000 aircraft and more than 200 warships. Joining the attack were forces from Italy, Hungary, Rumania and Finland. A total of 5 million men took part in the blitz attack along the entire Russian frontier that stretched some 3,720 miles. As an invasion force, history had never known such a huge army. "Almost all responsible military opinion," said Winston Churchill, "held that the Russian army would soon be defeated and largely destroyed."

Defining his war aims, Adolf Hitler told a conference of German generals, "Russia is to be abolished." The war, he said, was to be one of "annihilation." On the fate of Moscow he did not mince words: the city and every man, woman and child in it were to be destroyed. Hitler's chief propagandist, Dr Joseph Goebbels wrote in his diary: "The Fuhrer says that, be it right or wrong, we must win . . . for when we win, who is to question us about our method? We already have so much on our conscience as it is that we just have to win." Other members of Hitler's coterie, such as Alfred Rosenberg, spoke with contempt about "lower orders" of people. For the Hitler clique this included the entire Russian population of Slavs, Jews, gypsies and others.

At first it seemed true that nothing could withstand the ferocity of the German onslaught. The plan for the offensive against Moscow had been codenamed *Typhoon* to underline the crushing force of the blow. But it soon became clear that even if the German armies would ultimately win, they would not do so with impunity. The Russians began preparing for a massive defensive campaign. In Moscow more than 500,000 citizens began to build fortifications in and around the city. Up to a dozen volunteer divisions and almost ninety combat battalions were formed. As Hitler's armies pushed towards Moscow more than forty partisan groups taking their orders from Moscow operated behind enemy lines, disrupting enemy logistics and communications and sometimes tying up large bodies of German troops. (Such actions grew steadily in size so that, from 1943, it appears that up to 10 per cent of German troops on the Eastern Front were required to deal with the partisans.)

The initial stage of the war was extremely unfavourable for the defenders. Many Soviet generals and officials had realized that sooner or later Hitler would attack but the more perceptive knew that preparations for it were pitifully incomplete: that the Rusian armies, strong though they were, were not equal to the most prepared and powerful army ever assembled. Stalin apparently believed he had at least six more months of peace to build up his nation's defences. Miscalculations were therefore made in assessing the timing of the anticipated aggression. Obviously, this had an impact on the initial period of the war, a time when Russians had to "drink the bitter cup of retreat."

To this day it is puzzling why the Soviet Government and Stalin personally did not heed the many warnings of Hitler's coming invasion. Some of the most persistent came from London. But here the Russians seem to have been caught in a dilemma: could they trust Winston Churchill, a sworn enemy of Bolsheviks and one who had spoken frankly against them for two decades? Russian historians say that Churchill calculated that Hitler would be able to crush Russia; but that the longer that country held out against Germany, the better it would be for Britain. With this objective in mind, they claim, Churchill on 3 April 1941 warned Stalin about the danger threatening the USSR.

But there were other warnings of an imminent German attack, mainly from the offices of the US President Roosevelt, and from Russian intelligence officer Richard Sorge in Japan, who had access to the German Embassy in Tokyo. This access enabled him to read secret telegrams from Berlin. Sorge radioed Moscow the exact day and probable time of the invasion. Warnings also came from German deserters. Meantime, Russia in the spring of 1941 was feverishly at work on its Third Five-Year Plan (1938–42), building up industrial and military capacity. Of course the war interrupted it. The Fourth Plan did not begin operation until a year after the war.

The Nazi generals, conscious of their advantages and dizzy with their quick victories in Poland and Western Europe, based their plans on the concept of *Blitzkrieg*, or lightning war, which had already been so successful. Above all they counted on the shattering effect that a surprise strike by massed armoured, air and infantry forces would have, and banked on an easy thrust into Russia's vital centres. The generals hoped that the entire campaign would last not more than thirty or forty days; perhaps a little longer. American and British experts sided with the German estimates. An American historian, Frederick Schuman, points out that some senior military figures gave the Red Army no chance of escaping total defeat by Nazi Germany within six weeks (this from the US Army's General Marshall) or at most, three months (the opinion of the British Imperial General Staff).

Even some Western leaders who sympathized with the plight of the Russians felt at the outset that it would be foolhardy to help Moscow with war supplies since they would only land in the lap of the conquering Germans. Some of those who believed in an imminent Russian collapse had, in the years before the invasion, visited Hitler's Germany and were dazzled by massive night-time parades and over-whelming displays of military strength, not to mention signs of burgeoning economic power. But they dismissed other factors vital to the outcome of war: the strength of reserves and the character or morale of the population.

Hitler had statistical superiority in the beginning. In early 1941 Germany had the manpower resources of 290 million people and the raw materials and industrial capacity of nearly the whole of Europe at its disposal. German capacities in the output of metal, electricity and coal were approximately two or two and a half times greater than Russia's. When the invading armies occupied the USSR's western areas, which accounted for over 40 per cent of its population, and more than half of its industrial output and a third of its food production, Germany's advantages were even more glaring.

Taking advantage of their surprise attack and superior numbers – up to five to one in the sector of the main effort – Nazi troops advanced up to 155 miles by the night of 25 June and 372 miles by 10 July. The leadership was triumphant. General Franz Halder, Chief of the General Staff of the German Ground Forces, wrote in his diary on 3 July: "It would be no exaggeration to say that the campaign against Russia has been won in fourteen days." A little over a week later,

Hitler endorsed a plan to reorganize the Wehrmacht for carrying out new tasks: future operations against Britain and – a vaunted target for the future – America.

There was however, an early hitch or two. The stiff defence by the garrison of the frontier Brest Fortress showed at the start that Russia would not be an easy victim. Hitler's generals commented on the stubbornness and valour of the defenders, a circumstance that un-settled some officers who accepted the propaganda that Slavs were a "lower order" of species. Only two days after the invasion, General Halder wrote in his diary about the garrison at Brest: "There were cases when pillbox crews blew themselves up together with their pillboxes rather than surrender." Most of the garrison who held out for over a month after the fortress was enveloped chose death rather than surrender. Excavation of the ruined bastion after the war yielded evidence of the valour of its defenders. On the casement walls of the fortress were farewell messages from hundreds of the defenders. One of them is by an anonymous soldier who scratched with a bayonet the words: "I am dying but not giving up! Farewell, Motherland! 20 July 1941."

In a fierce battle at Smolensk (lasting from 10 July to 10 September) Hitler's Army Group Centre – the force battering its way towards Moscow – suffered heavy losses. Greater losses were suffered by the Russians; but at Smolensk for the first time since the war began the Wehrmacht was compelled, temporarily, to assume the defensive in its main line of advance. It was the first crack in the German armour.

By the beginning of the fourth month of the invasion the total Nazi losses exceeded 500,000 officers and men, whereas in the first two years of the Second World War the German armed forces had lost fewer than 300,000 troops in seizing nearly the whole of Europe. Although the Wehrmacht continued its successful drive in the summer of 1941, the Nazi High Command failed to reach its main objectives in the strategic directions of attack. It failed to capture Leningrad (now St Petersburg) and Moscow, and was unable to capture the oil resources of the Caucasus.

The Battle of Moscow was a landmark event in the first year of the Patriotic War. To capture Moscow was a matter of immense moral, political and strategic importance to the German leadership for they hoped that it would decide the outcome at one stroke. Hitler had concentrated in the Moscow sector more than a million officers and men, which was more than two-fifths of the infantry operating on the entire Eastern Front, and also three-quarters of the tanks, nearly half of the guns and mortars, and about one-third of his aircraft.

For their part, the Russians were determined to hold on to Moscow. Besides regular forces, the capital was defended by home-guard divisions formed by volunteers. Partisans actively operated behind enemy lines. Innumerable soldiers performed heroic acts in delaying or stopping the advance on Moscow.

The German troops fought fiercely but the defenders dug in with tenacity. The main blow fell on the 316th Rifle Division commanded by Major-General Ivan Panfilov and Major-General L. M. Dovator's cavalry group. The feat of twenty-eight soldiers belonging to Panfilov's division has become legendary. In November 1941 near the railway junction of Dubosekovo the small contingent of men kept some fifty enemy tanks from breaking through to Moscow, destroying eighteen of them. All twenty-eight of the men were given the title of Hero of the Soviet Union posthumously.

Although the Wehrmacht still retained its overall superiority, Russian forces launched a counter-offensive in early December. As a result, the Germans were thrown back from 62 to 155 miles from Moscow. This was the Wehrmacht's first defeat in the course of the war, and between January and April 1942 Soviet troops advanced some 186 to 248 miles to the west.

Terrible battles were waged around the clock. The Wehrmacht lost about fifty of its divisions. In the winter of 1941–2 the German land forces lost about 800,000 men killed and wounded. Russia's allies exulted. A year into the invasion (in May 1942) President Roosevelt said that the Russians were killing more Axis soldiers than were the forces of the other Allies combined. But Russian losses too were grievous. Each day of the war cost some 19,000 lives.

Losses of general officers were also high. More than fifty Soviet generals were taken prisoner in the first year of war.*

In the summer of 1942 the Wehrmacht made a bold attempt to alter the situation on the Russian front and prepare for an invasion of Asia. According to some historians, had Hitler achieved the desired results, the position of Britain and the USA would have seriously deteriorated. Edward R. Stettinius, a former US Secretary of State, observed that America was on the brink of disaster in 1942; that if the Russians had failed to hold on their front, the Germans would have been in a position to conquer Great Britain, overrun Africa and, in that case, establish a foothold in Latin America.

But the Russian strategies as well as their generals showed marked improvement after a year and a half of war, their greatest success coming at the Battle of Stalingrad, where after 200 days and nights, the struggle ended on 2 February 1943 with the surrender of the German Sixth Army commanded by Field Marshal Friedrich Paulus. Nearly everyone has heard this victory on the River Volga described as "the turning point of the war." But although it was pivotal, the battle exacted an appalling price in blood. In 1992 figures released by the Institute of Military History of Moscow's Defence Ministry said total Russian casualties amounted to almost 1,080,000 in dead and wounded. The German toll was said to be about 800,000.

But the battle touched off a triumphal mood among those Russians who managed to emerge unscathed. Indeed the victory lifted the morale of the Russian General Staff and that of its armies in the field.

For months the eyes of the world had been focused on the Volga conflict. No previous battle on the Eastern Front had so closely caught the world's attention. The victory had far-reaching implications. For instance, thousands of miles away Chinese Communist leader Mao Tse-tung assessed the outcome as being highly beneficial to China's

---

* A factor that cannot be ignored in seeking reasons for the early setbacks in the war was the loss of officers to the Great Purges of the late 1930s when the Red Army lost approximately half of its highest ranking officers – by any reckoning a "massacre at the top".

war against Japan. Significantly, when news of the defeat of Hitler's armies on the Volga was announced, the USSR for the first time began to be regarded beyond its borders as a formidable Allied power.

Meanwhile, Russian forces had mounted a counter-offensive in the Caucasus. Six months earlier the Nazi High Command had launched its Plan *Edelweiss*, aimed at seizing the Caucasus. German troops broke through to the Kuban area and the Northern Caucasus, compelling the defenders to withdraw south to the foothills of the Main Caucasian Range. It was at this point that the Nazi Command ordered the 4th Panzer Army north-east towards Stalingrad, depleting the German forces in the Caucasus. Fierce fighting in the Caucasus continued until December 1942 when the Red Army finally halted the enemy.

In their January offensive in the Caucasus the Russians inflicted heavy losses on the Germans, destroying some 200,000 troops, approximately 900 tanks and 2,000 aircraft. The success was mainly due to events on the Volga. The heavy German losses at Stalingrad prevented the Nazi Command from reinforcing its armies in the Caucasus so that Nazi forces never got beyond the foothills of the Caucasus mountains.

While the Battle of Stalingrad was still in progress and the Wehrmacht was within an arm's length of the River Volga the Russians had been buoyed by the news from North Africa of the British victory at El Alamein in October 1942. (Russian historian Dmitri Yefimov makes the point that many wrecked Nazi tanks and lorries were painted yellow because they were intended for action in the North African desert and were, therefore, quite conspicuous in the snow-covered plains near Stalingrad in the winter of 1942). British troops under General Montgomery had dealt a crippling blow to the Italo-German forces led by General Rommel. El Alamein cost the Germans and Italians 55,000 lives, 320 tanks and nearly 1,000 pieces of artillery. The official Russian view is that the victory, the first success of British forces in the North African campaign, deservedly entered the history books for its critical role in Allied operations in the Mediterranean theatre. Thereafter, the Allied landings in Sicily and the Italian mainland ended in defeat for the German and Italian forces opposing them and put Italy out of the fighting. There is, however, some Russian criticism of those who are thought to magnify Allied operations at the expense of Stalingrad. For example, according to Professor Oleg Rzheshevsky, head of the Department of War History and Geopolitics of the Russian Academy of Sciences, at El Alamein the British forces were up against Nazi units totalling less than 100,000 men, which means that the scale of operations was relatively small. By comparison, he notes, Hitler had more than one million men at Stalingrad by November 1942. Nevertheless, Rzheshevsky and his colleagues admit the brilliance and importance of the El Alamein victory.

After Stalingrad and the Caucasus many hard battles still lay ahead but the German defeats had made it possible to launch large-scale strategic offensives to drive the enemy from Russian soil.

In the summer of 1943 in the absence of a Second Front in France, Hitler sent fresh reinforcements to the Eastern Front, concentrating more than 200 divisions there. But in the fierce fighting at Kursk, Oryol and Belgorod, which started on 5 July and lasted for 50 days, 30 enemy divisions, including 7 armoured divisions, were routed. The Wehrmacht lost about 500,000 men, more than 3,000 planes and almost 1,500 tanks. Russian losses also were heavy.

At Kursk, one of the Second World War's biggest battles took place. Having put together whatever forces it could find and re-inforced them with new equipment, the Nazi High Command sought revenge for its defeats at Moscow and Stalingrad by making one final big-scale offensive on the Eastern Front, called the Battle of the Kursk Salient. More than four million soldiers, backed with thousands of armoured vehicles, guns and aircraft, clashed at Kursk. The Germans struck first. Wave after wave of tanks, including the latest "Tigers", battered against Russian defences. Despite the crunching pressure, the defending Russians stood firm and began an offensive of their own. This defeat precipitated the collapse of the Axis powers. As a result, say Russian generals, favourable conditions were produced for the Anglo-American landings in Italy in September.

Throughout 1942 and 1943 Stalin had pressed his Anglo-American allies to begin an invasion of France, opening up the so-called Second Front. Stalin's expectations were dashed in this period and he showed his resentment when Winston Churchill flew into Moscow in August 1942 and informed him that there would be no Allied invasion of France that year. The following year Stalin told his chief military liaison officer to the British Government that, "No matter how hard he kicks and balks, sooner or later, Churchill will be forced to open a second front in France." The officer, Admiral Nikolai Kharlamov, informed Stalin that there were many "second front supporters" in Britain, both in Churchill's Cabinet and among members of Parliament.

When Churchill informed Stalin on 6 June 1944 of the successful start of *Overlord* – the invasion of France – Stalin was effusive in congratulating the Allies. Anglo-American forces swiftly crossed the English Channel, taking the Germans by surprise and capturing a vital beachhead in Normandy. The tying up of Nazi armies in the East helped in the Anglo-American success. In the winter and spring of 1943/44 the Wehrmacht's mounting losses in the East forced the German High Command to send some forty additional divisions to the Russian front. By the time of the landings in France, almost three-quarters of the divisions of the Nazi bloc countries were fighting in the East.

Meanwhile, Stalin informed Churchill of the beginning, in late June, of a new general offensive by his armies. Churchill was highly pleased at this news, so much so that he gives almost three pages in his war memoirs to this pleasant exchange with Stalin. Four months later, Churchill spent a fortnight in Moscow and, after jointly addressing the most difficult issues, especially the future of Germany and Poland (in a spirit of "ease, freedom and cordiality"), he summed up his visit by saying that nothing prevented mutually satisfactory agreement among the Allies on these and other vital matters.

Russia's new general offensive in the summer of 1944 was called

Operation *Bagration*. It was another mammoth attack, also called "The Byelorussian Operation", and the Russian forces were joined by the Polish First Army under General Zygmunt Berling. The Russian plan called for the rout of Army Group Centre and the liberation of what is now the Republic of Belarus. Close cooperation with Belorussian partisans was also planned. The operation was triumphant. Siegfried von Westphal, one of Hitler's leading generals, has written of *Bagration*: "During the summer and autumn of 1944, the German armies suffered the greatest disaster of their history which even surpassed the catastrophe of Stalingrad." He said that only scattered remnants of thirty divisions escaped death or captivity.

The opening of the Second Front in North-West Europe had caught Germany in a ring of powerful forces, as Russia's armies continued to steamroller from the east while the Allies advanced from the west. The coordinated actions of the anti-Hitler coalition spelled doom for the enemy. Hitler's hope for an eleventh-hour falling out among the Allies towards the end of the war was also dashed.

The last decisive action of the Russians in the European sector was the encirclement of Berlin. Before dawn on 16 April 1945 powerful artillery strikes of the 1st Belorussian Front marked the beginning of the Berlin operation. Three hours later the artillery of the 1st Ukrainian Front opened up their own heavy bombardment. By the end of the day the main defence line of the enemy was pried open. The strategic offensive on the German capital was carried out by the 2nd and 1st Belorussian and the 1st Ukrainian Fronts (as these armies were called) on a frontage of nearly 300 miles. Russian striking power had never been stronger. The army employed 40,000 guns of all types, more than 6,000 tanks, and over 8,000 aircraft in penetrating the German defences and capturing the centre of the city.

On 20 April troops of the 2nd Belorussian Front launched an offensive, crossed the River Oder and pierced the enemy defences south of Stettin. On 25 April, the attacking units converged west of Berlin, encircling the defenders. On the same day, near Torgau, Russian soldiers crossed the Elba and established contact with units of the American First Army.

But fighting raged inside Berlin. The Nazi die-hards were routed only after heavy casualties on both sides. Skirmishes continued day and night as almost every street and building had to be stormed. Hand-to-hand combat also took place underground – in rail tunnels and in sewer and communications systems.

Finally, the Berlin garrison laid down their arms. All hostilities ceased at midnight on 8 May 1945 and formal ratification of the instrument of unconditional surrender took place in Berlin on 9 May. Britain's Air Chief Marshal Tedder signed on behalf of Eisenhower, Field Marshal Keitel for Germany and Marshal Zhukov for the Russians. Witnessing the signing was French General de Lattre de Tassigny. Zhukov records that Keitel's hand was shaking slightly as he signed copies of the document. The entire ceremony took 45 minutes.

CHAPTER 2

The Hero Fortress

Outside the frontier Brest Fortress hot air shimmers over the Eternal Flame and spring freshets flow gently around the inscription: "They fought to the death. Glory to the heroes." A hushed crowd of visitors is paying their respects to the hundreds of men and women who fell there in June 1941. They now lie together under a large granite slab. The names on the memorial include Lieutenant Alexei Naganov whose remains were found years after the war – with a cocked pistol in his hand, a round in the chamber – Senior Sergeant Grigoryan, Private Nur Sadykov, Senior Sergeant Botabai Suleimenov, Senior Sergeant Akaky Shevardnadze – the fortress was defended by soldiers of thirty nationalities. There are also – "Name Unknown", "Name Unknown" – dozens of anonymous heroes.

On 22 June 1941 people in the city of Brest, in what is now the Republic of Belarus, could see, if they looked up, dots of light moving in the blue-black predawn sky. These were Luftwaffe planes flying in cock-a-hoop to bomb Russian cities, with some pilots not bothering to switch off their lights, so confident were they of success. Most people, tired after a long summer day, were still asleep when the first salvoes thundered over the Western Bug, the river that separated the Russian and German forces. Suddenly explosions broke the silence. For the Russian defenders of the nearby Brest Fortress, it was the beginning of an inferno.

A twelve-year-old bandsman, Pyotr Kotelnikov, was in the fortress on the first day of war. He and other members of the band were scheduled to go to the city on that Sunday to be photographed in their new uniforms.

"When the shelling started," he says, "it seemed that all the shells and bombs were zeroing in on our barracks. We ran outside. Everything was ablaze. Something hit me on the head and I fell. When I came to it was quite light. Soldiers stood at the windows with guns. I was dizzy but I could walk so I started to bring them ammo. I learned how to load rifles and to prepare dressings for the wounded.

"The Germans were preparing a general assault and soon their machine-gunners penetrated the buildings after shelling and mortar fire. Hand-to-hand fighting started. They took us boys together with some soldiers to a POW camp. The conditions were hideous. The people were being starved. The day started with carts arriving at the camp onto which the POWs had to load the dead. Then they took them to the forest to bury the bodies."

Anastasia Arshinova was one of the women who helped defend the fortress. The wife of an officer and mother of two children, she was also an expert rider, sharpshooter and nurse.

On Saturday, 21 June, her seven-year old son went to the movies and came back very late. It seemed that no sooner had they gone to sleep than they heard a powerful bang. "A wall of the room opened up like a door, revealing the street outside," she says.

"I grabbed the children and fled from the house. Women were running to and fro and soldiers were firing machine guns. The sky was black with German planes. We set up a hospital on the HQ premises. We tore up red tablecloths into strips because it was impossible to reach the hospital, and we started to lay out the first wounded on the floor. We managed more or less with the dressings but the worst thing was the lack of water. The kids were bawling and the wounded died pleading for us to at least moisten their lips. It was unbearably hot. The place was full of smoke, soot and the stench of decomposing bodies.

"It was 272–327 yards to the river. Several women started to crawl to it but were killed. Then I set off with a machine-gunner covering me from above, suppressing enemy fire. Time seemed to stand still. Dead bodies floated down the river. I filled a water bottle and started to crawl back. Then I saw the machine-gunner get off the rampart – he was out of ammo. He was awful to look at. He looked at the water bottle that I was carrying and I knew that if I let him take it in his hands, he would drain it at a gulp. I told him there were so many little children and his wounded mates there. And, you know, I'll never in my life forget that soldier. He rejected my hand with the bottle and said: 'Take the water and give some first to the children and what is left to the soldiers.' "

In concealed positions, opposite the famous fortress, masses of Hitler's troops had been on battle alert since early morning, 21 June. They were hidden in the thickets that lined the Western Bug. These men were eager to move and so were their generals who were sure of enveloping the fort without much ado despite its strongpoints. In the event their over-confidence proved costly.

Protected by a system of drainage canals and the waters of two confluent rivers – the Western Bug and the Mukhavets – the fortress was actually at one time thought to be impregnable. The Russian engineers who built the fortifications after the war of 1812 had made Brest one of the strongholds of the Russian Army on the western border. They had built earthworks over 30 feet high that surrounded the fortress on all sides, stretching a distance of 5 miles. Where the earthworks stopped, moats were dug and flooded with the waters of the Bug and Mukhavets. The channels together with the moats formed four islands, four fortified blocks, which made up Brest Fortress. The barracks building with its 500 rooms could hold a garrison of 12,000 soldiers with enough provisions and military stores to withstand a long siege.

Brest had other strengths. The walls of the barracks, nearly 5 feet thick, could withstand large calibre shells. Along the outer barracks walls were towers with loopholes for firing. There were also huge cellars beneath the barracks, and under the cellars there was an extensive network of underground passages. Two gates, the Terespolsky and the Kholmsky, in the southern wing of the building, and a giant gate in the northern section, linked the inner courtyard by deep tunnels with bridges leading to the four well-fortified islands of the Fortress.

But – and this was the main drawback – the fortress had not been built for modern wars. With the advent of aircraft and explosive shells it had lost its so-called impregnability. Nevertheless, before the invasion two Red Army divisions were quartered on the territory of the Fortress, the 6th Orel Red Banner Division and the 42nd Infantry Division which had been formed in 1940 during the war with Finland. By far the best unit in the latter division was the 44th Infantry Regiment, commanded by Major Pyotr Gavrilov, a recent graduate of the prestigious Frunze Military Academy.

Gavrilov was destined to play a crucial role in the defence of the Brest Fortress. Possessing a broad face with high cheek-bones, a thick mop of dark hair and bushy eyebrows, he also had a stubborn, determined look in his dark eyes. He had volunteered for the Red Army in 1918 and took part in the civil war. At Brest, his superiors knew him as an exacting commander with exceptional will-power. Thanks to his severity, his men were well-trained. In the days and weeks ahead Gavrilov's deft hand could be seen again and again in the stalwart defence.

But the defenders were under another disadvantage: the Nazi invasion caught the fortress dangerously undermanned. By early summer some of the regiments, artillery and tank forces had been sent to camps in the surrounding country for summer training. Only the headquarters units and some maintenance troops remained in the fort. So when war broke out there were less than two regiments of infantry on hand. And there was another problem: many officers had spent the weekend at home. They were absent from the fortress.

Field Marshal von Kluge, commanding the German Fourth Army which advanced on Brest, hoped to capture the fortress before dinner. In order to do this he decided to give himself overwhelming super-iority in this sector. The army corps that was thrown into the zone opposite the Brest Fortress consisted of three fresh, reinforced infantry divisions. One of them had been the first to enter the ruins of Warsaw and had marched triumphantly into conquered Paris. Several times it had earned personal praise from Hitler himself.

All told, the numerical superiority of the Germans – at least ten to one – was exacerbated by the surprise of the pre-dawn attack. But the fortress was not entirely unprepared. On several occasions in the last few days Polish peasants had dared to swim across the Bug at the risk of their lives to warn Russian frontier guards of the intentions of the Nazi command. The records of one frontier detachment located near the Brest Fortress state that at 0100 hours on 22 June a turncoat German soldier swam across the Bug and declared that Germany was planning to attack Russia at 0400 hours that morning.

After the first salvoes were fired at the fort, Major Gavrilov's small detachment of the 44th was soon ready to reply; and when an hour later the enemy rushed the outer walls and the West Fort, they were met with powerful fire: here the German attacks were repulsed.

One of the first orders of business for Gavrilov was to ask the assistant surgeon, Raisa Abakumova, and other women in the fortress to organize care of the wounded, and this tall, attractive woman was seen many times dragging the wounded from under the enemy's nose. When bandages and medicines ran out she managed to find ways of alleviating suffering. Men's shirts were torn into strips for bandages, bits of board and broken rifle stocks were used for splints.

From the outset, the defenders of Brest Fortress, from commanders directing the defence down to the rank and file infantrymen, never spoke of defeat. They believed that the enemy would soon be beaten and hurled back across the state frontier and, besides, they were confident that at any moment help would come from Russian forces stationed nearby. In any case, along the 2,000-mile frontier stretching from the Barents to the Black Sea no fortress was more famous, better situated, or more strongly defended than Brest.

But what the men in the fortress didn't know was that Russian forces at the frontier were being swiftly overrun by powerful panzer attacks and the very units they expected to come to their aid were under constant bombardment from artillery and aircraft.

In the first days of the fighting in the north sector of the fortress, near the officers' quarters, the Germans captured a group of Russian soldiers commanded by a wounded battery commander of the 125th Regiment, Captain Vladimir Shablovsky. Several women and children were also taken prisoner, among them Shablovsky's wife and his four small daughters, the eldest of whom was eight years old and the youngest only eight months.

The prisoners were marched back to the rear under a strong guard of submachine-gunners. Wounded and exhausted, the prisoners could scarcely walk and had to support one another. Only one man knew that something was about to happen. Shablovsky had one arm in a sling and was carrying his youngest daughter in the other. On the way the column of POWs had to cross a bridge. When the prisoners reached the middle of the bridge, the captain kissed his daughter, handed her to his wife, and with a shout to his men – "Follow me!" – leaped over the railing into the water. Several of his men jumped after him. The German machine-gunners opened up madly and everyone who had jumped was killed in the water. It is quite possible that death was what they had sought. Wounded and exhausted as they were, it's doubtful they would have been able to escape by swimming.

The death of Captain Shablovsky and his men appeared to make a deep impression on the Germans. They immediately turned the column around and marched it back to the town jail. When, a day or two later, a group of women and children, who had been captured in the fortress, were being led across the bridge, the elderly German soldier who was guarding them told them how the Russian captain and his men had died; and his whole manner seemed to convey respect for the deathless courage of the fallen men.

By now the German generals directing the storming of the Brest Fortress were infuriated by the boldness of the defenders. More and more batteries were mounted on the banks of the Bug. The artillery barrage continued day and night, without a halt. Mortar shells ploughed up every inch of the fortress yard, scarring the brick walls of the barracks and tearing up the iron roofs. Aircraft dropped tanks of petrol as well as bombs. Walls that provided a shelter for the defenders gradually crumbled and it seemed no human being could exist amid the smoking ruins. But before long machine-guns and rifles would open up again from the debris, and those of the defenders who were still alive, though mostly wounded and suffering severely from burns, continued the unequal contest.

A week after the invasion, Hermann Schwarz, a German corporal of the 5th Company, 35th Motorized Division, arrived for the first time at the River Bug. He was headed for the front which was by then some 200 miles beyond the Brest Fortress. He wrote in his diary: "We reached the Bug at dawn. Many German graves can be seen, even mass graves with 5–7 men buried in them. The Russians defended well here."

At the end of June fighting was especially heavy in the vicinity of the East Fort. In the week since the invasion, by constant and increasing attacks, the Germans had succeeded in capturing the north and north-east earthworks of the fortress and in cutting off the company defending the West Fort from Major Gavrilov's main forces. But the remnants of this surrounded company went on fighting and a machine-gun in the blockhouse attached to the fort continued firing. Two other companies, which had been thrown back from the earthworks with heavy losses, reformed in the East Fort and under Gavrilov's command so strengthened their resistance that the Germans were obliged to resort to extreme measures to crush the remaining handful of defenders.

"It is impossible to approach the Brest Fortress with infantry", said German staff officers in their reports. Gavrilov's men standing in their trenches and in the horseshoe-shaped yard, armed with machine-guns and rifles, mowed down everyone who came within range. The enemy decided there was only one alternative: to starve the Russians out. To this end they kept up harassing fire from heavy mortars aimed at stopping the Russians from moving about the trenches or the main yard; they instituted close-range bombardment by tanks; and they broadcast surrender appeals by megaphone and by air-dropping of leaflets.

Further German reports, however, make it clear that these measures were mostly ineffective.

28 June: Shelling of the fort by tanks and siege guns was continued but apparently without success. Shelling by an

88 mm anti-aircraft gun achieved no result either. The tight ring around East Fort was restored. At night, captured Russian searchlights (and vehicle headlights) were used to light up the fort. But the Russians still answered every careless movement with fire.

29 June: At 0800 aircraft dropped a large number of 500 kilogram [1,100 pound] bombs. No result was evident but after the siege guns went into action some of the walls were seen to collapse.

In preparation for an offensive bottles and barrels of petrol, oil and grease were rolled into the trenches around the fort and ignited with grenades and incendiary bullets.

Those who compiled these reports neglected to mention one fact. Tear gas bombs were also thrown into the yard of the fort so that for several hours the whole garrison, including women, children and wounded were dazed by clouds of smoke and gas. Nevertheless, the German attacks continued to be driven off with bullets and grenades.

On 29 June the Germans presented the fortress with an ultimatum. Either the defenders surrender within one hour or the garrison would be utterly destroyed. Gavrilov assembled his men for a meeting. Only machine-gunners and observers remained on the ramparts. One after another the men stood up and swore to fight to the last, to die rather than submit to the ignominy of surrender.

It was clear however that the fortress could not hold out much longer. On Gavrilov's orders all staff papers were being destroyed so that they would not fall into enemy hands. It was also decided to bury the colours of the independent artillery battalion which was still in the fort. Meanwhile the term of the enemy's ultimatum had expired. German artillery opened fire, aircraft again began circling the fort. The unequal duel continued.

Only after the fort had been subjected to mass bombing, during which one of the planes dropped a bomb weighing 3,900 pounds that shook the city of Brest, when all the buildings of the fort had been destroyed and the inner yard was a sea of fire, were the German infantry able to storm the earthworks and penetrate its inner chambers. They took prisoner hundreds of women, children, wounded and a few exhausted survivors of the garrison. But though they searched every hiding place thoroughly, they were unable to find Major Gavrilov or his chief political officer who had been second in command during the siege. The Nazi officers figured the two men had committed suicide.

But Gavrilov had not been taken prisoner and had not shot himself. Trapped by German submachine-gunners, he was hiding in a dark cavern in the earthworks of the fort, which had been his command post for the last few days . . .

One of the last defenders of the citadel was Senior Lieutenant Ivan Potapov. He and his men continued to hold the Terespolsky Gate area for a few days, beating off attacks by machine-gunners coming from West Island. Ammunition stocks were very low, however, and Potapov decided to make an attempt to break through the enemy ring. But his plan differed from others who had tried before and met with disaster. The Germans expected a breakout in the north and concentrated their main forces in that area. However, they were unprepared for a breakout in the west, or south, and had left only small covering forces in those sectors.

Potapov decided to take advantage of this. His plan was to take his group and force the bridge over the Bug to West Island, then swim the side-channel of the river to the neighbouring island and from there make his way to where Russian artillery and tank units had been stationed up to invasion day. Potapov hoped the tankmen were still fighting in this area.

After one of the routine German ultimatums, when the defenders were given half an hour "for consideration" and enemy fire temporarily stopped, Potapov and those of his men who were still alive ran across to the barracks near Terespolsky Gate. At the moment when the ultimatum expired and the enemy began shelling the centre of the fortress with redoubled fury, Potapov gave the command. Leaping out of the windows and on to the bank of the Bug, the whole group rushed across the bridge to West Island. The men ran without firing a single shot so that the Germans did not immediately notice the breakout. By the time they realized what was happening and their machine-guns opened fire on the bridge, the greater part of Potapov's men had already taken cover in the bushes of the island and were making their way to the south-east.

A few minutes later they came out of the bushes and dived into the water. At that moment German machine-guns hidden in the bushes opened fire. The Bug was churned up by the fusillade, and one after the other the heads of the swimming men vanished below the surface. On the opposite bank the figures of enemy soldiers with dogs could be seen.

The breakout ended in tragedy. Almost all of Potapov's men were killed. Only a few managed to gain the opposite bank but most of them fell into enemy hands. Those who had not yet entered the water ran back to the bridge in an attempt to reach the cover of the fortress where it would be possible to continue to fight.

And fighting continued. But the defenders had ceased to exist as an organized whole and the character of the struggle changed. The defence was no longer unified. It had fallen apart and instead of unity there were individual pockets of resistance, even if they were fiercer than before. Everyone understood they couldn't break out of the ring. There was only one thing left for them: to hold out at all costs, to fight until help came from the east. Not abandoning hope they still expected help to come. But like stalwart soldiers, they would resist until they ran out of ammunition or had no strength left to fire their guns.

Meanwhile, German officers and men were stunned by the fierceness of the resistance. When, three years later, advancing Russian forces captured staff papers of the German 45th Division at Orsha, east of Minsk, they discovered a "Battle Report" on the fighting at the Brest Fortress during the last days of June 1941. Its final paragraph said: "Overwhelming attacks on the fortress were defended by a courageous garrison that cost us a lot of blood . . . The Russians fought with exceptional stubbornness and determination. They displayed superb infantry training and a splendid will to resist."

*   *   *

Together with Major Gavrilov hidden in a room beneath the earth-works was a frontier guard who throughout the siege had acted as his adjutant. Cut off from the rest of the garrison, they now ran from one chamber to the next, throwing hand grenades and firing back at the Germans with their last cartridges.

But the enemy had control of practically the whole fort. Gavrilov and his adjutant had little ammunition left and so they decided to try to hide until the Germans abandoned the fort and then it would be possible to make their way north-east out of the fortress towards the Belovezhskaya Pushcha – a large virgin forest and wildlife sanctuary – where they hoped partisan units were already in action. They were lucky in finding a safe hiding place.

During the early days of the defence Gavrilov had ordered his men to dig a tunnel in the earthworks. A hole was made in the brick wall of one of the chambers and some of the men began taking turns in digging the tunnel. The earthworks turned out to be made of sand, however, and the work had to be abandoned as the tunnel roof kept falling in. But the hole in the wall remained and behind it there was a deep passage that entered the thick earthworks. It was this shelter that Gavrilov and his adjutant chose as their hiding place just as the voices of the Germans who were searching the neighbouring chambers reached their ears.

Having crawled into the narrow passage left by the defenders, both men began digging. The loose sand yielded easily and they gradually began to move away from the hole in the wall, Gavrilov burrowing to the left, his adjutant to the right. They worked with haste like moles, blocking the tunnel behind them. Nearly half an hour passed before the enemy soldiers entered the chamber, by which time the two Russians had managed to dig about 3 yards away from the entrance hole along the inside of the wall.

Through the wall Gavrilov could hear the Germans talking to one another as they searched the chamber. He held his breath, knowing that a single movement might give him away. The Germans had apparently noticed the hole, for they stood around it for several minutes discussing something. Then one of them fired a burst into the hole with his submachine-gun. They were quiet for a moment, listening, and when they were satisfied that there was no one there, went on to examine the other chambers.

Gavrilov spent several days in his burrow, in absolute darkness. He did not know if it was day or night outside. Hunger and thirst began tormenting him. He had two stale rolls in his pocket and though he only nibbled them, they were soon gone. He discovered a way of alleviating thirst by putting his tongue to the brick wall of the chamber. The bricks were cold and there seemed to be drops of moisture on them. Sleep helped him to forget his hunger and thirst, but he slept only in snatches, afraid of giving himself away by a careless movement or groan. The Germans were still in the fort, he could still hear their voices; and once or twice enemy soldiers entered the chamber.

At this point Gavrilov didn't know whether his adjutant was alive behind the barrier of sand that separated them. He was afraid to call him, even in a whisper, for the Germans might be close by. One false move would ruin everything. There was only one thing to do: he must force himself to wait until the Germans were gone. It was the only chance of escaping and continuing the struggle. In spite of his hunger and thirst, he never forgot about fighting back and more than once he ran his fingers carefully over the loaded pistol and the few grenades that remained in his pockets.

Now German voices were heard less and less often and at length everything seemed to grow quiet. Gavrilov decided it was time to move out when a machine-gun started firing on the top of the earthworks, just above his head. By the sound he knew that it was a Russian light machine-gun. But who was using it – his own men or the Germans?

For a long time he lay in an agony of doubt. From time to time the gun fired a short burst. The gunner seemed to be trying to save ammunition and this gave Gavrilov a vague feeling of hope.

At last he made up his mind and called to his adjutant in a whisper. He received an answer. The pair crawled out into the dark chamber and the first thing they did was to drink their fill from a well that had been dug there. Then with their grenades at the ready they peeped into the narrow yard of the fort. It was night but quiet voices could be heard from above. They were speaking Russian.

It turned out there were twelve Russian soldiers with three light machine-guns on the earthworks. Like Gavrilov, they had managed to hide when the fort was taken. After the German submachine-gunners had left, they had emerged from their hiding place and once again taken up defence positions. During the day they hid in the chamber and at night they fired on any enemy soldiers who happened to come near the fort. The Germans thought there was no one in the fort and had not yet discovered that it was from there that the machine-gun bursts were coming, particularly as there was inter-mittent firing going on everywhere. The machine-gun in the West Fort's blockhouse was still active, shots could be heard from the officers' quarters, and a crackle of firing, now faint, now stronger, came from Central Island.

Gavrilov now decided it was time to try and lead the whole group out towards the Belovezhskaya Pushcha.

By day they left only an observer on the wall, but at night they all went up there, and even opened fire, if the chance presented itself. This continued for several days. The fighting did not cease and groups of German soldiers frequently appeared so that it was still impossible to leave the fortress. The worst thing was that they had nothing to eat. The men's meagre supplies of rusks had run out and they were desperately hungry. Their strength was waning. Gavrilov was think-ing of making a desperate attempt to break out when unexpected events upset all his plans.

Unnoticed by the observer, a group of German submachine-gunners arrived at the fort during daylight. The Germans immediately discovered the Russian soldiers. Gavrilov was dozing in a corner of the chamber when shouts came from the yard outside.

"Russ, surrender!" the enemy shouted. This was followed by grenade explosions. The Germans were few in number and most of them were soon killed, but some escaped.

An hour later the fort was surrounded. The first attacks were repulsed. But the Germans brought up mortars and field guns and soon there were killed and wounded among what was left of the little group of defenders. Then came an attack from all sides and the enemy won by sheer weight of numbers. The German submachine-gunners gained the top of the wall and the yard below was at the mercy of their grenades.

Once again the burrow in the wall was their hiding place. But this time there were three of them: Gavrilov, his adjutant and another soldier. Fortunately, night had fallen by this time and the Germans did not risk searching the chambers in the darkness. But Gavrilov realized that as soon as morning came they would search every inch of the fort and might easily discover his hiding place. Something had to be done right away.

After whispered conversations they crawled cautiously out into the chamber. It was deserted. The yard of the fort was also deserted. But when they crawled to the fort gate they saw campfires with German soldiers sitting around them only a short distance away. The enemy was waiting for the dawn, having surrounded the fort to make sure that none of its defenders escaped.

Escape, even if it were possible, could only be achieved by fighting. On Gavrilov's word of command each of them would throw a grenade at the Germans sitting at the campfire, then all three would scatter in different directions, the adjutant to the south, the soldier to the east, and Gavrilov to the west. Gavrilov's direction was the most dangerous, for German troops frequently moved along the road leading from the North Gate to Central Island.

The three shook hands and agreed that if anyone was lucky enough to remain alive he should make his way to their hoped-for salvation in the forest sanctuary.

Gavrilov whispered the order "Fire!" and they all threw their grenades.

Time passed. Gavrilov could not remember how he got through the line of German outposts. His mind registered only the crash of the exploding grenades, the cries of the German soldiers, the whistle of bullets over his head, and the deep enveloping darkness of the night, even darker now after the bright light of the fires. He ran with all the strength he could muster, gripping his pistol and his second grenade. Behind him he could hear shouts and the sound of running feet. His brain cleared for a moment when he ran across the road, which just then happened luckily to be deserted. He stopped for a second to recover his breath and at that moment a burst of machine-gun bullets whistled over his head.

The bullets came from an unknown Russian machine-gunner firing from the blockhouse at the West Fort. Alerted by the shouts and the firing, he had opened up with long bursts, aiming apparently at the light of the campfires. Gavrilov had thrown himself flat by the wall of a ruined building to avoid being hit. But without knowing it, the machine-gunner had saved him. The Germans who had been hunting for him came under fire and Gavrilov heard them shout at each other and turn back.

Fifteen minutes passed and all was quiet again. Pressing his body to the earth, Gavrilov crawled in the direction of the outer wall, gradually getting further and further away from the road. The night was so black he did not see the wall until he came up against it. It was the brick wall of one of the chambers in the earthworks. Groping for the door, he went inside.

For a whole hour he worked his way around the dripping slimy walls of the chamber. Then he realized where he was. Before the war this had been a stable for the regiment's artillery horses. Now he knew that he was in the north-west sector of the fortress, and he was glad because it was nearer the forest sanctuary that was his goal.

He went outside and climbed cautiously over the earthworks on to the bank of the moat. The sky was already growing light in the east and before doing anything else he lay face down on the bank and for a long time drank from the stagnant waters. Then he started wading across to the other bank.

Suddenly he heard German voices in the darkness and stopped dead, staring ahead of him. Little by little he began to make out the dark outlines of tents on the opposite bank, then a match flared and the red glow of a cigarette appeared. A German unit was camped on the far bank. He stepped silently out of the water and crawled on his hands and knees back to the fort's earthworks. Here he discovered a low door and, on entering it, found himself in a narrow corner chamber with two firing slits facing in opposite directions. A passage ran from the chamber into the bowels of the earthworks. He followed the passage and once again found himself in the stable.

Now it was distinctly lighter. He had to find a safe hiding place for the day. After a little thought he chose the corner chamber. Its walls were thick and the two firing slits might prove useful. If the Germans discovered him, he would have a good view to defend himself. He examined the chamber again and found one thing about it that worried him. It offered no hiding place. The enemy had only to glance through the doorway and they would spot him at once.

Then, thinking of all possibilities, he remembered something: near the door of the chamber there were mountains of dung that had been dumped when the stables were cleaned. Making haste he began carrying armfuls of dung and dropping them in a corner. Before morning came his hiding place was ready. He burrowed into the heap of dung and covered himself up, leaving a narrow slit for observation and keeping his five remaining grenades and the two loaded pistols (one Russian, the other German) at hand.

All next day he lay in seclusion in his malodorous berth. German soldiers walked close to him, urinating on the bank of the canal and talking to one another. Once a group of them walked through the chambers to the stable. Gavrilov gripped a pistol in readiness but they paid no attention to the dunghill in the corner.

Night came and he again went down to the bank of the moat and drank. On the other side he could still see the dark shapes of German tents and hear the voices of soldiers. But he decided to wait until they went away, particularly as the firing in the fortress seemed to be abating — a sign that the enemy was crushing the last pockets of resistance.

Gavrilov had had no food for three days. His hunger became so acute that he could bear it no longer. It occurred to him that near the stable there should be some sort of fodder store where perhaps he would find barley or oats. He groped about the stable for a long time until his hand touched several lumps of a hard substance. He bit a piece off one of the lumps and found that it was edible. It was fodder cake for the horses: a mixture of grain, chaff and straw. It eased his hunger and in his plight even tasted good. Now at least he had a supply of food and was prepared to wait any length of time until the road to the dense forests was clear.

For about five days everything was all right. He ate the fodder cake and at night drank the water from the moat. But on the sixth day he paid for his abnormal diet. He felt severe pains in his stomach which increased hourly and became unbearable. All that day and the following night he had to bite his lips to muffle the groans that might give him away. Then he fell into a kind of stupor and forgot about time. When he snapped out of it he felt extremely weak; but although he could hardly lift a finger he still reached out for his pistols and grenades.

Unfortunately for him, the Germans must have heard his groans. All of a sudden he was awakened by voices close by. He saw through a spy-hole two submachine-gunners standing over his dung-heap. And, as if by magic, as soon as he saw the enemy he recovered his strength and forgot his stomach pains. He felt for one of his pistols and released the safety catch.

His movement in his burrow apparently alerted the Germans because they began kicking the heap of dung. Gavrilov lifted his pistol and with difficulty squeezed the trigger. It was an automatic pistol and within a few seconds he had emptied the magazine. There were screams and a clatter of boots as the Germans rushed to the door.

He mustered his strength and stood up, shaking off pieces of dung. This was, he decided, going to be his last fight, he was so exhausted and ill that he felt death would be a release. Carefully, like a tradesman laying out his tools before a job, he arranged his five grenades near him and gripped his service pistol.

The enemy did not keep him waiting long. Within minutes machine-guns started firing at the window slits. Luckily the slits were so placed that he was safe. That is, unless a bullet ricocheted.

Then he heard the Germans shouting to him to give up. He guessed they would now creep cautiously along the walls towards the door and he waited until he heard them up close. Now through the window slits he hurled two grenades, one to the left, one to the right. The Germans scattered; he heard groans that told him his grenades had done their work.

But within half an hour the attack was repeated and again he used his grenades. The Germans fell back, but now he had only one grenade left and his one remaining loaded pistol.

The enemy suddenly changed tactics. While Gavrilov watched the window slits, there was a burst of submachine-gun fire and one German appeared in the doorway. Gavrilov threw his last grenade. Another German thrust the barrel of his gun through one of the slits, but Gavrilov fired twice and the barrel disappeared. At that moment something flew in through the other slit and hit the floor. A flash of flame filled the chamber and Gavrilov fell unconscious to the ground . . .

So impressed was the enemy by his endurance and defiance of death that they let Pyotr Gavrilov live. They took him to a sprawling camp for Russian POWs being assembled south of Brest, which had a hospital staffed by Russian army doctors who had been captured in the opening days of war. Some of the doctors who survived imprisonment tell that on 23 July 1941 that is, thirty-two days after the invasion – a whole month after the Germans surrounded the Brest Fortress – a wounded Russian officer was brought to the hospital. The man was in critical condition, being wounded in several places. He had a thick beard and he was covered with dust and filth. He was too weak to swallow food so he was fed artificially to save his life. The injured officer was Gavrilov. The German soldiers who brought him to the hospital said they had discovered him in one of the chambers of the fortress and that even though he was barely alive he had held out against heavy odds for hours.

For the next three or four days German officers visited the camp hospital to look at the survivor; apparently they couldn't believe such courage was possible.

Pyotr Gavrilov survived the war, spending four difficult years in a German prison camp. Coming home after the war he moved together with his wife into a little white cottage surrounded by grapevines in Krasnodar, not far from the warm waters of the Black Sea. After the war, he resumed his rank of major and was appointed commandant of a POW camp in Siberia for Japanese soldiers. It is reported that with the horror of Nazi concentration camp experience fresh in his mind, Gavrilov made his camp for the Japanese a model one, doing what he could to improve conditions for the POWs. As commandant he helped prevent an epidemic of typhus among the prisoners and is said to have put a stop to injustices committed by Japanese officers in distributing supplies among enlisted men. For his even-handedness, Gavrilov later received letters of thanks from former Japanese prisoners.

After the war Gavrilov was given military honours and made a "hero" of his country. He lived out his last years at his cottage near the Black Sea tying up and pruning his grape vines. When he died in 1975 he was, according to his wishes, buried in the garrison cemetery of Brest Fortress.

Gavrilov, however, had not been the last defender of the Brest Fortress. Even as late as August shots and grenade explosions were heard coming from the cellars; and some of the invaders met their death among the ruins of the citadel. Small groups of Russian officers and men went into hiding in the deep cellars and proved so dangerous to the enemy that the Germans feared to go alone into the fortress they had captured. Finally, citizens of Brest learned that the German High Command had given orders that the fortress cellars be flooded with water from the Bug River. This meant death for the few undefeated defenders of the Brest Fortress. Mostly they remained anonymous heroes.

But other amazing stories were told by the people of Brest and surrounding villages; how months after the Germans took possession of the fortress individual Russian who had hidden among the ruins occasionally fired shots during the night. Some local citizens said that during the winter of 1941–2, when the occupying troops drove people to the fortress to clear the rubble, they sometimes saw wraiths in ragged Russian uniforms darting among the ruins. They saw scrawled on the half-demolished walls defiant slogans such as: "Death to the invaders!"

An extraordinary story is told by Alexander Durosov, one of the defenders of the fortress who was a sergeant major in the 84th Regiment and, after the war, settled in the town of Mogilev, a few hundred miles east of Brest. Durosov was taken prisoner after being wounded and spent several months in a POW camp near the fortress. In the spring of 1942, when he had recuperated from his wound, he was assigned to work in a labour gang in a German hospital in Brest. He heard the following story.

A small group of Jews from the ghetto established by the Germans in Brest also worked with the prisoners. They suffered no less humiliation than the Russian POWs. In the group was a violinist who before the war had played with a jazz band in the city's restaurant. One day in April 1942, ten months after the invasion, the violinist was late for work in the hospital, and when he finally arrived he told his friends what had happened.

On the way to the hospital he was overtaken by a German Army vehicle with an officer seated in it. The car braked sharply and the officer called to the violinist:

"*Jude!*"

The man pulled off his cap.

"Step into the car."

He got in and they drove to the Brest Fortress. The car stopped on Central Island, close to where the positions of the 333rd Regiment had been.

A deep hole had been tunnelled among the ruins and around it stood a platoon of submachine-gunners with their weapons at the ready.

"Go down into the tunnel!" barked the officer. "Find the Russian still hiding in the cellars. He refuses to surrender and keeps on firing. Persuade him to come out and surrender. Tell him we won't shoot

The German invasion of Russia. The invading troops put many towns
and villages to the torch.

The wartime slogan on a Nazi signboard says: "The Russians must
die so that we may live."

Brest Fortress today. The black spots are the preserved pock-marks
caused by Nazi gunfire.

Moscow looks deceptively close as German soldiers see the dim outline of city
buildings through their binoculars.

Tickets for sale for a famous wartime concert. In the summer of 1942 a packed audience of off-duty soldiers and half-starved civilians attended the Leningrad premiere of Shostakovich's Seventh (widely known as "The Leningrad") Symphony, despite the fact that the city was blockaded. The poster advertises the event.

This "Road of Life" over frozen Lake Ladoga brought food and supplies to blockaded Leningrad but famine prevailed as the food received was hardly able to feed hungry citizens.

Walking calmly to the gallows, the teenaged partisan, Zoya Kosmodemyanskaya, is followed by German soldiers. The placard around her neck has the inscription "Incendiary".

Zoya in death, her breasts mutilated. She was tortured and hanged in 1942.

Pilot Nadya Popova flew almost 1,000 combat missions against Hitler's armies in an aircraft made of plywood and canvas. Here she wears her Gold Hero Medal.

Mila Pavlichenko, the acclaimed woman sniper who felled over 300 enemy soldiers, lies in ambush.

General Vasily Chuikov, one of the celebrated Russian commanders at the Battle of Stalingrad, examines a rifle belonging to ace sniper Vasily Zaitsev (right).

Alexander Pokryshkin (with aviator's cap) shot down 59 enemy planes during the war. After the war he rose to become an air marshal.

A Russian cavalry charge in deep snow at the Battle of Moscow in December 1941.

him. But if you fail don't come back because I'll personally shoot you!"

The violinist, overcoming his fear, climbed down the hole with difficulty and found himself in a dark underground passage. Slowly he groped his way, meanwhile calling out who he was and why he had come, hoping the Russian would not fire.

But a shot rang out and the violinist flung himself flat on the damp earth. The bullet missed him. Then a faint voice ahead of him said:

"Come closer, don't be scared. I only fired in the air. That was my last cartridge. I was going to come out anyway because my food ran out long ago. Help me, I can barely move."

The violinist got up and went forward. In a minute he came across a wraith-like figure sitting by the wall. The man put his arms around the violinist and pulled himself up. They made their way to the entrance of the tunnel, the emaciated soldier leaning heavily on the violinist's shoulder.

After they scrambled out of the hole, the unknown soldier closed his eyes for the light blinded him and he dropped to his knees, completely exhausted. Germans troops stood around, regarding him with curiosity. The tunnel-dweller had difficulty in standing up; he had a heavy, matted beard which made it impossible to tell his age. It was also impossible to see if he was an officer because his uniform was in shreds. An ambulance was called.

Not wishing to show his weakness, the soldier attempted to stand, but could not do so. The German officer gave an order and one of his men put a tin of meat and biscuits down in front of him, but he didn't touch the food. Then the German officer asked him if any more Russians were left in the tunnel.

"No", the unknown soldier gasped. "I was alone . . . I fired my last cartridge and you can shoot me if you want . . ." He was swaying back and forth, his feet were swollen and frost-bitten, and there was a faint trail of blood following his feet. When the ambulance arrived, it was too late. He was dead. In 1944, when the fortress had been retaken, an article about the "last defender" of Brest Fortress mentioned this soldier who had spent ten months alone in the cellars of the fortress. No one knows how he survived so long. The article said that the unknown soldier had "defeated death with death".

After the war a large memorial complex was built at the Fortress, including a tall tetrahedral bayonet that rises toward the sky. Giant evergreen trees, like sentinels, stand today outside the main entrance to the Fortress. The thousand pock-marks on the red brick facade which were made by enemy bullets and shells in June and July 1941 still remain and give the fort a kind of religious sanctity. Twenty years after the war the Brest Fortress was awarded the honorary title of "Hero-Fortress".

CHAPTER 3

Shopping in Berlin

For a designer of airplanes, no news could have caused a more profound shock. Alexander Yakovlev, "father" of the famous YAK-1 and YAK-3 fighter planes, had just heard that by noon on the first day of war Russia had lost 1,200 aircraft – 300 destroyed in aerial battles, 900 caught on the ground. At one stroke Hitler had attained mastery over a significant part of Russia's air space.

But there was another problem for the Russians to ponder: the apparent inadequacy of the fighters and bombers on hand to cope with Hitler's Luftwaffe. When Nazi fighters and bombers began demolishing Polish targets in September 1939, the Soviet Air Force was *even then* noticeably short of comparable aircraft. One of Yakovlev's colleagues, Leonid Kerber, has said frankly that up to the time of Operation *Barbarossa*, Russia had no combat aircraft to equal Hitler's.

It would be Yakovlev's responsibility to help reverse the balance of power in the air between 1941 and 1944.

Alexander Yakovlev was a Russian patriot. He wrote in his memoir: "I had a deep love towards Russia and pride in my people and their history, their great leaders and generals – Peter the Great, Suvarov, Kutuzov." On the other hand, Yakovlev was far from parochial in his tastes: he liked to read foreign authors, his favourites being Daniel Defoe, Jack London, Rudyard Kipling, Ernest Thompson Seton, Mark Twain and James Fenimore Cooper. From his reading he became an admirer of trail-blazers and explorers such as

Columbus, Bering, Amundsen, Nansen, Livingstone, and Miklukha-Maklai. Books also gave Yakovlev a deep interest in technology and radio engineering.

It was Yakovlev's interest in building model aircraft ("I had no time in school for games or play") which started him on his career as an aircraft designer, culminating in 1943 when his fighter planes figured prominently in the summer campaigns of that same year – the year that Russian planes took command of the skies over the Eastern Front. Looking back on his early life, he says: "I had always dreamed of accomplishing something difficult in life."

Before the war, Yakovlev made a number of invaluable working visits abroad: in 1935 to Italy; in 1936 to Britain (to attend the Royal Air Show), and to France; and to Germany in 1939. Yakovlev proved himself a keen observer of all types of aircraft and as a consequence his frank opinions were listened to in the Kremlin.

He flew to Italy in a four-engine TB-3 bomber designed by Andrei Tupolev. In those days these acclaimed bombers showed the world that Russia was an up and coming air power. Yakovlev was unimpressed by the Fiat aircraft plant because of its apparent technical backwardness. Examining some planes made by Caproni, he noted that they were unoriginal in design and that the work in progress consisted mainly of improving already existing types. Mussolini was waging war in Africa and Caproni, with remarkable pragmatism, agreed with Yakovlev, saying, "To fight Abyssinia [Ethiopia] you don't have to have modern planes. What's the use of squandering money?"

The Royal Air Show, held at Hendon Airport outside London, opened with air races of various types of planes. They took off simultaneously, circled over the airfield and landed. Visitors were shown flying machines dating from the first years of the century, including a biplane made by the Wright brothers, the monoplane designed by Louis Bleriot,★ and others. To Yakovlev's eyes they looked more like "kites" or "bookcases", than real airplanes.

★ In July 1909 Bleriot, a pioneer of aviation, made the first aeroplane flight across the English Channel.

The primitiveness of the early planes stood out starkly when the latest fighters and bombers appeared. Yakovlev was duly impressed by an aerobatic stunt in which five British fighters were tied together with ribbons before take-off. The flight of the quintet was in perfect unison and the planes, noted the Russian designer, landed without snapping a single ribbon.

Yakovlev records two more of what he calls "stunts": In the first, a fighter pounced on a bomber, its machine-guns rattling away. The bomber was set on fire and tongues of flame and a black trail followed it in the sky. But the real-life effect had been done with brilliant lights. The bomber seemed to have crashed to the ground wrapped in flames but, in reality, it disappeared behind a hangar and spectators saw a column of artificial smoke and flame billow into the sky.

The second stunt was criticized by Yakovlev as a "decadent symbol of the British Empire". A "mob" of what appeared to be native people burst onto the airfield from a concealed hiding place. In white burnouses they rushed at the viewing stands shouting and howling. The spectators appeared to be frightened; but at that very movement fighter planes shot out over the roof of the hangar and, flying low over the airfield, "strafed" the troublemakers with machine-guns and showered them with small bombs. The attackers were "wiped out to a man". Yakovlev sarcastically referred to this as the "humane treatment" of others by a great power.

The next day, at its own airfield, the De Havilland Company organized a display of the latest types and designs of British aircraft, engines, equipment and armament for the officials of many countries. On display were fighters, bombers and passenger planes. Many foreign aircraft engineers and designers climbed inside the aircraft, examined them and fired questions at pilots and mechanics. Being a designer, Yakovlev was attracted by the "stream-lined light planes" such as the Miles training and sporting aircraft and also the twin-engine Monospar plane which at that time was a technical novelty.

Finally – and of supreme importance to the visitor from Moscow – were the fighters. Among them were two new monoplanes: the

Hurricane built by the Hawker Company and the Supermarine Spitfire, the latest product of the British aircraft industry. These were the same Hurricanes and Spitfires which a few years later became the backbone of RAF Fighter Command defending Britain in 1940 against what Yakovlev called "Goering's air pirates".

Yakovlev noted that in 1936 visitors were restricted from a close examination of the Spitfire because it was supposed to be a British military secret. The plane was roped off and no explanations were given about it. Later, says Yakovlev, he learned that the designer of the Spitfire was Reginald Mitchell. To his regret, he says, he did not meet the famed British designer who was at that time severely ill. In his memoir, Yakovlev pauses to give credit to these superb aircraft and the men who flew them: "In the 1940 Battle of Britain Hitler's air force suffered heavy losses from these combat planes flown by courageous and skilful pilots."

Disappointment greeted Yakovlev on his arrival in France. He visited the Renault-Caudron plant in the suburbs of Paris and noted the "primitive methods" that were used in making parts and assembling aircraft. Despite the achievements of Caudron planes in winning speed records in 1934–5, somehow few of them found their way into the French Air Force. According to Yakovlev, an opinion prevailed in France that as many types of aircraft should be created as possible so that the best could be selected from among them. The French market, he says, was thus "swamped" with too many new types of planes and, therefore, the work of serious designers was impeded. The result, according to Yakovlev, was that when war with Hitler broke out, France had no aircraft that could stand up to the best German planes.

In the late summer of 1939, at a time when Germany and Russia were still joined by a non-aggression pact, Yakovlev and General Ivan Petrov, himself an expert in aircraft design and an experienced pilot, visited Berlin as members of an economic mission, although their real purpose was to see aircraft and related plants. As their train stopped at various German stations, en route to Berlin, the Russian guests noted the sullen faces of the German people and the gloomy atmosphere of the stations. Yakovlev records that the windows of their train were heavily curtained. In Germany during the space of a few weeks the two Russian experts record having actually visited between them 200 plants of different types. At that time Germany was engaged in a fierce air battle with Britain and was blacked-out at night.

In Berlin life came to a standstill from nine o'clock in the evening until morning in anticipation of British raids. Theatres and restaurants closed down and streets became deserted as people hurried off to the accompaniment of the wailing of sirens. But during the day things looked quite different as children were about and people queued up at food shops. Most of the men wore the uniform of the army, the SS or the police. Some wore "those brown coats with swastika arm-bands."

Yakovlev was stunned by the militarization and racial theories of Nazified Germany. He saw a popular German illustrated magazine with its cover showing a soldier with a hand grenade in one hand and a pistol in the other against the background of a ruined city. The picture caption said: "Warsaw is ours!"

One picture especially etched itself in Yakovlev's memory. It showed a dying German soldier, kneeling under a tree, resting his head in the lap of an angelic-looking maiden. The caption beneath the picture said: "The supreme calling of each German is to die for his Führer." On the opposite page was the picture of a heavy German gun with its crew around it, while smoke billowed from buildings on the horizon. That, says Yakovlev, was the "psychological treatment" fed to every rank-and-file German citizen. This went on hour after hour, day after day, instilling in them "the spirit of destruction", something which Russians were to become familiar with during Hitler's "Operation *Barbarossa*."

Yakovlev admits, along with his colleague Leonid Kerber, that he was surprised at first that the Germans allowed the Russian visitors to see their aircraft industry which after all was one of the most secret branches of their armed forces. But after a while the clue to the mystery was supplied by the Germans themselves.

This happened when the Russian design experts were invited to visit an aircraft plant in Oranienburg, north of Berlin. The plant was in perfect order. It took, Yakovlev says, advance planning and official applications in order to inspect such a plant; and when they arrived everything was already prepared for them. After the Oranienburg visit the head of the plant suggested that Yakovlev write down in the guest book his impressions and opinions of what he had seen. Yakovlev turned the pages to see who had previously signed the book. There were signatures of designers from the United States, Britain, France and Japan. The director of the plant especially wanted Yakovlev and Petrov to see the French entry, made by the Air Force Commander-in-Chief. It said: "A magnificent plant which does honour and glory not only to the builders of the plant but to the whole German aviation industry."

"Yes," Yakovlev agreed, "your plant deserves praise."

But the director then gave him a "sly look", saying openly that the German intention was to make the French general realize and not forget that German air power was far superior to that of France. The Germans, Yakovlev explains, tried to implant in the minds of all visitors the seeds of fear of the German war machine and to induce a degree of "panic" in their minds. This panic, he claims, helped Hitler defeat others.

In Germany Yakovlev met Willi Messerschmitt, the designer of the famous fighter plane of that name. Yakovlev describes him as tall and lean, laconic and morose, with eyes that were "clever but angry". Messerschmitt, he says, put on a "show of cordiality". The Russians visited important aircraft plants at Augsburg and inspected a twin-engine plane in addition to the pride of the German fighter forces, the allegedly invincible fighter, the Messerschmitt-109. The conversation then turned to the latest model, the Messerschmitt-209, which was surrounded by a veil of secrecy that prompted the Germans to speak in whispers of its high performance. Naturally, the two Russian visitors wished to see the new plane. But when it was wheeled out onto the field it was not at all what Yakovlev and Petrov had expected to see. It was an experimental model, an attempt to convert a racing plane into a fighter. Yakovlev says he judged the project a failure and believed work on the aircraft had been suspended. Later that same day the Russians spoke openly about their impressions of the new plane. Messerschmitt's face reddened and he became agitated before admitting that what had been shown was not the Me-209. He then ordered the real Me-209 to be brought out.

However, the visitors' opinion was again negative; they thought this aircraft too was still in a "raw state" and would need considerable refinement before it would make a combat fighter. Messerschmitt was stung by the frank criticism of the Russians and, Yakovlev says, "got into a white heat".

"You don't like it? All right, that's your business. But I think the machine is good!" In Yakovlev's opinion Messerschmitt was vehement and was "guilty of a breach of etiquette". But it may have been simply German outspokenness that was too much for Russian sensitivities.

Heinkel, another German aircraft designer, was completely different from Messerschmitt. While the latter was tall and youthful, Heinkel was short and elderly. Both men were in Russian eyes "big capitalists" who owned several aircraft plants in Germany. The Heinkel firm produced the twin-engine Heinkel-111, which became the chief tactical bomber of the German Air Force. In 1937 it had been used to bomb Spanish towns during the civil war; it was later used in the blitz against Poland in 1939 and, still later, against Belgium and France. The Russian guests could not know that on 22 June 1941 the Heinkel-111s would be the first German planes to drop bombs on Soviet soil. But this bomber, according to Yakovlev, was unable to defend itself well and later became a "sitting duck" for Russian fighters.

Unlike Messerschmitt, who did not conceal his aversion towards Russia and was reluctant to show off his planes, Heinkel pretended that he was telling his guests more than his government wanted him to; and at times he lowered his voice to a half-whisper, as if sharing secrets with them.

Heinkel demonstrated his latest fighter, the Heinkel-113, another machine Yakovlev and Petrov did not rate very highly. To them it looked fine in the air but seemed greatly hampered by its "bad" operational qualities.

Next, the Russians visited the Junkers company and were shown the twin-engine Junkers-88 bomber which lasted throughout the war, giving satisfactory combat and flying performance for the Luftwaffe. Yet from 1944 onwards, claims Yakovlev, pilots who flew the Ju-88 suddenly "became panicky" during encounters with Russian fighters. Henceforth they took part in bombing raids only under a "heavy cover" of Messerschmitt and Focke-Wulf fighter escorts.

The Focke-Wulf plants were run by Kurt Tank who had formerly been a pilot for Hermann Goering. At an aircraft plant in Bremen, Tank was introduced as the plant's director, chief designer and chief test pilot all in one. Of middle-height with an athletic build, Tank impressed his guests as "the typical Prussian militarist". Both his cheeks bore scars of student duels, a tradition at Prussian schools, the scar being regarded as a token of courage. As Yakovlev neatly phrased it: "The scar was the visiting-card of the true Prussian Aryan."

During the visit Kurt Tank climbed into the cabin of a trainer and demonstrated some aerobatic flying. The fact that Tank did the flying himself made a big impression on his Russian guests. Afterwards, Tank invited them to dine with him, leading the way to the workers' canteen where he offered them seats at the common table.

"Don't be surprised," Tank said. "I always eat here."

Yakovlev admits that it was an "interesting experience" to have a meal in the workers' canteen rather than in a posh directors' dining room. Tank seemed to be saying, says Yakovlev, "Look at me, I'm a democrat." But in Yakovlev's estimation, Tank was a braggart. At a diplomatic reception he told three Russian engineers, including Yakovlev, that he had designed a superb fighter plane capable of flying at 434 mph, which was exceptionally fast in those days. He promised to show it to the Russians next time they visited his plant, but he cautioned them not to tell anybody, as he expressively put his fingers to his lips.

Later on, in Bremen, Yakovlev reminded Tank of his promise. But Tank said the plane had had an accident the previous day and therefore could not be shown to the visitors. Yakovlev said he and his colleagues did not mind seeing the plane "as it was", but Tank declined. The wonderful new plane later proved to be the Focke-Wulf-190. Its speed was reported to be far less than Tank had said and, says Yakovlev, it was brought down many times by Russian fighters during the war.

General Petrov, who accompanied Yakovlev on some of their visits to German aircraft plants, says that before they left for Berlin, Stalin had told them: "It is extremely important that we know the daily output of their aircraft." Petrov found out that it was eighty-four a day. But, says Petrov, "We couldn't believe that figure because our own production barely amounted to twenty aircraft daily. But no matter how much I checked and rechecked it, the figure came out the same." This and the other information collected by Petrov and Yakovlev proved helpful to Soviet defence planning.

But it wasn't merely information the two men were after. Shown Hitler's latest warplanes, the Russians drew up a shopping list, putting one of each type of aircraft on the list to take back to Moscow. Strange as it seems, the Germans agreed to sell them the planes, with two conditions: payment in cash and permission for a German delegation to visit at least one aircraft plant in the Soviet capital. When Hitler heard about this deal he is said to have exploded in fury, ordering a full investigation and stiff penalties for those involved. Yakovlev mentions a report reaching Moscow in 1942 which said that the Luftwaffe general who approved of the Russian "shopping list" was in such trouble that he shot himself.

Yakovlev says that during his visit to Germany he got to know Hitler's war machine fairly well, especially its air force. Postulating a future war, he saw a difficult road ahead, one involving the most intensive battles. The aircraft designer knew that of the major world powers Germany's armed forces were in the eyes of many, "the perfect war machine".

Yakovlev was also disturbed by explicit anti-Semitism. He noted that the regime taught its people to hate and despise other nationalities and did this openly. He saw taxis display the sign "No Jews"; and at least some movie houses posted notices saying, "No tickets are sold to

Jews." On boulevards, Jews were assigned special benches which faced away from the walks. "*Fur Juden*", they said. The paradox of a highly cultured and prosperous nation persecuting a minority was for Yakovlev incomprehensible.

Yakovlev made another visit to Germany as a member of a high-level delegation headed by Prime Minister V. M. Molotov at the end of 1940, when he found Berlin blacked out at night and all activity stopped in anticipation of British bombers. The story goes that when an air raid occurred and Molotov was led to a shelter, a senior German official confided to him, "England is finished". Molotov is reported to have replied: "If that is so, what are British bombers doing over Berlin and why are we in this shelter?"

In 1940 serious difficulties were encountered by the Russians in operating aircraft in winter conditions. Because airfields were not then cleared of snow, skis were fitted on all planes. But the skis could not be retracted which resulted in a great loss of speed and, argued Yakovlev, such a loss could not be compensated. Stalin accepted this and decreed that the airfields must henceforth be cleared.

Three months after the invasion an Anglo-American mission arrived in Moscow – it was September 1941 – headed by Lord Beaverbrook for Britain and Averell Harriman of the United States. Yakovlev was present at the Kremlin talks. The Russians wanted to know what the Allies could give them and how soon; the Allies, says Yakovlev, wanted to know how long the Russians could hold out. Beaverbrook, he asserts, kept trying to find out to what extent the Russians could draw off German forces to the East so as to give Britain a chance to mobilize her resources for a long struggle.

As to receiving aid from the Allies, Yakovlev contends that the British were inclined to furnish Russia with Hurricane fighters, which he says were by that time "outdated" and could not stand up against the Messerschmitt. When the British were asked about the more modern Spitfire, an aviation expert attached to the British delegation named Balfour said the plane was still on the "secret list" and could not be exported. "Thus," claims Yakovlev, "the talks yielded no tangible results."

But Yakovlev paints too bleak a picture. Granted the truth about the Hurricanes, there was another quite positive side to the talks, and the reaction of Maxim Litvinov, the former Foreign Minister who acted as chief interpreter, showed how truly pleased the Russians were at the outcome. There was (according to the British) an astonishing scene in the Kremlin when, to item after item of equipment asked for by the Russians, Harriman said "Agreed" and Lord Beaverbrook said "OK", and Litvinov, unable to restrain himself, rose up and slapped his thighs. (Harriman himself recalled in my interview with him in 1975: "On our return from Moscow, Beaverbrook and I recommended maximum possible supply of war material, raw materials and food to support the Russian effort. Shipments began promptly and increased under lend-lease as our production gained momentum.")

In January 1942 Yakovlev was appointed deputy in charge of the Aviation Ministry. He now had to combine his design work with his new administrative job. Usually he spent the first half of the day at his design bureau and at an aircraft plant; and in the afternoon he would go to the ministry and work there until two or three in the morning. At that time the entire aviation industry was struggling to re-equip the Air Force with more modern planes.

Stalin, according to Yakovlev, put much faith in air power and kept abreast of aviation developments. Anything which disrupted the smooth running of his Air Force made him furious. The Supreme CIC knew the "vital statistics" of all the major warplanes, Russian and foreign. Once, when the American politician Wendell Willkie was visiting Moscow, Stalin complained to him that the United States and Britain were sending Russia inferior planes and withholding the best models. He said Russia needed more advanced aircraft than the P-40s and Hurricanes that were being sent as part of lend-lease aid. He also complained that when the Americans were about to deliver to Russia 150 advanced-model P-39 Aerocobras, a plane the Russians greatly admired, the British saw them first and grabbed the lot for themselves.

It is probable that Stalin regarded Yakovlev as his top aircraft designer*, and Yakovlev's notes on their meetings, mainly when Russia was embroiled in war, reveal aspects of Stalin's character, including his well-known irascibility.

27 April 1939. This was Yakovlev's first of many visits with Stalin at the Kremlin and he admits to being nervous. ("I shall not forget my first impression as long as I live.") Two lieutenants checked his pass, then gave a snappy salute. He mounted red-carpeted stairs and was greeted by Stalin's secretary, who asked if he was Yakovlev the designer. He was ushered into Stalin's office at 6.00 p.m. sharp, a fact that impressed him, since punctuality was not usual among his colleagues and friends. He was surprised and slightly disappointed by the simplicity of the dictator's office. It was a big room with a vaulted ceiling and plain white walls with panels of light oak. In the corner was a glass show-case with Lenin's death mask; to the left was a grandfather clock. Across the floor was a large desk with a heap of papers alongside a model of the aeroplane flown by Russian pilots (in 1937) over the North Pole to America. To the right was a large bookcase containing works by the icons of Marxism.

Stalin and his colleagues queried Yakovlev on his new bomber aircraft, the BB (for "*Blizhny Bombardirovshchik*" or short-range bomber). He remembers that Stalin used the word "miraculous" in describing the BB, as its speed was 62 mph above that of the earlier types of plane using the same engines and bomb load. Asked how the greater speed was obtained, Yakovlev said it had to do with aerodynamics and the rapid strides in aviation science. In addition, the weight of the BB had been reduced.

In the early summer of 1941, shortly before the invasion, Stalin asked Yakovlev and his colleagues how military planes were camouflaged in other countries. Learning that the Germans, Americans and British used three colours in camouflaging aircraft, so as to blend with the landscape, Stalin accused his own designers of carelessness.

---

* There were other talented aircraft designers, besides Yakovlev. They included Andrey Tupolev, Artyom Mikoyan – brother of Politburo member Anastas Mikoyan – N. N. Polikarpov, Mikhail Gurevich and Sergei Ilyushin.

Camouflage paint had been prepared, he said, but nothing was done with it. Stalin branded those involved as "irresponsible bureaucrats" and gave them three days to prepare orders concerning the use of aircraft camouflage.

Visiting the Kremlin shortly after the invasion, Yakovlev was asked by Stalin to build a fighter aircraft with a special engine. Yakovlev agreed and gave its projected speed, ceiling and range. When he asked how soon Stalin wanted it, the reply was, "With all possible speed. Could it be finished by New Year's Day?" Yakovlev explained that he lacked experience in building fighters, and besides it took the Americans two years to produce a new fighter. "But you're not an American", Stalin rejoined, and he asked Yakovlev to show what a young Russian engineer could do. "Prove your mettle, and if you do, I shall have you in for a cup of tea." (To this Yakovlev replied like a good trooper: "If it must be done we shall do it without fail.")

In March 1943 Yakovlev was invited to the Kremlin in connection with an engine built by Vladimir Klimov, the VK-107. Yakovlev reported that his colleague, S. A. Lavochkin, had produced a new model of his LA-5 which had performed well in flight tests. Stalin said that nevertheless the flying range of the plane was insufficient, adding that it must not be less than 620 miles. Then he compared British Spitfires and American Aerocobras. When Yakovlev heard Stalin quote figures for the Spitfires, he suggested that he was speaking of a reconnaissance model which had a range of over 1,240 miles but carried no guns; that this was not a fighter plane. Stalin turned on him: "I'm not a child, am I? I'm talking about the fighter, not the reconnaissance plane. Spitfires have a greater range than our fighters, and we must catch up in this respect without fail." Yakovlev, although certain that Stalin was in error, coyly held back from replying, saying only that he would "take the necessary steps."

Yakovlev was present at the Kremlin when Stalin was meeting with engineers who had worked on the heavy tank, the KV, many of which had broken down at the height of the battle at Kharkov. It turned out that the improvements on the tank demanded by the military were unfeasible. Stalin angrily charged the engineers with irresponsibility, telling them they must use their brains when setting out to improve a combat vehicle; that when they added to the thickness of the tank's armour or increased its fuel supply they should remember that the tank became heavier but was still powered by the same engine. In the case of the KV, extra weight had put too much strain on the engine and the vehicle had lost its cross-country mobility and manoeuvrability. Beware, he said, of "unwarranted and irresponsible" demands.

Dismissing the tank engineers, Stalin turned to Yakovlev, saying that the "tank problem" also concerned him. All too often, he said, there were people eager to give advice on planes, but it was the designer who would be called to account. He concluded: "It is difficult to make a good machine, and very easy to ruin it. And it is the designer whom we shall hold responsible."

In June 1943, Stalin lost his temper again when a new problem grounded the mainstay YAK fighter planes. Preparations were then underway for one of the war's biggest operations, just a few weeks off. But the YAK planes had a serious wing defect. Senior Air Force officers were shaken when the paint used on the aircraft cracked under certain atmospheric conditions, causing the fabric of the wing to peel from the frame, and resulting in many crashes. Yakovlev was summoned to the Kremlin. Never, he says, had he seen Stalin so enraged. "Our whole fighter plane force is out of commission," Stalin thundered. "There have been a dozen cases of the skin separating from the wing. The pilots are afraid to fly. How has it come about?"

Stalin then revealed that an "important operation" was being held up because it could not be carried out without the highly durable and fast YAK fighter planes. He evidently meant the impending Battle of Kursk, the biggest operation in the summer of 1943, and one of the largest of the war.

Again Stalin barked: "How did it happen? How could you produce several hundred planes with such a defect? Do you know that you have put the entire fighter plane force out of commission? Do you know what a service for Hitler you have performed? You are Hitlerites!"

There was a long silence. Yakovlev recalls that at last, after walking back and forth near his map table, Stalin calmed down and asked in a businesslike tone: "What are we going to do?"

An associate of Yakovlev who was present stammered out that all planes would be "fixed" at once.

"What do you mean? Within what time period?"

"Within two weeks," said the associate.

"You're not fooling me?"

"No, Comrade Stalin, we'll do it."

Yakovlev was aghast. He was sure the repairs would take two months. But the deadline was accepted, and Stalin, still irate, ordered a military commission to investigate and punish the offenders.

Before he left Stalin's office, Yakovlev was again rebuked, but this time in a more subdued tone: "Doesn't your self-esteem suffer? How do you feel? You're being made a fool of, your plane is being sabotaged and you just stand by."

Yakovlev parried his accuser meekly. "Comrade Stalin, I feel terrible as I fully realize the damage this misfortune has caused. But I swear that in the shortest possible time the defect will be corrected."

To put things right, Yakovlev and his design team worked without let-up and managed to complete the repairs within two or three days of the start of the famous Orel-Kursk battle of July 1943. In that battle Hitler, aiming to blast the Russian frontlines, sent up 150 bombers escorted by hundreds of fighters. Aerial fighting raged, each side using planes of advanced design. Yakovlev's team supplied the YAK-7B while Semyon Lavochkin produced the LA-5 and LA-7 attack planes. The Russians also used Ilyushin-2 attack planes. Meanwhile, the Luftwaffe was bolstered with new Focke-Wulf 190-A fighters and Henschel-129 bombers. In six days, according to Russian archives, the Luftwaffe lost over 1,000 aircraft. Hundreds of Russian planes were also reported destroyed. Yakovlev has recalled that on the third day of battle several hundred Russian fighters and bombers wiped out the Nazi main line of defence, destroying lengthy tank columns before they had a chance to engage the Russian ground forces. On 12 July the Russians began a successful counter-offensive.

*   *   *

In his memoirs, Yakovlev looks at the war and offers his own reasons for the crushing setback to the Soviet Air Force at the beginning of the war. There were:

1. Miscalculations made in the 1930s, an over-estimation of the role of the bomber force and underestimation of other types of aircraft. At the start of the war the USSR regarded heavy bombers as the main, decisive element in its air force and continued to produce them in large numbers.

2. The "evil" of complacency especially in regard to the frontiers. Hundreds of aircraft had been lined up at airfields close to the border.

3. The fact that throughout the 1930s there were only two large design bureaus in the Soviet Union, one specializing in bombers, the other in fighters; and each enjoyed a monopoly in its field.

4. The fact that aircraft plants were scattered over the European parts of the country and that nearly all of them were located west of the River Volga, with only a few of them east of the Volga and, therefore, out of reach of the Luftwaffe.

Yakovlev enters the arena of controversy by defending Stalin against widespread condemnation for failing to make good use of the two-year "breathing space" offered by the non-agression pact with Berlin, signed in August 1939. Yakovlev calls such views "irresponsible". Throughout this period, he contends, many new planes were undergoing tests and he and his colleagues prepared "midnight reports" every day for the CIC. Critics, however, blame Stalin for not doing enough and also for sending shipments of strategic materials to Nazi Germany before the war, including oil and special metals needed for armaments.

Yakovlev's aircraft received lavish praise throughout the war and he was showered with government awards. He was raised to the rank of general and also became deputy chief of aviation. If Yakovlev was stunned by the loss of so many pilots and planes at the beginning of the war, he could exult at the end of it. Then, thousands of young Russian pilots were flying the combat planes that he and his colleagues had designed; and the enemy which once seemed all-powerful in the sky had relinquished command of it.

CHAPTER 4

The Night Witch

"At first no one in the armed services wanted to give women the freedom to die," said the much-decorated veteran pilot Nadezhda ("Nadya") Popova. Hitler's armies had just invaded Russia and experienced pilots were in demand, but women were not permitted to engage in direct combat with the enemy. But when their country was assaulted by Germany, Russian women, like their men, craved the "right to fight and die" for the Motherland.

The poet Yulia Drunina, writing about the many attempts of women to enlist for frontline duty, said that the Army "did not welcome us girls with rapture" but, instead, sent them home. However, the danger in which the country found itself finally brought the government round; and Russian women achieved the right to engage the enemy in the air and on the ground – with certain conditions. For instance, women were not allowed to fight in the trenches, or to operate tanks. Nevertheless, in a short period of time, the number of Russian women at war on various fronts – including anti-aircraft gunners and gunners on merchant ships – swelled enormously and brought to mind the Amazon warriors of ancient Greek myth.*

* Women quickly attained rough equality with men. By 1944 Russian women accounted for almost 50 per cent of all military doctors and 23 per cent of the medical orderlies. Many women were snipers and thousands served in the air defence forces. Under the hail of bullets, nurses and orderlies dragged or carried thousands of wounded soldiers off the battlefield to medical aid stations. The Tatar hero-poet Mussa Jalil – fought as a soldier, was captured and executed in a Berlin prison in 1943 dedicated his poem "Death of a Girl" (written in April 1942) to a fallen nurse who had saved a hundred wounded men on the field of battle. The poem has these lines:

> A hundred other lives her young life saved
> Before it flickered out in battle gore . . .
> And yet the glory of her dying spurred
> A hundred other hearts to deeds of valour.

Popova got her chance to engage in combat and, after four years of war, she was well on her way to completing a thousand missions – an extraordinary number in any air force. Speaking to guests in her well-appointed Moscow flat on the eve of the new millennium, Popova, then seventy-seven years of age, said that women of diverse professions had been anxious to meet the enemy as equals with the men to drive the invaders from Russian soil.

Popova spoke so softly and in such a relaxed manner that it was not easy to associate the speaker with the intrepid young woman who over half a century before was climbing into the open cockpit of a small aircraft and taking off to make bombing runs against Nazi targets.

In the opening days of the invasion, the Luftwaffe destroyed over a thousand planes, many of them sitting in neat rows on the ground, while the Wehrmacht pierced the Russian state border at dozens of points from the Black to the Barents Sea. Hundreds of older-model Soviet planes were shot down. After a series of failed attempts by women to join the Air Force, a celebrated pilot and friend of Popova, Marina Raskova, finally made a direct appeal to the Kremlin and was granted permission to form three all-women bomber regiments. But there was a stipulation that women should fly light bombers and only at night. A fighter regiment was also approved. The order was entitled, "The Formation of Women's Air Force Regiments", and dated 8 October 1941, four months after Hitler's armies thundered across the Russian frontier.

Popova was ecstatic. She had had pilot training before the war, and in 1938 had also attended a school for parachutists, during which time she performed many jumps. Her friend Raskova was killed early in the war when her plane crash-landed, but Popova went on to become a seasoned bomber pilot, and was commander of the 2nd Women's Regiment from 1941–5. There was not a single male in her regiment. "The Germans knew all about us. They called us 'night witches'. In fact, the Germans spread stories that we were given special injections and pills which gave us a feline's perfect vision at night. This was nonsense, of course. What we did have were clever, educated, very talented girls. All were volunteers. We had no generals; mostly we had low ranks due to the fact that we were relatively small units compared to the giant-sized armies fighting at the front."

"Our missions," continued Popova, "were especially tough because we had open cockpits in our light bombers. Often we abandoned our parachutes because we flew so close to the ground that parachutes would have been useless." Generally the girls flew at an altitude of only 2,600 to 3,270 feet; the minimum was 1,962 feet. "If we flew lower," said Popova, "we could have destroyed our own planes with the impact of our bombs."

The plane the girls used – the PO-2 – was not originally a bomber but a trainer. It was a small two-seater biplane made of plywood and canvas with a maximum speed of 110 mph. The planes, nicknamed "ducks", had no armour protection and very primitive navigational equipment. But when modified and given special bomb racks, the PO-2 could carry a bomb load of nearly 800 pounds. It also had a few advantages. A PO-2 was easy to control and was steady in flight. It did not need special airfields but could land on a road, a village street or the edge of a forest. Due to its slow speed it was rarely used in daylight as it would be easy prey for the much faster German fighters; but at night its modest speed and ability to fly at very low altitudes made it possible for these girls to hit objectives in the immediate enemy rear with great accuracy. The PO-2 also had a unique advantage. At a large angle of attack and with the engine stalling, the little biplane could dive and gain speed as it came close to the ground, then nose up at full throttle, thereby causing pursuing enemy fighters to crash.

But although the manoeuvrable PO-2 was the "favourite brainchild" of its designer, Nikolai Polikarpov, the open cockpits were a serious drawback in the long winter months. Popova recalled: "It was so cold flying this plane in winter that our cheeks and nose often froze. Of course, we wore fur-lined helmets, and we had fur boots and gloves. But still our fingers and legs ached when temperatures dropped well below zero." Popova remembered that during some flights the girls had to use their bare hands to tear free the bombs that would get stuck under the ice-covered wings. The problem was that sometimes the air regiment used bombs that had been captured from the enemy and their lugs didn't properly fit the PO-2 bomb racks.

"It was," said Popova with much understatement, "not an easy job."

There was, incidentally, no discrimination in the ration of vodka between fighting men and women. Before a mission, each woman pilot and navigator was entitled to a small glass of vodka.

Popova remembered "those helpless moonless nights. . . . We had no special equipment for night flying and so we dreaded clouded nights or terribly bad weather. And almost every time we flew we had to sail through a wall of enemy fire while the Germans tried to blind us with their searchlights."

Particularly tough was the battle for the Caucasus. After countless aerial battles in the region, the women pilots were assigned to what they called "maximum nights" – that is, very difficult nights when it was necessary to fly as many sorties as possible, sometimes up to fifteen. Later, in Poland, the women flew more sorties than that: Popova recalled one particular night, in December 1944, when she and her fellow pilots flew up to eighteen sorties each, and the regiment as a whole flew 300. They took off from a temporary airstrip located a bare four miles from the front line, taking as many bombs as possible with no room for parachutes. The mechanics, who were also girls, prepared each aircraft for a new flight in a turn-around of five to seven minutes. "That night we really had our hands full." Several times her plane was hit by German bullets. Once she counted forty-two holes in her PO-2. Luckily the engine was not hit; otherwise she would have crashed. A number of times the fast-flying Messerschmitts attacked them but they managed to elude their pursuers. Popova admitted that her greatest fear was being wounded and forced to crash-land in enemy-occupied territory. For her, to be killed was one thing, but to be wounded and taken prisoner was far more dangerous.

"I lost many of my close friends in the war, especially in the Taman area on the Black Sea," said Popova. "I remember once we were successfully bombing the German positions there. I was the lead plane and there were four enemy fighters following me; and then the Messerschmitts hit four of our own planes that were behind me. It was the first time the Germans used the speedy Messerschmitt fighters against us 'ducks'. At that time, thirty-seven of our girls perished in the air." Today many city streets are named after these heroic women pilots.

Nadya Popova's Moscow flat is lined with photographs of her fellow pilots and navigators, including many who fell in battle. Several photographs show a stunning nineteen-year-old pilot standing smartly alongside members of her regiment. It is Nadya Popova herself. There are also pictures and models of various wartime aircraft as well as photos of her late pilot-husband. On various shelves are souvenirs of her postwar visits to countries in Europe and Asia.

Here is Popova recalling one of many perilous night flights:

It was a very dangerous mission in the middle of the second year of the war. But as a result we destroyed two bridges, a train with military equipment, and several artillery positions, in addition to bombing German troop concentrations. At our headquarters our radio told us that our cities were still being captured one after another by the invading armies. So for us girls it was a very depressing period. After completing a number of night missions, I was called to HQ in the morning and asked to take on a special mission. Our high command needed more information about the position of the front line which was not far from Rostov-on-the-Don, near the Azov Sea. My task was to check on the location of the enemy, identify the various kinds of units, and then write up a report. Yes, you can call it an intelligence mission. I flew at a very low altitude, 320 feet maybe 650 feet, which was dangerous. I was skirting the shore around the north-eastern corner of the Azov Sea. I saw lots of birds and ducks. The tension was very high. I was observing the ground but also craning my neck to see around me because enemy planes were always hovering about. Suddenly, one of the struts between the wings was hit by a duck. I felt the impact, thinking it was a German shell. But it was a duck. So I reached out and dislodged the unfortunate bird and tossed it away. I continued my mission, jotting down information on the map which was on my lap. Our own troops were behind me, there was a river in front of me and a small bridge spanning the river that was loaded with marching troops. It was the summer of 1942. At first I thought they were friendly troops. But when I came nearer they turned their machine-guns in my direction and started shooting at me. I saw tanks with swastikas on their sides. Quickly I banked to avoid being shot down and managed to get away. I put all this data on the map: troops, tanks, artillery. Yes I was jittery. But I had no time to think of danger. Only when I landed and reported to HQ, did exhaustion overtake me. I sat down on the ground, took off my helmet and told my commander that, somehow, I was still alive . . . As the Russian saying goes, maybe I was "born in a *rubashka*" [a Russian blouse]. Which means, to be born under a lucky star.

Anyway, three hours passed after that mission and I had collapsed on my bed. But again I was called to HQ. I trotted over and the commanding officer told me I had been chosen for another special mission. This time I was told to deliver a message to our troops. As I approached my plane, still feeling fatigue, I was thinking that maybe this time I might not return.

I took off and landed at an airstrip close to our troops. There were no effective communications then, so you had to land your plane and personally hand over the orders or other messages to the troop commanders. All went well. But on taking off I saw two Messerschmitts flying above me. Because of the background of wheat fields, it was easy for them to spot me. Just then I heard the clatter of machine-guns firing at me. I quickly turned left and right to elude their fire. I was then flying at an altitude of only 320 feet. But they hit my wing and I saw a spurt of flame. It was not, thank God, the petrol tank. I was really lucky. I flew straight back to my airstrip and, landing at the end of it, jumped from the plane before it came to a halt, meanwhile watching the flames envelope the fuselage. I ran as far from the plane as possible to avoid the blast. Meanwhile my plane continued moving slowly and the Messerschmitts, still following me, kept on shooting, finally completely destroying my little PO-2 plane. But I wasn't in it.

In the autumn of 1942 Popova was ordered to bomb an enemy crossing on the River Terek, near Mozdok. Her regiment was based in the Cossack village of Assinovskaya. The crossing was carefully guarded by the enemy who had numerous anti-aircraft guns and searchlights. The route took her over snow-covered mountain peaks, some of the highest in Europe. In preparing for the flight, Popova and her navigator, Yekaterina ("Katya") Ryabova, made a thorough study of weather conditions. The girls paid special attention to the fact that at that time of year it was nearly always very cloudy over the mountain passes. It was risky to fly under the clouds because they hung low over the mountain peaks. So for safety reasons pilots were compelled to fly above the clouds.

"What if we start to climb right at the airfield?" thought Popova. She mentioned this to her navigator and they agreed to this procedure. The night was very dark and cold. They took off, gained the necessary altitude and followed a set course. About half an hour elapsed. "We are approaching the pass," the navigator, Ryabova, said. This meant they were close to their target. But the cloud cover was becoming heavier. Ryabova stopped reading the map and shouted:

"Visibility is zero!"

Although they couldn't see the ground, according to their calculations they were over the target. Again they checked their data. They couldn't be mistaken. Meanwhile, the wind was slashing the canvas covering of their plane. With the ground concealed in darkness, precision bombing was out of the question. Popova tried different altitudes as the girls searched for an opening in the clouds. Only the smallest gap was needed. Again and again they changed altitude, veered, and began circling again. Popova's nerves were strained to the limit. Her eyes hurt from constantly peering into the darkness. Should they drop the bombs at random? But that way they might do only minimal damage, if any, to the enemy. But their task was to destroy the bridge crossing. Both girls felt they must carry out their assignment without fail.

Once again they searched for an opening and at long last found one Popova dived through it. She and Ryabova saw a barely visible ribbon of water traversed by the thin lines of the bridge. At that instant shell bursts were heard. Unmindful, Popova steered the plane to the target. The PO-2 dropped its bombs and the girls returned to their base.

Early in 1943 a major operation was taking place on the Taman Peninsula, close to the Crimea coast, between the Black and the Azov seas. Russian sailors who were fighting on land badly needed supplies and Popova's "night witches" were called in to help.

Marshal Georgi Zhukov, who was the Deputy Supreme Commander-in-Chief, has commented on the importance of this operation: "The elimination of the enemy on the Taman Peninsula was of great significance." In his memoirs Zhukov mentions the "heroic" sailors of the Black Sea Fleet who were fighting, along with the infantry, on a small Taman bridgehead against the Wehrmacht's well-equipped force of up to 200,000 men.

"There was nothing to do but help our sailors," said Popova. She recalled taking on complex missions with the Black Sea Fleet which involved eight crews from her regiment. "We were at Gelenzhik aerodrome on the shores of the Black Sea. It was very difficult flying there on dark nights. On the right side were forests and mountains; on the left the Black Sea. There were very few places to land. If you were shot down you had to plop into the sea.

"Although we had special life jackets, they were really a joke. You could not rely on them. If you landed in the water, the life belt couldn't keep you right side up; you might find your legs sticking up and your head under the water, like a duck upside down. Thank God, I was not shot down over the water."

Popova's orders were to supply the sailors. Bomb loads were

replaced with special canisters filled with water, ammunition, food and medicines – whatever was needed to fight on the ground. "We saw radio messages saying our sailors were out of fresh water and foodstuffs and their ammo was almost gone. So our urgent task was to take these supplies to them. Our boys were near Novorossisk harbour on the Black Sea. In flight, there was water on one side of us and mountains behind us. Turkey was across the sea – about 250 miles – to the south. The difficulty was having to drop supplies with pin-point accuracy at night. This depended first of all on ability and experience. It was reported by radio that our soldiers occupied only several buildings in the city. The rest were in German hands. A far greater force of the enemy was squeezing the Russian sailors and soldiers on the tip of the peninsula, which was called *Malaya Zemlya* ["Little Land"].

"So first of all it was necessary to find where our boys were, which position was ours, which the enemy's. Before the mission, we looked at the map and saw how much of the city of Novorossisk was ours. When we flew low we were immediately shot at. So we climbed to a higher altitude and approached the front lines. I then reduced speed and came close to the ground above the buildings where our sailors were supposed to be. I asked Katya, my navigator, if those were our buildings. Suddenly I saw a blinking light on the ground. It was 10 p.m. I said, let's drop our canisters here. I knew that if I made a mistake by only a dozen or so metres the canisters would fall into enemy hands. Do you understand? I checked everything and we were successful. But it was another hard night."

Popova thanked the stars for helping guide her mission. "Luckily a few stars were out. But, you know, there is such a thing as night vision. So that if you fly very low you can faintly make out the roads and buildings, that is, the outlines of the buildings. Also, because there was a constant crossfire between the opposing forces, we saw flashes of light from which you could roughly identify ground positions. But all the time my navigator was shouting: 'We are too low! We may hit the ground. We are too low! Only 100 metres . . .' Still, we managed to drop our well-padded canisters on target."

A few seconds later they were not so lucky.

"After the drop the Germans started shooting at us. I put on speed and tried manoeuvring to avoid being hit but bullets struck my right wing. We wanted to get out of there fast but enemy fire increased against us. Their fire was accurate, too. A bullet ricocheted off my helmet and hit my hand. I thought: If I fall into the hands of the enemy, it is curtains for me. I must land anywhere except on the German side. But the only 'safe place' was the Black Sea. I veered in that direction but a German ship started shooting at me. So I continued flying low, along the beach, and our luck held out: we reached our aerodrome. I remember that the base was camouflaged, that there were no lights. But suddenly three bonfires were lit and I landed near one of them. Switching off the engine, I took off my goggles but remained in the cockpit; I was too numb to climb out.

"After a minute a colonel arrived from our main air base and stepped on our wing. He knocked on my helmet and said, 'Popova, Popova, thank you, thank you! The sailors say thank you. At 10 past ten they got the supplies.' At that moment the tears came to my eyes."

The next morning Popova looked at the damaged wing and counted forty-two bullet holes. Turning to her navigator, she said: "Katya, my dear, we will live long."

I met Nadya Popova three times. After our first meeting I was invited to her flat to see her collection of war books and photographs. Her library also contained the collected works of dozens of Russian and foreign authors, mainly classics of the nineteenth and early twentieth centuries. In addition there were seven or eight thick photo albums and she showed me all of them.

After the war Popova married a pilot who, like herself, was awarded the highest combat medal, the gold star. For almost two decades Popova held a job as flying instructor. Many of her fellow women pilots married and had children, and some, like Popova, became flying instructors, while their children became doctors, journalists, diplomats and, of course, pilots.

Popova, who devoted her youth to the defence of the Motherland, was sensitive to unfeeling criticisms of Russia by foreigners, and understandably saddened by the deterioration of Russian society that was so apparent in the 1990s.

"I belong," she said, "to the generation of Russian people, many of whom gave their lives in the war, who believed our sacrifices ensured the future happiness of our people. We were born in the twentieth century. We are students of that time. We lived with hope, with honest labour."

She showed me an article written by a close friend, Yevgenia ("Zhenya") Zhigulenko, whom she called "a symbol of our whole regiment". Zhigulenko was a pilot-commander who logged a total of 968 missions. Twice shot down, she too was awarded a gold star hero medal. In the article, Zhenya remembered the shattering effect of the war. "Flying was very frightening. After completing a mission your teeth would chatter, your knees would shake and sometimes you didn't even have the energy to talk. We would take off ten or more times a night." After the war Zhenya became a script writer and film director. In the article she said that many years after the war, in her dreams, she would find herself aloft once again and under enemy fire. But the dream was more frightening than the real thing because, she said, in the dreams she was helpless. In a real-life situation, she was able to operate the controls of her plane.

Over coffee, Nadya Popova produced a copy of the official document that had authorized the formation of the three all-women regiments of night bombers and the one fighter regiment. It reads, in translation:

Order of the Peoples Commissar of Defence Number 0099, 8 October 1941, Moscow.

Subject Formation of Women's Air Regiments.

1. For the purpose of utilizing women in the air force, I order the formation and preparation for combat, first, of the 586 Fighter Air Regiment using the YAK-1 plane.
2. The 587th Air Regiment of bombers using the SU-2 plane.

3. The 588th Air Regiment of bombers using the U2 plane.
4. The commander of the air force will complete the above-mentioned air regiments with the planes, pilots and specialists from women volunteers, and receive assistance from various public organizations.
5. The training of the pilots using the new planes will be organized and carried out along with the formation of the regiments. The volunteers will first be assembled in Moscow. Navigators will be trained by the commander of the 2nd lvanovskoye Higher Navigators' School.
6. The main suppliers of equipment to the armed forces, and the heads of the various branches and departments of the armed forces, shall ensure that the women's regiments are outfitted with all necessary supplies.

"The Germans called us 'night witches'," said Popova. "Yes, we practised our 'witchcraft' almost from the first to the last days of war."

CHAPTER 5

Stalin's Son

When war broke out, Yakov Djugashvili, Stalin's son by his first wife, rang up his father and told him he was leaving for the front. He was then a Senior Lieutenant in the Red Army. There was an absence of small talk. Stalin was laconic. "Go and fight!" he said. A month later Yakov was taken prisoner by a fast-moving German panzer group.

From all accounts he conducted himself honourably during his captivity, refusing to cooperate with the Germans or do anything to dishonour his country or family. There is evidence Yakov died a hero.*

Yakov Djugashvili had received few privileges in life; his accomplishments derived mainly from his own exertions. He was a serious youth, interested in Western as well as Russian literature. He knew several foreign languages and was said to be able to read books in the original English, French or German. He held a university diploma in what would be the equivalent of liberal arts or the humanities.

For Russian soldiers the worst nightmare was to be taken prisoner by the Germans. Time and again their political instructors (commis-

---

* Some of this information comes from Stalin's grandson, Evgeni Djugashvili, an historian, who is Yakov's son. I first met him in Moscow in November 1999. Evgeni says that Stalin in his relations with his three children was "even-handed", although he was slightly more attentive to his daughter, Svetlana, especially during her adolescence; that he was too busy with "state affairs" to give much time to his sons, Yakov and Vasily. Vasily, the younger son, became an Air Force general after the war, quarrelled with his father, and, after Stalin's death, his irascible temper, drinking, and womanizing led to frequent clashes with his superiors until his own death in 1962. One of Zhukov's Air Marshals, Sergei Rudenko, who knew Vasily well, told me in an interview in 1985 that Vasily took advantage of his father's name and position and "ruined many lives".

sars) would harangue the soldiers about the folly, even sinfulness, of surrender. It was not bravado that led many soldiers to shoot themselves with their last cartridge when faced with capture. A book of diaries and letters of German soldiers describes an episode that occurred during the early part of the war. Two Russian officers smoking *papirosas* (Russian cigarettes) were slowly moving towards German lines through a crop field. When ordered to stop and raise their hands, they shot each other through the mouth. At the frontier fortress at Brest, a last shout was often heard: "Good-bye, comrades! Avenge my death!" – followed by a shot.

But Yakov, a victim of concussion, was already a German prisoner. In the opening weeks of war tens of thousands of men like himself, hungry, sleepless, wounded, many shell-shocked, had been taken prisoner. If he thought about it (and Yakov had ample time for thinking) he understood that being a POW was tantamount to a death sentence. Being under constant surveillance, escape for him was simply out of the question. No doubt he knew his captors would try to use him for propaganda purposes.

But there was no way Yakov would cooperate with the Germans, according to his son. Says Yevgeni Djugashvili: "Yakov was steeped in patriotism, not only love for his own republic [Georgia] but for 'greater Russia'. When Yakov was captured, Stalin was sure his son, who'd grown up in Georgia, would never betray his Motherland, that he was a true son of Georgia. Stalin was himself a Georgian. His first wife, Yekaterina Svanidze, was a Georgian. Yakov came from a pure Georgian line. So he was reared in patriotism. And devotion to the [Russian] Motherland was in his blood . . ." (The most famous example of Georgian loyalty to the Russian state was that of Prince Pyotr Bagration, a hero-general who was mortally wounded in fighting against Napoleon during the invasion of Russia in 1812. Bagration told his men: "Russia is our mother. With your breast you must bar the path of the enemy.")

After the Germans had lined up their prisoners, including Lieutenant Yakov Djugashvili, an SS officer barked: "All Commissars, Communists and Jews, step forward!"

A few men broke ranks. The SS man stepped up to one prisoner and stuck a pistol in his belly.

"Why don't you step out? You're a Jew."

"I'm not," was the reply.

Then some men in the ranks shouted: "That's Stalin's son. He's a Georgian."

Yakov, with his black hair, black eyes and dark jowls, had the handsome, swarthy look of a majority of Caucasian males. Due to the Nazi racial policy, dark-complexioned prisoners fared the worst. In any case, tens of thousands of POWs, no matter what their complexion, whether Russian, Ukrainian or Georgian, fell victim to execution squads. Some of these soldiers, says German historian Hans-Adolf Jacobsen, were killed because they were circumcised or had "certain facial features" that doomed them.

As a prisoner, Yakov's position became progressively more desperate. According to some accounts, he felt that by being taken captive he had failed his father and, therefore, even if the Germans released him (that is, exchanged him for a German officer held by the Russians) he would return home in disgrace. To Stalin, the very idea of surrender was odious. The military commissars – the political indoctrination officers – not only sought to lift the fighting spirit of soldiers, but always spoke of the harmfulness of surrender.

But in the initial stage of the war large numbers of Russian soldiers could not escape the powerful enemy pincers and were compelled to surrender. In the first two years of the war the biggest losses in terms of POWs occurred in the following battles: Belostok-Minsk, August 1941 – 323,000; Uman, August, 1941 – 103,000; Smolensk-Rostavl, August 1941 – 348,000; Gomel, August 1941– 30,000; Demyansk, September 1941 – 35,000; Kiev, September 1941 – 665,000; Luga-Leningrad, September 1941 – 20,000; Melitopol, October 1941 – 100,000; Vyazma, October 1941 – 662,000; Kerch, November 1941 – 100,000; Kharkov, May 1942 – 207,000. The vast majority perished in POW camps.

Shortly before Yakov's capture, the Germans had dropped propaganda leaflets over Russian lines urging troops to defect and not to lose their lives "for nothing". One of these leaflets said: "Avoid senseless bloodshed in the interest of Jews and Commissars! If you abandon the defeated Red Army and cross to the side of the German Armed Forces, German soldiers and officers will render assistance to give you a good welcome, feed and arrange a job for you."

After Yakov's capture, the Goebbels propaganda office put out a new leaflet:

To Red Army soldiers. Follow the example of Stalin's son! He has surrendered and is a prisoner. He is alive and feels fine. Why do you want to die when already the son of your leader gave himself up and is our prisoner?

Peace to your tormented Motherland!

Stick your bayonets in the earth!

Yevgeni Djugashvili says the Germans moved Yakov from one concentration camp to another, that the German propagandists even created a "false Yakov" in the camps. "The Germans found many Yakov look-alikes in each camp. Our intelligence service actually lost trace of the real Yakov because there were too many false 'German' Yakovs."

A German officer who interrogated Stalin's son wrote: "Yakov Djugashvili knows the English, German and French languages and gives the impression of being a highly intelligent person."

The following is a verbatim record of the interrogation of Stalin's son made by Major Walter Holters on 18 July 1941:

Holters: Did you surrender of your own accord or were you taken by force?

Stalin's son: I was taken by force.

Holters: In what way?

Stalin's son: On July 12 our unit was surrounded. There was heavy bombing. I tried to reach my men but was stunned by a blast. I would have shot myself if I could.

Holters: Do you believe that your troops still have a chance of reversing the war?

Stalin's son: The war is still far from ended.

Holters: And what if we shortly get hold of Moscow?

Stalin's son: You will never take Moscow.

Holters: Why are there commissars in the Red Army?

Stalin's son: To raise fighting spirit and give political guidance.

Holters: Do you believe that the new government in Russia is better suited to the needs of workers and peasants than the Tsar's government?

Stalin's son: I have no doubts at all about that.

Holters: When did you last speak to your father?

Stalin's son: I rang him up on 22 June 1941. Upon hearing that I was leaving for the front he said, "Go and fight."

SS officers made several futile attempts to enlist Yakov's cooperation. They asked him to write to his father or at least send him a radio message. Yakov refused. So counterfeit letters were prepared giving glowing accounts of "Nazi hospitality". The following is an example:

"Battery commander Senior Lieutenant Yakov Djugashvili has written to his father Joseph Stalin: 'Dear father, I'm in a prison camp. I am well. I will soon be transferred to an officers' camp in Germany. I'm treated well. Wishing you good health, regards to everyone. Yakov'."

A photograph, taken at this time, shows an unshaven Yakov wearing a full-length coat. He appears to be talking freely to two German officers. This particular photo was widely disseminated and used as propaganda.

A truer picture of Yakov emerged from another interrogation, this one carried out by intelligence officer Wilfred Strick who said that all attempts to gain advantages from Yakov had failed. Strick gave this description of Yakov: "He has a fine intelligent face with sharp Georgian features. He is self-possessed and carries himself well. He last spoke to his father over the phone before leaving for the front. He flatly rejects any compromise between capitalism and socialism. He refuses to believe in Germany's final victory."

The Germans brought Yakov to Berlin where he was apparently put in the hands of Dr Joseph Goebbels' Ministry of Propaganda. As before, attempts to "turn" Yakov failed. Then, in December 1941 he was sent to a camp for ordinary prisoners. In the archives may be found the recollections of ex-prisoner Alexander Uzinsky: "Yakov had lost weight, was black in the face and a heavy dismal look came from his sunken eyes. He was wearing a much worn greatcoat and a torn army shirt. One of the camp guards came up to him with a bucket of red paint and began to paint the letters 'SU' [*Sowjetunion*] on his chest, back, shoulders and even on his trousers. Stalin's son said for all to hear: 'Let him paint the words – The Soviet Union is my motherland!' This defiance shocked the guards. Such words were usually punishable by death."

Yakov was transferred to a camp in Nuremberg, then to one in Lubeck where a large number of Polish officers were held captive. Friendly Poles shared some of their Red Cross food packages with Yakov once a month. The Germans denied to Red Army officers and non-commissioned officers any of the limited privileges granted to other prisoners under the Geneva Convention on POWs. However, some Polish orderlies, taking pity on Yakov, gave him a newer coat to replace a ragged one, and a pair of boots. A Polish officer remembers Yakov saying that if he never saw Russia again, to get word to his father that he never betrayed his country.★

In February 1943 the Battle of Stalingrad ended in victory for the Russians and the surrender of Field Marshal Friedrich Paulus and his Sixth Army. History books say that Berlin secretly offered to ex-

★ Regarding Soviet prisoners in Nazi camps, some observers contend that the USSR totally abandoned its soldiers who became prisoners of Nazi Germany, refusing even to send them food through the Red Cross. But the problem was a complex one. Would the Nazi regime have allowed Russian POWs to receive food parcels even if Moscow had sent them? All indications point to the contrary. First, the extermination of a large part of the Russian people was the keystone of Hitler's Eastern campaign. For this purpose, the Nazis set up an "industry for killing" both Soviet civilians and soldiers. The twenty-odd Nazi concentration camps set up mainly on German and Polish territory had about 700 branches, close to 100 of which were situated on occupied Soviet territory. Some four million Russian prisoners-of-war and more than six million civilians died of hunger, torture, or ended up in camp crematoria. It is thus clear that food parcels sent from Russia to the Third Reich for distribution to Russian POWs would have been stolen.

change Stalin's son for Paulus. Stalin, according to the conventional view, spurned the offer, declaring, "Soldiers are not exchanged for marshals."

Not so, says Yakov's son, Yevgeni. He concedes that an exchange offer was made by Berlin and that it was rejected. But, he asserts, Stalin's actual retort was, "And what would other fathers say?"

The death of Yakov in April 1943 was witnessed by Harry Naujocks, a German Communist and prisoner at the Sachsenhausen prison camp. This is his report:

> Yakov Djugashvili (Stalin) was haunted by his hopeless position. He was often depressed and refused food. He was terribly affected by Stalin's statement that there were 'no prisoners of war, only traitors to their homeland' which was repeatedly broadcast over the camp radio. Maybe this prompted him to the fateful act. He began looking for a way to die – and found it. After dark on April 14, 1943, Yakov refused to go back to the barracks and started running into the "dead zone" (where the guards had orders to shoot without warning). The sentry fired. Yakov died instantly. Then his body was thrown onto the electric fence. They said the prisoner had, "Attempted to escape." The remains of Stalin's son were taken to the camp crematorium.

Few Russian POWs fared any better. According to the German historian Jacobsen, of some four million Russian prisoners, more than three million perished in the POW camps.

Yakov's half-sister, Svetlana Alliluyeva, who fled to the West after her father's death in 1953, says that in the summer of 1945, shortly after the war ended, Stalin broke a long silence over Yakov. The Germans, her father told her, had "shot Yasha". He said that a letter of condolence had arrived from an eye-witness, an officer who had been a fellow prisoner with Yakov. Svetlana says her father took the news badly and could say only a few words.

Here is a concise summary of Yakov's life by his son: "The tragedy of Yakov was that he did not have a mother's love. Stalin's first wife, Yekaterina Svanidze, died when her son, Yakov, was two months old. She was twenty-four. So he took milk from another woman. As to his father's love and care, he received just a little bit. His father as the leader of the nation was very busy and could not pay much attention to Yakov."

While Stalin was still alive a Georgian film maker produced a two-part feature film about the war, with an heroic account of Yakov before and after being taken prisoner. Stalin rejected the film. After seeing a private showing, he said, according to Yevgeni: "The time is not ripe for showing this. Delete all episodes that mention Yakov."

CHAPTER 6

Zoya's Execution

In order to crush the fighting spirit of the Russians, the Wehrmacht set up a reign of terror in the occupied territories But instead of cowing the people, the terror fuelled their resolve, causing a rising scale of resistance behind enemy lines. Partisan fighting became the leading form of resistance. There were more than 6,000 partisan units operating during the war with a total strength exceeding one million. Of this number, one young girl became a legend in the eyes of her comrades when they learned about her fate at the hands of the Nazis.

She was Zoya Kosmodemyanskaya. The name is derived, like many Russian surnames, from the Christian names of saints – Kosma and Demyan – (Cosmos and Damian).

Zoya was born on 13 September 1923 in the village of Osinnovy Gayi, in the province of Tambov, known for its muddy roads, fine horses and wolf packs. Russian writings about Zoya do not fail to mention her "peasant origin" but her mother, Lyubov Timofeyevna, was a schoolteacher and Zoya herself was remarkably well read for an eighteen year old. In one of the notebooks she left behind, there were written names of writers and titles of books, with crosses against those she had read. They included Pushkin, Lermontov, Tolstoy, Dickens, Byron, Moliere, Shakespeare, Goethe. She had copied out quotations from some of the writers she admired:

"Everything in man should be beautiful: his face, his clothes, his soul and his thoughts." (Chekhov)

"In character, manners; style, in everything – it is the simple that is beautiful." (Longfellow)

"Lies are the religion of slaves and bosses . . . Truth is the god of the free man!" And: "A book is, perhaps, the most intricate, the greatest miracle of all the miracles created by man on his road to the happiness and might of the future." (Gorky)

"Reading a good book for the first time is like gaining a great sincere friend. To read what you have read again is like meeting an old friend once more. To finish reading a good book is like parting with one's best friend, and who knows whether one will meet him again." (A Chinese adage)

Zoya had copied out large extracts from *Faust*, including these lines, a chorus in praise of Euphorion:

> My slogan now –
> Is battle, the cry of victory.
> Yes! On my wings
> I will soar there!
> I will soar into the fire of war,
> Into battle I will soar.

There were also quotations from *War and Peace, Anna Karenina* and *Hamlet*. And as if she were able to divine her own tragic end, she wrote an essay about the Russian folk hero Ilya Muromets that included these lines: "The people treat him with love and affection, and weep for him when he is wounded in battle. When the 'wicked infidel' overcomes him, the Russian earth itself gives him strength." And on another page of the same essay: "And now, centuries later, the people's desires and aspirations have come true: our land has its own worthy defenders from among the people . . . Not for nothing does the song say, 'We are born to make legends true.' We are making wonderful legends come true, and the people sing of their heroes with the same deep love as they once sang of Ilya Muromets."

Zoya was fond of Beethoven's music, according to her mother, and never missed a chance to hear him. Goethe's war poem (from *Egmont*) which Beethoven set to music, she knew by heart and often recited. After reading *Othello* she jotted down this comment:

"*Othello* depicts the struggle of man for the lofty ideals of truth, of moral purity; *Othello*'s theme is the victory of genuine and great human emotion."

In her notebook there was also a passage of the kind calculated to touch the soul of every true Russian: "I love Russia, my heart bleeds for her, and I cannot even imagine myself anywhere but in Russia." (Saltykov-Shchedrin)

Zoya's mother felt "a blow straight at the heart" when after her daughter's death she read on the last page of a notebook the words from *Hamlet*:

"Adieu, adieu, adieu! Remember me!"

It had all begun for Zoya at a partisan training camp in the autumn of 1941. (Some of the following details were supplied by Klava Miloradova, Zoya's friend and a fellow partisan.) There were ten girls in the room all volunteers. Although they were in the same class, studying weapons and explosives, they did not know one another by their real names. Zoya was using the name "Tanya".

It was in this period that Moscow was in the greatest danger and volunteers were being sent through the frontlines from Moscow to assist the partisan detachments. The girls were called up one by one before a Major Sprogis, who asked them: "Are you frightened? You won't lose your nerve now, will you?" And he added: "You still have a chance of quitting." But he emphasized, "Afterwards it will be too late. Now, please come into my room one at a time."

Each girl went into the major's room where they were questioned and a final decision was made. Zoya, who had just celebrated her eighteenth birthday was one of the first to enter the major's room and she came out in just a few minutes in high spirits. After most of the girls had "passed the test", revolvers were distributed and the members divided into groups.

A few days later, on 4 November, several small groups drove out to Volokolamsk, west of Moscow, where they would cross the front line and penetrate into the rear of the enemy. Their job was to lay mines on the Volokolamsk Highway. Each group consisted of two girls.

Before parting the girls buoyed themselves up. Zoya said: "If we fall let's fall like heroes!" Zhenya replied: "How else?"

In the dead of night, very quietly, they crossed the front line. Then Zoya and her new partner, Klava, were sent out on reconnaissance. Full of tense excitement, they had not gone more than a hundred paces when two German motorcycles appeared from nowhere, speeding past within a few yards. The girls got on their knees, mindful of the rustle of the autumn leaves. After 2 miles they came back into the dense forest to report that the coast was clear. Now a group of boys went ahead and began to lay mines as the girls kept watch. Even before they finished the job they heard the roar of engines getting louder and louder. Everyone ran, crouching, into the woods. They had hardly stopped running when an explosion boomed out. Everything flared up for a moment. Then silence descended. A second explosion rang out, and another.

The different groups made off through the thick of the forest and stopped to rest only when it was light. Then because it was National Day, 7 November, they congratulated each other. At midday Zoya and Klava went to a main road used by armoured columns and scattered sharp spikes – they would pierce the enemy's tyres. The girls worked efficiently together. They came to be regarded as excellent scouts. But they were warned not to forget for a moment that they were at work behind enemy lines.

The following day they were given a new assignment. The composition of the groups changed and the girls were becoming friends. The group commander was a man named "Boris", a former teacher, who was calm, spoke little, and as might be expected of a teacher, was rigidly prim. Sometimes he would tell the boys when he heard them using obscenities: "Boys, you can swear your heads off, but you're none the wiser for it, and neither is anybody else."

The young partisans now went deeper into the enemy's rear with bottles of petrol and grenades hanging from their belts. This time they had to fight their way out but no one was hurt. But the next day they had their first real battle when they were caught in a crossfire.

Someone said in an excited whisper: "Lie down!" Everyone

dropped to the ground. When the firing ceased the scouts crawled as far as possible from the danger zone, only then realizing that three of their members were missing.

"I'll go back and see if there are any wounded," Zoya told the commander.

"Whom will you take with you?" asked Boris.

"I'll go alone."

"Wait. Let the Germans quiet down a bit."

"No, it will be too late then."

"All right, go."

Zoya disappeared into the forest. The others waited and waited but she did not return. An hour passed, then another and a third. Everyone thought Zoya had been captured or killed. But just as dawn was breaking, she came back, loaded with weapons, her hands covered with blood, her face darkened by exhaustion. She reported that their three comrades were dead. She had crawled up to them and taken their weapons. One of the dead was a girl, Vera, and she had taken from a pocket a photograph of her mother and a little notebook containing poetry. From another, Alexei, she recovered some letters.

The group made a camp-fire deep in the forest from dry fire twigs which made no smoke. They warmed their hands and heated tinned food. As there was no water anywhere, they were hounded by thirst.

Now danger increased. They moved on to the village of Petrishchevo where enemy forces were concentrated. As they went they cut communication wires. At night they reached the village which was surrounded by a dense forest. The commander detailed one of the boys for sentry duty. The others sat around a camp-fire, eating their rations: half a crust, a lump of sugar, a small piece of dried fish. The first snow began to fall. They seemed hemmed in by huge snow-covered fir trees.

Zoya began to recite a poem by Mayakovsky, about building an enormous garden town. He was one of her favourite poets.

After the new area had been reconnoitred, Boris told Zoya: "You'll stay here on duty." Zoya objected.

"Please send me out on a mission."

"Only boys will be sent on missions."

"Difficulties ought to be shared equally. Please!"

Zoya's "please" was a softly-phrased demand. Boris gave in and sent her on her mission – into the heart of the enemy-occupied village. She took along her Russian revolver, called a "Nagant". When she returned she seemed transfigured. She had set fire to a stable and a house. Others remember her saying, "You feel completely different when you are doing a job like this, right in the lair of the enemy."

With the commander's permission she went to the village of Petrischevo a second time. After being absent for three days all hope was lost that she would return.

Pyotr Lidov, a journalist, visited Petrischevo a few weeks after Zoya's death, when a Russian counter-offensive regained the village. He spoke to all the villagers who knew anything about Zoya. While the tracks were still fresh he uncovered the following details of her death.

In Petrishchevo from ten to fifteen German soldiers were billeted in every house. The owners were obliged to huddle in corners or on a shelf over the stove. Food supplies in the village were confiscated. It is said that the greediest of the lot was the Nazi interpreter who subjected the inhabitants to indignities, often beating young and old indiscriminately.

One night someone cut the telephone lines; and soon after that a stable in which were seventeen horses belonging to the German troops was destroyed. The following night a partisan wearing a hat, fur jacket, quilted trousers and felt boots visited the village again. A knapsack containing bottles of gasoline was slung over the partisan's shoulders. Just as the partisan stooped to strike a match, a sentry pounced from behind. There was a struggle in which the soldier struck a revolver from the hand of the partisan and gave the alarm. The partisan was taken prisoner, and it was then that the Germans discovered that their prisoner was a girl, quite young, tall, olive-skinned, with dark, lively eyes and dark hair, brushed high on her head. The girl was stripped and pummelled with fists. After about twenty minutes she was led through the village barefoot and clad in her underwear to the house where the enemy had its headquarters. Here they were informed about the capture of the young female partisan and they decided her fate. The interpreter meanwhile informed the Russians who owned the house that it was planned to hang the prisoner publicly the next morning.

The following is Lidov's newspaper account of Zoya's interrogation by a German officer and her subsequent torture and death:

"Who are you?"

"I won't tell you."

"Was it you who set fire to the stables?"

"Yes it was."

"Why did you do it?

"To destroy you."

"When did you cross the front line?

"On Friday."

The Russian couple who lived in the house told Lidov that under interrogation, Zoya was heard to say, "I don't know" and "I won't tell" many times. Then came the sound of a strap whistling through the air and its sharp smack against her body. It seems four men had taken off their belts and were beating the prisoner. Maria Sedova, who lived in the house, says she counted more than one hundred lashes. She says hardly a murmur came from Zoya.

A German sergeant, Karl Bauerlein, who was present at the torture and was later taken prisoner, wrote in his deposition:

The young Russian heroine remained tight-lipped. She would not betray her friends . . . She turned blue with the cold, blood flowed from her wounds, but she said nothing. After her torture there was a large purple-black bruise on her forehead, and weals on her arms and legs. She was breathing heavily. Her hair was dishevelled, and sweat had glued her black locks to her brow. Her hands were tied behind her. Her lips were bloody and swollen. She had evidently bitten them when her captors had tried to wring a confession from her.

During the torture, two younger German officers, apparently finding the beatings intolerable, retired to the kitchen and remained there until it was over.

After the interrogation Zoya was taken partially clad and barefoot, through the snow, to another house accompanied by a squad of soldiers. Soon the soldiers who were billeted in the house arrived and surrounded the girl and began to torment her. Some of them punched her with their fists, others held lighted matches under her chin, while one of them punched her on the spine. The owner of the house pleaded with them to stop torturing the girl in consideration for the children who were present. But the pleading was in vain. Then a sentry ordered Zoya to walk in the snow barefoot until he himself was cold and decided it was time to turn back to the warmth of the room.

The next morning soldiers began to erect a gallows in the centre of the village. Zoya was marched to the scaffold with a sign around her neck saying, "Incendiary". More than a hundred German soldiers were assembled and the villagers were ordered to watch the execution. But some, after standing for a while, slipped quietly away so as not to watch the hanging. Some of the German officers took cameras out of their leather cases.

Under the noose hanging from the arm of the gallows were two boxes placed one on top of the other. The executioners placed the girl on to the raised platform and put the noose around her neck. At this moment one of the officers came closer and aimed his camera at the gallows.

Zoya took this opportunity to shout to the villagers:

"Why do you look so downcast? Be brave, comrades. Fight, smash, hound the enemy!"

A soldier tried to make her close her mouth. But she continued:

"I am not afraid of dying . . . It is great to die for one's Mother-land."

The executioner then kicked the box from under Zoya's feet.

The box slid on the snow. The crowd swayed back. There was a shriek and, says the reporter Lidov, "The echo bounced off the icy wall of the distant forest."

Officers snapped pictures of the lifeless girl whom they knew as "Tanya". The face of this young Russian girl, unforgettable even in death, on a rope, her face brushed with white frost, was captured for posterity by a single close-up photo. When the unit which executed Zoya was later captured, including the officer who had taken the close-up, the photo was circulated throughout Russia.

A leading novelist wrote a dramatic play about Zoya. A composer wrote an opera. Sculptors made statues of her and a Russian movie-maker produced a film. The photograph of this girl, tortured and hanged, her breasts mutilated, caused mass indignation wherever it appeared.

Zoya's body hung for a whole month in the village, swaying in the wind and sprinkled over with snow. According to local witnesses, when occupying troops passed through the village, they surrounded the scaffold and amused themselves around it for a long time, roaring with laughter. Then on New Year's Eve enemy troops stripped the clothing from the hanging body and subjected it to indignities. For another day Zoya's body, pierced and slashed with knives, hung in the centre of the village. Then an order was given for the gallows to be taken down. Zoya's body was carried on a peasant sledge to a frozen pit outside the village. The torn noose was still around her neck.

Lidov gives this unforgettable description of her face: "Her eyes, arched by the black wings of her eyebrows, were closed; her long lashes lay on her olive-skinned cheeks, her lips were tightly pressed and her high forehead had a purple tinge of suffocation. Her handsome Russian face still preserved its integrity and freshness of line. An imprint of profound rest lay on it."

Zoya's mother, Lyubov Timofeyevna Kosmodemyanskaya, learned the news about her daughter in the worst possible way. She saw a newspaper photograph of her daughter with a rope around her neck. But before this she had heard a conversation on the street that made her uneasy. In her biography of Zoya she wrote, "I was riding in the streetcar on the day the article about 'Tanya' by Pyotr Lidov was published in the newspapers. I had not read the paper but all around me I could hear people saying: 'Tanya', 'Tanya', and telling about the brave deed this girl had done, about her extraordinary will-power. It did not even enter my head that this Tanya was my own daughter. Only, I began to worry, thinking of Zoya and wondering how she was getting on at the front. I hoped that if she should ever have to come face to face with danger she would be as strong as this marvellous Tanya. And then it turned out that this Tanya was indeed my very own Zoya."

Zoya's mother went to liberated Petrishchevo on 13 February 1942. "I don't remember very well how we got there," she says. "I remember only that the asphalt road did not go as far as the village, and we had to push the stalled car for almost 3 miles. I was taken to a hut but could not get warm. The cold was inside me. Then we went to Zoya's grave. They had already dug up the grave, and I saw her.

"She was lying with her arms straight down by her sides, her head thrown back, with a rope around her neck. Her face, which was perfectly calm, had been beaten unmercifully. There was a large dark bruise on her cheek. Her body had been pierced repeatedly with a bayonet. The blood had dried on her breast. I knelt down beside her and looked. I drew aside a lock of her hair from her clear brow – and again was struck by the calm serenity of her torn, disfigured face. I could not tear myself away from her; I could not turn my eyes away."

Then a woman in an army uniform came up, gently took her hand and helped her to her feet. She was Zoya's friend Klava. She cried as she told Zoya's mother everything she knew.

A short time later Zoya's mother spoke on the radio about her daughter.

"Zoya was a surprisingly courageous and developed person. I am older than she, more experienced, yet she helped me to bear failures or difficulties with courage. When Zoya told me she was leaving for the front, I admit I could not hold back my tears. It was all so unexpected for me and I found it hard to grasp immediately that my only daughter, so young, was going off to war . . .

"That night, Zoya was so happy, elated and excited . . . We had a particularly good heart to heart talk. The next day she let me accompany her to the streetcar stop. She carried only a small kit-bag that I had recently bought for her . . .

"One thing rejoices me. Zoya will not be forgotten. She will live in my heart as long as it beats. But she will live in the hearts of others when I shall no longer be alive. And perhaps your children too will remember her with kind words."

In October 1943, Russian troops sighted the enemy's 197th Infantry Division which included officers and soldiers who had tortured Zoya. When they next went into battle the troops read the prepared slogans that were printed in the military newspapers and in leaflets which said: "When you go into attack, remember Tanya!" (The newspaper stories called Zoya by that name.) "Smash the enemy for Tanya! Show no mercy as they showed none to her!" "Go into battle as avengers of Tanya!"

In short shrift the troops routed the enemy division. On the body of a Wehrmacht officer killed near Smolensk, were five photographs of Zoya's execution.

Zoya's younger brother, Alexander, a tank commander, was killed in action in Germany one month before victory day.

Pyotr Lidov who first wrote about Zoya died on the battlefield in 1944 while shooting at enemy bombers.

CHAPTER 7

The Blockade of Leningrad

In early September 1941 Hitler's armies cut the last roads leading into besieged Leningrad and, in the words of poet Olga Bergholtz, "the noose of the blockade tightened on the city's throat". Leningrad (now St Petersburg) was Russia's second biggest city, its biggest seaport and was extremely important as a focus of heavy industry: steel, loco-motives, machine engineering and electrical equipment. It had the largest rubber plant in Europe.

The blockade prevented all but a trickle of food and other supplies to enter the city. A typical family were the Savichevs who all died of starvation, one each month, their deaths recorded in a notebook by a ten-year-old schoolgirl, Tanya, who herself succumbed in 1943. There were interminable aerial dogfights over the city and naval actions by immobilized ships, including the revolution-era cruiser *Aurora*.

The "noose" remained for almost 900 days. Hitler used every means to destroy the city including on some days sending in its direction more than 1,000 bombers at a time. German troops never entered the city but the human toll from the siege was heavy: more than half a million civilians perished. The invaders plundered nearby historic cities, destroying the eighteenth century palace at Pavlovsk that had been built by Catherine II. Peter the Great's summer residence was also gutted and its 114 gold-trimmed fountains smashed.

After August, the only way for food convoys to reach the starving citizens was the "road" (christened "The Road of Life") across Lake

Ladoga. The road also had to supply ammunition and provisions for the troops defending Leningrad. By the middle of September the situation worsened. The city was virtually encircled by the Finns in the north, the German-occupied Baltic area in the west, and by other powerful Wehrmacht units to the south and close to Lake Ladoga in the east, with only a narrow strip of the lake's southern boundary remaining in Russian hands. All able-bodied citizens rose to defend the city. Leaving their ships to fight on land, thousands of sailors from the Baltic Fleet took oaths to defend Leningrad "to the death".

At the end of September the city was subjected to continuous artillery bombardment and air raids. The poet Anna Akhmatova gave a radio address. "My dear fellow-citizens," she began, "Mothers, wives and sisters. For two months now the enemy has been threatening our city with capture and inflicting severe wounds on it." She mentioned the historic figures and writers associated with the city such as Peter the Great, Pushkin and Dostoyevsky. Their city, she said, "is threatened with disgrace and destruction". She added, "Like all of you, I only live by my unshakable faith that Leningrad will never bow down to the Nazis. This faith is made stronger when I see women defending the city with such simple valour and enabling ordinary human existence to continue . . . when I see women stand on the roofs during air raids, watching for incendiaries . . ."

Leningrad was a vital strategic objective in the plans of the German High Command. It assigned Army Group north the task of taking the city. So optimistic were the Nazis that they had in advance appointed officials in charge of the "final days" of the city after its capture. As a sign of German efficiency, special passes were printed for cars entering Leningrad.

A Nazi document (the Directive of German Naval Headquarters of 22 September 1941) said this about the city: "The Fuhrer has decided to erase St Petersburg from the face of the earth. It is proposed to approach near to the city and to destroy it with the aid of an artillery barrage from weapons of different calibres and with prolonged air attacks."

In July the Germans' first attempt to capture the city was foiled by the resistance of the Leningrad garrison which was supplemented by 160,000 volunteers who enlisted in the People's Corps. The second enemy attempt, made in August, also failed. Early in September enemy troops made an all-out assault, preceded by a relentless bombardment. Russian Defence Ministry archives reveal that for almost 30 months an average of 245 shells fell daily on the city.

D. V. Pavlov, a civilian who was a witness to the siege recalls a particularly bad day: "The houses, streets, bridges and people, plunged in darkness as there was no electricity, were suddenly illumined by sinister flames. Dense clouds of black smoke rose slowly to the sky, filling the air with an acrid smell. Fire brigades, self-defence groups and thousands of workers fought the fires in spite of fatigue after a full working day. Their efforts tamed the flames gradually, and the fires died. But the warehouses where the food was stocked, continued to burn. The fire there raged for more than five hours."

Meanwhile Leningrad's food stocks dwindled rapidly and there was a sharp reduction in rations. The fate of the city now depended wholly on the water route along Lake Ladoga. Due to the blockade daily bread rations were cut to ½ pound for workers, engineers and technicians, and ¼ pound for office workers, dependents and children – barely enough to keep a normal person alive. During the blockade half a million people perished from hunger.

One of the fire watchers on the roofs during the first months of the siege was the composer Dmitri Shostakovich who had joined a voluntary fire brigade. He kept watch on the roof of the Conservatoire, where he was also a part-time teacher. On the same day that a local paper carried the headline, "The Enemy is at Our Gates", Shostakovich delivered a radio address. Anti-aircraft guns were heard booming in the background as he told listeners about his new musical work: "An hour ago I completed the second part of my new work. If I manage to complete the third and fourth parts of this composition and if it turns out well, I shall be able to call it the Seventh Symphony." He added: "All of us are soldiers today, and those who work in the field of culture and the arts are doing their duty on a par with all the other citizens of Leningrad." In early October at the insistence of local authorities Shostakovich and his family were evacuated from the beleaguered city and he completed his famous symphonic work a few months later far from the tumult of battle.

Plans were made for its premiere in Leningrad, although among the victims of the siege were members of the city's symphony orchestra. During rehearsals, in the summer of 1942, reports were written by Yasha Babushkin on the health of the orchestra. One of his reports – updating an earlier one – says: "The first violin is dying, the drum died on his way to work, the French horn is at death's door . . ."★

Nevertheless this wartime performance of the 'Leningrad Symphony' was not only a triumph in musical art but it was a "first" in musico-military history. Despite conditions of near starvation in the city, the hall of the Philharmonia where the performance was held – the date was 9 August – was packed. Those attending the concert noted that the guns were strangely silent on both sides. What happened was that the Commander of the Russian forces guarding the city, General L. A. Govorov, informed about the concert, ordered his artillery to fire hundreds of salvoes prior to the concert against the enemy's weapons emplacements. Thus, the performance took place virtually uninterrupted.

Hitler's armies had expected to enter the city on 5 July 1941 but those plans did not materialize. However, besieged Leningrad suffered beyond description. In the winter of 1941–2 the city was immersed in darkness, without electricity; transport stood frozen in the streets, and water had to be drawn in cans from the icy River Neva. Citizens were so weak they could not carry the water-filled cans; instead they used hand sledges. Many breathed their last as they queued for their bread ration – a tiny slice of bread. Before the enemy finally closed a ring

---

★ Shostakovich's work aroused great interest abroad, especially in the United States and Britain. Many conductors vied for the privilege of being first to conduct the symphony. In June a microfilm of the score had been flown to America. On 19 July Arturo Toscanini performed the Seventh Symphony in New York to a radio audience. But the first overseas performance was held in London on 22 June 1942, when it was broadcast over BBC Radio, Sir Henry Wood conducting.

around the city the valuable paintings and other art exhibits of the Hermitage were evacuated, being placed on hundreds of railroad cars and sent off to safety beyond the Ural Mountains.

The blockade continued from September 1941 to the last week of January 1944 – nearly three years.

After the war, poet Olga Bergholtz, who remained in Leningrad during the entire blockade, visited the Piskarevskoye Memorial Cemetery where nearly half a million civilian defenders of the city lie buried, including her husband. She says that she, who had endured the blockade, was shaken by the mile-long rows of burial mounds with concrete markers and the laconic inscriptions: "1941", "1942" . . . Says Bergholtz: "Nearly half a million nameless heroes – the population of a whole city – lay buried here."

One day in the 1960s passersby saw a strange event taking place next to a cathedral in Leningrad. With rifles in their hands, a dozen people in civilian clothes, half of them women, had rifles at the ready and fired off a graveside salute. On closer scrutiny it was observed that all twelve wore Second World War combat medals on their chests. Spectators were puzzled until the mystery was solved. The deceased was an Orthodox priest; and next to the cross on his chest was pinned a war medal.

Father Fyodor, the priest, hailed from the tiny village of Zapolye in the Pskov region, not far from the Baltic states of Estonia and Latvia. The whole region had been under Nazi occupation during the war.

Zapolye was then (as now) an ordinary village with tiny vegetable gardens, small houses and a solitary church. On arrival, the enemy had posted signs detailing penalties for failure to obey the "new order". Two members of the village council were hanged at once in the square in front of the church as a warning. As a consequence the villagers found safety by making themselves scarce. During the war such a withdrawal by the inhabitants of a small occupied village was not so unusual. For example, there was the western Russian village of Timkovochi where Hitler's army attempted to stamp out partisans and their supporters. The German commander, a Captain Keil, warned the population that for each German killed "the first ten Russians we come across will be shot, irrespective of sex or age". That very night, the entire population of Timkovochi took to the woods. Then, partisan detachments raided the village, killed or wounded the enemy garrison, blew up fuel and food dumps, took prisoners and captured machine-guns and rifles.

Outside Zapolye early in the war, a partisan detachment that had been formed behind enemy lines had heard a rumour that the local priest, Father Fyodor, speaking from the pulpit, had condemned the invaders as "barbarians". If this was true, it was an important piece of news. But it had to be verified. Four members of the partisan detachment were summoned by the leader who asked them directly:

"Are there among you any who believe in God?"

Some of those assembled were embarrassed at the question.

"This is no joke," said the leader. "I ask you again: who among you is familiar with the church service? We will be taking part in an important action soon and we must make contact with the priest of Zapolye, Father Fyodor. My orders are that you must treat the priest with courtesy. Do not stir things up so that the congregation will have suspicions against him. Whatever you do, be extremely cautious."

Two partisans were chosen to meet the priest and at dusk on that same day they stealthily entered the village and knocked on the priest's door. It was opened by the priest himself. Father Fyodor was about sixty years old and wore round spectacles tied with a string to keep them on. He had a kind, intelligent face, a flowing white beard which gave him a regal appearance, and wore an old cassock. With a simple gesture he invited his guests in.

The two visitors were uncertain how to begin. If necessary they must try to convert the priest to their "partisan faith". One of them made a tentative beginning:

"Citizen priest! Is it true that you have told your parishioners to pray for the speedy return of our army?"

"I eagerly wait for it," said Father Fyodor.

"But we ask you: What can you do to help?"

The priest removed his glasses, wiped them, and said:

"My religious orders forbid me to spill human blood and hold weapons in my hands. But in these days of foreign occupation, if I could get hold of a rifle, I think I would start shooting."

The two partisans liked what they heard. They thought it over for a moment; then one of them said:

"We have enough people who can shoot. But if you really want to help us, we have a more important job for you. Those people who have remained in the village live in fear under the enemy occupation. They have no news at all about the situation on the fronts. If we provide you with official news bulletins, will you agree to pass them on to the people?"

Father Fyodor agreed even though he knew that if the Germans found out that he was reading from the pulpit news emanating from Moscow, it was an offence punishable by immediate death by firing squad.

The summer of the invasion and brutal occupation passed into autumn. The village turned into a sea of mud, rendering the roads impassable to vehicles and pedestrians alike. Cold rain pattered on the roofs which in normal times would have kept everyone indoors. But despite the weather, the citizens of Zapolye filed to the church daily. They even took their children, covering them with shawls.

In the church, glimmering with candles, Father Fyodor offered words of consolation and hope among the prayers. But then, in the same sing-song voice, he read out official news bulletins about the war. Nobody knew where the priest got these reports. Did he keep a hidden radio receiver? Some parishioners became frightened at first and questioned their priest's boldness, knowing the grave risk he was taking. But within a short time the villagers began flocking to the church, as hungry to hear news from the front as they were for their daily bread. Sometimes parishioners who didn't catch a few sentences asked the priest to repeat what he had just said. For a time all went well.

But Zapolye had a "headman", or village leader, and it didn't take him long to guess where the news reports were coming from. It was clear that partisans were in the habit of visiting the local church. He wondered if he himself could identify them and he at once began to look closely at the churchgoers. However, he saw no unusual movements among the parishioners who prayed piously and received Father Fyodor's blessing. All the services were conducted with dignity and nobody received special attention from the priest. Yet every day when the time came Father Fyodor took out a neatly folded piece of paper and read out the war news from Moscow. And this was behind the German lines.

The headman, a collaborator, was no fool. He knew that he had to proceed carefully since there was no enemy garrison inside the village itself. One day he set out on foot to visit the Nazi commandant about 12 miles from Zapolye. But something unforeseen happened to him and he never returned. Nor did any Germans come. And then winter arrived.

When the first snows fell an SS unit suddenly arrived in the village. Soldiers broke into homes and dragged people outdoors. They had suspicions about Father Fyodor and demanded to see the priest. They entered the small church but nowhere could he be found. Before departing they set fire to the church along with the entire village of Zapolye.

But the SS unit was completely unaware that a "reception committee" was waiting for them outside the village in the form of a well-armed partisan group. On the way back to its base the SS troops were ambushed and wiped out. The partisans then conducted their own search for Father Fyodor but they also were unable to find him. While the church was burning some persons said they saw the priest making his way through backyard paths to a distant farm. Another thought he had left the day before. Weeks passed and all decided that the elderly priest had died. Although he was remembered gratefully by the village people, with the passage of time they gradually forgot about him.

Then one day, a partisan accompanied a white-bearded man to headquarters. The man, who demanded to see the leader, was Father Fyodor. With his string-tied spectacles and beard he was instantly recognized. The priest bowed to the partisan leader and, taking a rucksack off his back, emptied it on the desk. Gold coins, silver and melted pieces of gold icon frames fell out. "This is for you, my dear brothers. I've brought you about 500,000 rubles. This money was collected from people in many villages; the gold comes from our church which the enemy burned to the ground. This wealth belongs to the people who collected it. They have requested that you use it to build a tank unit to be named after our Russian hero Dmitri Donskoi."

The partisans smiled with appreciation and expressed their thanks to the brave clergyman.

It wasn't until 1944 that the Russians liberated the Pskov region. At that time Father Fyodor was summoned by Alexei, the Metropolitan of the Leningrad Region who later became the Patriarch of Moscow and all Russia.

"You have received a great honour because so many of the people recognize you as their pastor," the Metropolitan said.

Thanking him, Father Fyodor told his superior about something that was troubling him. The military authorities wanted to bestow a medal on him. "May I, a priest, wear a military medal next to a holy cross?"

A smile appeared on the face of the Metropolitan. "The recognition of your merits not only by the church but also by the nation is the greatest happiness for a priest who devotes his thoughts and his life to his people. You have my blessings."

Father Fyodor returned to his parish. From that day forward one could always see on his chest next to his cross a military medal with the inscription, "Partisan in the Patriotic War". And when he died many years later, partisan veterans gathered to honour him as one of their own and gave him a rifle salute. Father Fyodor, gallant though he was, was not unique among the clergy. Orthodox clergymen remained for the most part unshakably loyal during the war and opposed to Hitler, their patriotism rising above past grievances towards the Communist regime. Nazi ideology was contemptuous towards the basic religious precepts of love and magnanimity, while the Kremlin, still atheist to the core, wisely softened its attitude to religion and formed a working alliance with the Orthodox Church, thereby facilitating its active support.

Father Fyodor, gallant though he was, was not unique among the clergy. There were numerous instances of Orthodox priests engaging in anti-Nazi activities, even taking up the rifle in emergencies. In occupied Cossack villages, it was said that priests were among the best and bravest informants for the partisan cause. There is an eyewitness story, told by a middle-aged woman, about how she went to confession in the Kuban Cossack region, and as the Orthodox priest bent down a revolver fell from beneath his robe. He quickly picked it up, put it back into his cassock and said: "These are evil times, little sister, and when the German Nazi Antichrist is among us, even a priest must carry a gun."

CHAPTER 8

The Snipers

Vasily Alexandrovich Zaitsev

Russians, male and female, made excellent sharpshooters. An official document mentions that Senior Sergeant Feodosy Smolyachkov picked off 125 of the enemy with just 126 bullets. In the very first days of the war Nina Petrova, a forty-eight-year-old factory worker, went to the front as a sniper to defend Leningrad. She felled over a hundred Nazi soldiers. There was also a very skilful sniper named Vasily Zaitsev.

At the height of the Battle of Stalingrad, Vasily Zaitsev's name became widely known not only to the city's defenders but also, it is reported, to the Nazi High Command. His sharpshooting had become a painful thorn in its side. During the struggle for the city Zaitsev had put out of action one enemy after another until the toll grew to over 300 officers and men. Alerted, the German side took countermeasures. An order was issued to "find and kill the Russian hare". (The surname Zaitsev is derived from the Russian word *zayats*, meaning hare.)

Russian sources claim that a German who was taken prisoner revealed under interrogation that "a certain Major Konings"*, chief of a snipers' school in Berlin, had arrived in Stalingrad with the order to eliminate "the hare", to Colonel Anatole Batyuk, Zaitsev's divisional commander, was in high spirits.

* See Source Notes on p. 254.

"They've sent a major – a small fry for our boys," he said jokingly. "Anyway, this enemy super-sniper must be snuffed out." Then he added a serious note. "But be cautious, Vasily; use your brains." Zaitsev, holding a senior captain's rank, had already won a handful of medals for bravery and marksmanship. Short, compactly built, with a chubby face and dark brown hair, he was well-liked both as officer and sharpshooting instructor.

"Certainly," said the laconic Zaitsev. But he thought: "That's easier said than done." After all, according to the prisoner, Berlin had sent the head of a sniper school to hunt him down.

Zaitsev had already learned to read the Germans' "hand" and he could distinguish without too much difficulty – by the mode of fire and use of camouflage – between experienced snipers and novices. He could also pick out "cowards" from those who were unyielding.

But almost a week had passed since the Berlin super-sniper was supposed to have arrived; and so far the visitor was a total mystery. Assuming this distinguished opponent had arrived, it was obvious that Zaitsev was now facing someone of equal skill and determination. He began the most patient day-to-day observations which, however, produced no definite results. It was even hard to say on what sector of the front the "Berlin ace" was now operating. Most likely he changed positions often and was himself equally cautious in pursuing Zaitsev.

Without discontinuing his search, Zaitsev began to analyze his own experience and that of his fellow marksmen in order to find a solution. Experience told him that he could not count on success without the help of his comrades in the trenches: riflemen, machine-gunners, sappers and signalmen. Usually after an enemy sniper was discovered and his location determined, Zaitsev chose a fellow soldier, gave him a spyglass and, himself peering through a trench periscope, indicated a distant object and slowly led the man's eyes from one reference point to another. When this "spotter" actually saw the enemy sniper and realized how well he had camouflaged himself, only then did he become a dependable assistant.

But there was more preparation involved than that. It was necessary to set up sham positions, create dummy snipers, and make use of camouflage. In doing this, Zaitsev studied each soldier to see his capacities. He knew that sometimes a person shows initiative and boldness in action, but because he is too hasty he will not make a good assistant; or the person may have wildly contrasting moods. Such a man could not be relied upon when it came to a prolonged snipers' duel.

As to enemy snipers, their character was more difficult to determine. In general, Zaitsev classified all German snipers as "stubborn". But he had settled on his own method for dealing with them. First he prepared a realistic dummy; then he placed it somewhere without being noticed and, afterwards, started to move it. This was necessary because a dummy must, like a person, change poses. Positioning himself beside the dummy he would then settle into his own well-camouflaged position.

Predictably the following sequence of events would occur: the enemy sniper fired at the dummy, but it remained "alive". Then his "stubbornness" showed itself. The German sniper fired a second shot and prepared for another; but as a rule he himself was then caught in his opponent's sights before he could squeeze off the third.

Years of observation and training taught Zaitsev lessons that meant the difference between life and death. He knew that experienced enemy snipers arrived at their front-line positions under cover of fire, invariably accompanied by two or three helpers. In the presence of such a sniper, Zaitsev usually pretended to be a novice – or sometimes an ordinary soldier – so as to lull his opponent's vigilance. Occasionally part of his strategy was to poke fun at him. After each shot he provoked his antagonist by showing the results of fire on conventional bull's-eye targets that are used at a firing range. The enemy sniper would quickly get used to this diversion and turn his attention away from Zaitsev's dummy target. But as soon as he switched his attention to other targets, Zaitsev instantly took the place of the dummy. This took only a few seconds. Tossing the dummy aside he would deftly catch the enemy's head in the cross-hairs of his telescopic sight, and this would usually put an end to the duel.

In his preparatory work, Zaitsev subdivided detection of an enemy target into two stages. The first stage began with studying the opponent's defences. Then he learned when and under what circumstances his own men had been wounded. Medical orderlies were vital in this respect. They would tell where a wounded man had been found. Arriving at the spot, Zaitsev asked eye-witnesses for additional details about the wound; and in this way he discovered the enemy sniper's plan of fire.

The second stage was "pinpointing the target". So as not to get himself caught in the sights of an enemy sniper, he reconnoitred the terrain using a trench periscope or battery commander's telescope. He knew that the optical sight of a sniper's rifle, or field glasses, were inadequate for this purpose. Also, experience showed that if previously the enemy had shown animation but, afterwards, the same enemy did not betray a single useless movement, Zaitsev was facing an expert.

This is the reason Zaitsev never failed to tell his colleagues that they must study the situation and talk about it to the men, but must never become emotional over what was tormenting them. He was fond of saying, "In sniping one has to live according to the popular saying: look before you leap." To prepare a deadly accurate shot you had to combine effort and ingenuity, to study the opponent's character and strength, discover his weak points and only after this set about ending the pursuit with one good shot.

Zaitsev's instructions to new snipers were strict: "As soon as you come to the forward edge, conceal yourself like a stone and observe, study the terrain, compile a chart and plot distinctive marks on it. Remember that if in the process of observation you have revealed yourself by a careless movement of the head, betrayed your presence to the enemy and not managed to hide in time, you have made a blunder and, for this, you will receive a bullet through your head." That is why in training snipers Zaitsev always gave concealment and camouflage top priority.

Now the "sniper from Berlin" would have to be outwitted or drawn into a difficult struggle so that it would become impossible for him to extricate himself. Zaitsev had to think of clever shams, how to distract his opponent's attention, annoy him by intricate movements, and in this way make him glassy-eyed, perhaps even muddled.

But Zaitsev had to admit the truth: so far, it appeared, the enemy sniper had outwitted the Russians.

Then one day the elusive "Berlin sniper" broke the telescopic sight of a Russian sniper named Morozov and wounded Zaitsev's friend Shaikin. Both men were experienced snipers and had often come out on top in complex and difficult engagements. Now there was no longer any doubt that they were closing in on the quarry they were searching for.

At dawn the next day Zaitsev went with his colleague Nikolai Kulikov to the positions where their fellow snipers had been the previous day. The enemy's forward line of defence was well known to Zaitsev who had been studying it for days on end. He saw nothing new. Now the day was ending. Suddenly a helmet rose up over the enemy trench and slowly moved along it. Should he shoot? No. He knew this was a ruse because the helmet swung unnaturally. It was certainly carried by the enemy sniper's assistant while the expert himself was waiting for the "Russian hare" to betray himself by a shot.

Zaitsev and his assistants waited in vain until dark.

"Maybe he left long ago," Kulikov said as they left their position under cover of night.

But Zaitsev would not be deterred. By the skill the enemy showed in not revealing himself the whole day, he was reassured that the super-sniper had to be there. The situation called for special vigilance.

Another day passed. The vital question was: whose nerves would prove stronger? Who would outwit whom?

The next morning began as usual. The darkness was melting away and the enemy positions were becoming more visible with each passing minute. A mini-battle started up nearby. Shells whistled through the air but the Russian snipers, their eyes glued to their optical sights, were not interrupted in their observation of what was happening in front of them.

"There he is, I'll show him to you with my finger," suddenly shouted a political officer above the din. For a split second he rose above the breastwork; but that was enough. Fortunately, the bullet only grazed his scalp.

Zaitsev thought: Only an expert sniper could fire like that.

He scrutinized the enemy positions for a long time but could not find the ace's lair. For many days he had studied the enemy's forward line; so well, in fact, that he immediately noticed every new shell crater and every new breastwork that appeared. He saw nothing new or suspicious. But by the speed with which the previous shot had been fired he concluded that the "Berlin sniper" must be somewhere directly in front of them.

He continued his observation. To the far right was a disabled tank and to the left a pill-box. Was the sniper in the tank? No, he told himself. An experienced sniper would not take cover there. In the pillbox, then? Again, no. The gun-port was sealed tightly.

Where was he then?

Between the tank and the pillbox, on a flat surface just in front of the Wehrmacht's line of defence, lay a large sheet of corrugated iron with a small heap of broken bricks on it. It had been there for a long time and Zaitsev had become used to it. He mentally placed himself in the enemy's shoes and asked: Where is the best place for a sniper's post? Why not a foxhole beneath the iron sheet? Probably it had communication trenches leading to it. Most likely, he concluded, the Berlin sniper was there, under the sheet of iron in no-man's-land.

But now he must test his hypothesis. Putting a glove on a small plank he slowly raised it. The enemy swallowed the bait.

"Very well," Zaitsev thought. He cautiously lowered the plank into the trench in the same position in which he had raised it, then examined the bullet hole. It had no slant; the bullet had gone in from dead ahead. This meant he was right: the ace from Berlin was under the iron sheet. Now the question was how to lure him out. At least the edge of his head had to be visible. But his opponent was unlikely to abandon this convenient position. Now, however, the "hare" knew the other's character well enough.

Night came. Zaitsev and his assistants did not sleep. They equipped a new sniper's post and each took up positions in it before dawn. Enemy troops were now firing sporadically. Mortars were aimed at a pontoon bridge on the Volga. Flares soared into the air. Now Russian artillery opened up and the mortars were silenced. Then Luftwaffe bombers appeared. The sun rose. Kulikov fired a random shot to draw the sniper's attention. Zaitsev had decided to lie in wait for the first half of the day because in the brilliance of the sun their optical instruments could betray them. In the afternoon their rifles were in the shadows while the direct rays of the sun fell on the German's position.

As they watched, something glistened near the edge of the iron sheet. It might have been just a splinter of glass or a telescopic sight. Kulikov started to raise a decoy helmet as cautiously as only the most expert of snipers can do. The Berlin sniper fired. Kulikov rose for an instant, gave a loud shout and fell . . .

The enemy must have thought that at last the "chief hare" he had been hunting for a week was silenced because half of his head suddenly protruded from under the iron sheet. The "hare" fired. The head sank but the optical sight of his rifle continued to glisten in the sun.

As soon as it grew dark Russian forces launched an attack in the same sector. At the peak of the fighting Zaitsev and Kulikov dragged the dead "Berlin super-sniper" from under the iron sheet. They kept his rifle as a souvenir and delivered his documents to the divisional commander.

Mila Mikhailovna Pavlichenko

On a foggy morning in the spring of 1942, an unusual snipers' duel was underway on a Crimean battlefield. The duel had already lasted almost three days. Pitted against the enemy sniper was a twenty-two-year-old Ukrainian woman, Sergeant Mila Pavlichenko. She survived the marathon ordeal but had a warning for others: "I would not advise anyone to catch a sniper's eye. If you do, you practically have no chance of survival."

Here is what happened. Mila had concealed herself in a tree outside the city of Sevastopol. In her arms was her sniper's rifle cocked and ready. Mila was well camouflaged, she thought, but suddenly a bullet whistled above her head. Ten seconds later another bullet struck the tree trunk above her shoulder. A thought flashed through her mind: "Fall down as if dead . . ."

She fell down from a height of 10 feet to the ground and lay in that position until the German sniper got tired of observing her. By midday the fog had cleared but Mila still lay prostrate behind thick bushes. Her head had grown heavy, she had a tickling in her throat, and her clothes became soggy. Worst of all, her arms ached. She had spent most of the day hugging the ground. Then Mila, fighting back fatigue, peered into the enemy's forward line of defence and, as the fog lifted, she suddenly saw the object of her pursuit. The German sniper was slowly moving in her direction.

Mila decided to trick her opponent. As soon as his head disappeared behind a hillock she left her shelter and crawled over to another bush. But long inactivity had made her body grow heavy, even clumsy. Nevertheless, she held her rifle in front of her and kept her eyes glued to the telescopic sight. Then, unexpectedly, her eyes "caught" her opponent. It seemed to her the German sniper was looking right at her. Each moment was precious. Which of them would triumph? She pulled the trigger. By the merest fraction of a second she had forestalled her adversary. But not being sure of the result, she lay on the ground and waited for an hour or more to elapse. No answering shot came. Mila looked into the telescopic sight and this time saw the enemy's lifeless face. After waiting a little longer she crawled over to the luckless enemy. Taking a small notebook out of the sniper's pocket she read: "Dunkirk". Next to it was a figure. The German had killed more than 400 French and British soldiers. The sniper had started his "killing game" in Western Europe in 1940. Two years later he had been sent to the Crimea. Mila took his rifle and started back to her own lines.

Before her narrow escape in the Crimea, Mila's marksmanship during the defence of Odessa, located on the Black Sea coast, was the talk of the entire coastal navy. In those days men couldn't believe that the famous sharpshooter was a slim, attractive and slightly-built woman. At Sevastopol a burly sailor, after meeting her, told his shipmates jauntily: "Now there's a woman for you! By the looks of her she's just a dragonfly; but by the way she shoots she's a tiger!" Mila became the best-known sniper of the war and appeared in a documentary film made by the well-known cinematographer Roman Karmen.

Using a standard Model 1891/1930 Russian rifle with telescopic sight, Mila's combat score rose as she kept a bead on her foe, finally dispatching over 300 enemy soldiers, many of them accomplished snipers themselves.

A student of history at Kiev University when war began, Mila walked into a military registration office, said she had completed a course at a sniper's school and requested front-line duty. While a student she had joined a volunteer group working closely with the armed forces that included a women's sniper school. Mila was assigned duty as a sniper in the 25th "Chapayev" Rifle Division named after a hero of the Russian Civil War. As she explained, "What began as my hobby became my profession in the army."

In the third year of the war, General Ivan Petrov issued Mila, now promoted to lieutenant, a certificate as sniper-instructor. In Moscow, Mila was received in the Kremlin and included in a delegation of front-line soldiers that was invited to America by Eleanor Roosevelt, wife of the President. During a visit to Chicago, Mila attended a luncheon where she was asked to deliver a two-minute speech in front of a large audience. At that time – it was 1943 – America and Britain had not yet opened a Second Front in France and the Russians never missed an opportunity to taunt their Allies.

On the platform, Mila, looked slight in her army officer's uniform. She spoke briefly into the microphone, but these few words brought the house down. "I am twenty-two years old and have already destroyed 309 enemy soldiers who have invaded my country." After a pause she added in a soft voice: "I hope you will not hide behind my back for too long."

The crowd froze for a moment. Then the auditorium filled with laughter and applause.

Mila made a tour of England and Wales in 1943 that produced a few gasps. In London she was invited to parties in stylish restaurants and her reaction to them was not flattering. A few of her hosts were taken aback when she asked them straightforwardly: "Are you at war, or aren't you?" Mila, it should be noted, had recently visited Stalingrad and seen its utter destruction.

Britain's Home Authorities took Mila around to different parts of the country, including a look at industry in South Wales, and then up north where trains were late and unheated, where there was a stringent black-out and nothing to eat or drink in the bars and buffets. But this she thought was "swell" – it being concrete proof of a country truly at war. She also inspected bomb damage in London's East End and stopped at an Auxiliary Fire Station where she "tested" the boys to see if they could actually turn out in sixty seconds in the event of an alarm. In fact she was so conscientious in her sight-seeing tour of Britain that the authorities confided later that they could well believe her prowess on the killing fields because she had very nearly *killed them*.

Meanwhile, the Anglo-American media began paying attention to Mila. British and American journalists dubbed her "The Queen of Fire" and "Sniper Number One". On the Eastern Front, however, German soldiers had a different sobriquet for Mila: the "Russian Valkyrie". According to Norse mythology the Valkyries visited a battlefield and chose who was to live and who was to die.

Fyodor Matveyevich Okhlopkov

In this war of Titans, something new appeared – a group of unflappable, self-reliant men from the remote reindeer regions of Siberia whose skills at tracking animals in the taiga and tundra were now put to use in hunting enemy soldiers. These were the Yakuts who, as every Russian knows are born sharpshooters.

Fyodor Matveyevich Okhlopkov was a hunter from the tiny Yakut village of Krest-Khaldjai which is so far off the beaten path that when he joined the army it took him one week by sleigh from his home to the nearest railroad station. Then he had to travel 2,000 miles to Moscow.

Fyodor smiled easily and he had the healthy, oval features and dark eyes usually associated with people of the Far North. Yakuts are famed for their eyesight. The Yakut hunter, like the Eskimo, will never lose the trail of an animal (meat is a staple diet) either on grass, moss or stones. And when it came to Fyodor's shooting skills, few in the world could match him. I have seen this Yakut skill with my own eyes. A few winters ago while travelling in Siberia I watched an impressive display of Yakut marksmanship as well as reindeer-racing outside Yakutsk, the Yakut capital.

With war underway, Fyodor and his brother, Vasily, and their many army friends arrived in Moscow on a cold winter morning. They marched through Red Square with rifles on their backs, past Lenin's Mausoleum, and went straight to the front. It was time to get down to business; the time of music and patriotic speeches which they had listened to back home was over.

The 375th Infantry Division, to which Fyodor belonged, was formed in the Ural region and went into action as part of the Twenty-ninth Army. Fyodor and Vasily were at first issued with light machine-guns. Their regiment stopped for a short rest in the forests near Moscow where they saw fresh Siberian divisions marching towards the front line. A snowstorm raged and they saw the reality of war: mounds of frozen Russian and German dead, now covered with a white shroud of freshly-fallen snow.

Early the next morning after an artillery preparation the troops went into the attack. The Okhlopkov brothers were in the first line of the advancing battalion. Now and then they lay on the prickly snow to fire a short burst or two at the enemy. These were their first steps in the war, and they were testing their skills and their weapons. In a fierce battle lasting two days, the ground changed hands several times and their division managed to cross the River Volga over ice that was broken by enemy artillery shells. It was a victory but at a high price. The division lost many officers and men and an explosive bullet fired by a German sniper killed Vasily Okhlopkov who died in his brother's arms.

Fyodor could not hold back his tears. Standing at the side of Vasily's body, his head bare, he made a pledge: he would "open an account" of the enemy for his lost brother.

And so a new career as sniper began for Fyodor Okhlopkov. Already his marksmanship had been noticed by the regimental commander who urged the other men to follow Fyodor's example. As a sniper, there was many a lull in action but the task was never dull. Constant danger added to the excitement. Rare courage, poise and self-control were prerequisites, added to superb eyesight.

Fyodor also had a good knowledge of plant-life, which came in handy in the trenches. He knew the healing properties of different herbs, berries and leaves and was skilful in treating certain ailments, even possessing some secrets that had been passed down from one generation to another. So in 1942 when he received three separate wounds on 2 March, 3 April and 7 May he refused to go to the field hospital. Clenching his teeth against the pain, he scorched the wounds each time with the flame of a burning pine splinter. (Those who happened to see the cult 1988 Hollywood fantasy, *Rambo III*, could watch actor Sylvester Stallone apply the same type of "home remedy" – a burning splint – to an abdominal wound.)

In the evening of 18 August, Fyodor, who had temporarily left his sniper's duty and joined an assault on a small, burnt-down village, was wounded for a fourth time, and it was severe. Blood streamed from him and he lost consciousness. Two fellow soldiers carried him to the edge of the forest where there was a cover of bushes and trees. Then medical orderlies took him to a battalion medical aid station and from there he was evacuated to a military hospital miles behind the front.

Upon recovery, Fyodor was sent to the 234th Regiment of the 178th Division whose commanding officer was pleased to learn that Okhlopkov was a sniper. The enemy, he was told, had an expert marksman on that sector who in a single day had killed seven Russian soldiers with seven shots. Fyodor was ordered to put the enemy sniper out of action. After a brief preparation, Fyodor set out at dawn the next day. From his experience he knew German snipers favoured sitting in trees; he himself preferred a position on the ground.

Now a most dangerous game began – a duel to the death between expert marksmen. His opponent, Fyodor thought, must surely have chosen a pine tree with a forked trunk. So he riveted his gaze on a suspicious tree and scrutinized each bough. He looked hard for some sign of the sniper who, he knew, was also looking for him. The "iron rule" was that victory would come to the man who first sighted his adversary and pulled the trigger.

It was arranged that at exactly twelve minutes past eight a steel helmet would be raised from the Russian firing trench at a distance of 109 yards from Okhlopkov. At that instant a shot came from the forest ahead; but Fyodor failed to locate the flash and he continued to keep the pine tree in his field of view. Then, suddenly, he caught a glimpse of light close to the trunk. It seemed that for a fraction of a second a glint of the sun had touched the bark and then disappeared immediately.

It was apparent that the German sniper was perched in the tree. Fyodor looked intently at the spot but could detect nothing. Strict patience was now necessary so as not to betray his own position. Should his foe expose himself Okhlopkov must finish the duel with a single shot. If he missed, the enemy would, Fyodor knew, do one of two things: he would either disappear altogether or start firing back. In Fyodor's experience he seldom had a second chance at the same target.

A half hour had now elapsed since the German fired his shot at the decoy helmet. Now at the same spot a glove was raised, then another. This was an effort to simulate the movements of a wounded man trying to rise from the ground, tugging at the breastwork. The enemy took the bait and aimed his rifle, at which point Okhlopkov saw in the boughs a part of his face and, also, the tiny black spot of the gun barrel. (As his commanding officer was fond of saying, "Okhlopkov has marvelous eyes".) He got off two shots and a body fell to the ground, head first.

In the course of the first week with his new division Fyodor eliminated eleven enemy soldiers. This was reported by the observation posts who witnessed these "dangerous games".

Fyodor's "account" grew on his brother's behalf. Here are a few chronological listings from the divisional records: 14 March 1943– 147; 20 July – 171; 2 October – 219; 13 January, 1944 – 309; 23 March – 329; 25 April – 339; 7 June – 420. After that, Okhlopkov added nine more snipers to his list, making a grand total of 429.

Meanwhile, he was presented with numerous awards and decorations for his achievements.

Some time later, Fyodor's unit was in the forward skirmish line. This was, he thought, the best place for a sniper. If he saw a flash of light this would betray to him the position of an opponent's machine-gun, which he then must silence.

In the last week of October 1943, in a battle near the village of Matveyevo, Okhlopkov put twenty-seven enemy soldiers out of action. His friends were surprised at his luck on the battlefield, saying: "Fedya's life seems to be insured. He is immortal."

Now, Fyodor would sometimes "hunt" at night, firing at the red-hot ash of cigarettes, at a distant voice he happened to overhear, or the clank of a weapon, mess-tin or helmet.

An army newspaper of that time (*Zashchitnik Otechestva* – "Defender of the Homeland") said this about the super sniper: "Fyodor Okhlopkov has taken part in the hardest battles. He has the sharp eye of the hunter, the firm hand of a miner and a warm heart. The enemy who is caught in his sights is a dead man."

Though he was almost always at the front, he had time to give advice to others who wrote letters to him. He gave these tips to a young sniper:

- Don't try to imitate others.
- Work out your own methods of fighting the enemy.
- Seek new positions and new methods of camouflage.
- Don't be afraid to go to the rear of the enemy lines.
- Don't try to use a spear when you need a needle.
- Unless you can see a way out, don't enter.

Sometimes he also took young snipers with him to forward positions. From there they could learn the elements of combating enemy snipers. Fyodor would say: "In our business anything can serve a useful purpose: a damaged tank, the hollow of a tree, the frame of a country well, a stack of hay or straw, even the oven of a burnt-down house or a dead horse."

Once he pretended to be a corpse in no man's land, where he lay for a whole day among other soldiers who were really dead; and, because they had already lain there for some time, they were making him feel ill. From that unusual position he caught an enemy sniper who had hidden behind a drain pipe. Enemy soldiers did not notice where the shot had came from, and Fyodor, lying quietly till night set in, was able to crawl back to his own lines.

Fyodor's division was transferred to the First Baltic Front where the entire situation and scenery changed. But he continued to "hunt" every day for enemy soldiers, many of whom were snipers. It is testimony to his marksmanship that, in the many duels he fought with enemy snipers, he was not wounded even once. The twelve wounds and two contusions that he suffered came when he joined offensive and defensive operations fighting with the infantry. But though each of these wounds sapped his strength, he always returned to the front.

However, luck was against him on 23 June 1944. In fierce fighting to liberate the town of Vitebsk, north of Minsk, Fyodor had joined an assault team and in the battle he was shot through the chest. Evacuated to a military hospital deep in the rear, he did not return to the front again.

The war ended and Fyodor Okhlopkov regained his health in a Black Sea spa. Once he revisited the battlefields where he had fought as infantryman and sniper. The earth that was scorched and scarred by war had healed and there were now crops and wild flowers. Among the graves he visited was his brother's. Vasily had been killed at a Volga crossing. His body, like countless others, had returned to the Russian soil.

Nina Alexeyevna Lobkovskaya

In one of the photographs of Nina Alexeyevna Lobkovskaya, a white scar runs down her cheek, the "souvenir" of a sniper duel that took place in the summer of 1943. Notwithstanding the scar, the photo shows a young woman with a pleasant, cherubic face with a slightly turned-up nose. The black and white photograph shows Nina clutching her trusty sniper's rifle.

About the scar, Nina says: "My opponent in the duel happened to be an experienced sniper. I tracked him for a long time but I could not get him to betray himself. I took note of several places where he could have been and continued my observations. Meantime, I felt very uncomfortable, and my legs were numb. I moved just a little bit and, apparently, my rifle jiggled so that the lens of my sight reflected the sun. That moment the German sniper fired at me and I felt sticky blood trickling down my cheek. I felt no pain. The bullet had struck the metal rim of the sight and ricocheted into my face. As I wiped away the blood I thought I knew where to look for the enemy. I lost no time crawling to another foxhole. Taking my spare rifle I prepared to fire. The enemy sniper was sure the duel was over. As he was leaving his foxhole he appeared above the breastwork and I fired. Next morning a prisoner confirmed that the day before their ace sniper had been killed.

"But such duels were rare," Nina stresses.

When war broke out Nina Alexeyevna was a sixteen-year-old student living thousands of kilometres from the front-line. But she knew from the start about the horror of war. She knew that soldiers' families in her neighbourhood were receiving more and more *pokhoronkas* – official notices of a soldier's death. It was then that she decided to go to the front and "take revenge" on the enemy. Meanwhile, her father had gone to the front when the war began and was killed in 1942.

Nina and a girlfriend went to a local military office and requested to be sent to the front.

"What can you do?" an officer asked them.

The girls remained silent.

"All right, then. For a start, learn to bandage the wounded, operate a radio set, and fire a rifle. Then we'll see . . ."

In the summer of 1942 Nina received her secondary school diploma. But she was particularly proud of another certificate – Excellence in Marksmanship. That was the result of painstaking sessions on the rifle range.

Then one day Nina took part in a shooting contest. A few hundred girls competed in shooting and knowledge of assembling weapons. Nina and her friend Olga scored highest. As a result both girls were given the opportunity to attend a Women's Sniper School in Moscow.

In her diary Nina records how she felt about her sniper's lessons:

"As soon as I started studying I realized that the mere desire to fight the enemy was not enough. You had to have skill, too. Women are said to be more patient than men and, therefore, make good snipers. But we discovered that being a sniper is a difficult art and we mastered it only after months of daily lectures and training. We would go to the firing range at dawn and return after dark, tired and dirty. In winter it was not easy to crawl with a heavy rifle through snow and try to hit the target when your fingers froze on the trigger. It was equally tough performing long marches with a full pack on your back."

Nina's instructors drummed it into the girls that good camouflage was the difference between life and death for a sniper. A pair of snipers would be given two hours to dig a firing trench in a forest or field and to camouflage it according to the terrain. After a careful check the platoon leader would often make the girls dig another trench and camouflage that one too. One day they enjoyed a good laugh when the commanding officer held an examination in camouflage. No matter how hard he tried, he just could not locate the cleverly concealed foxholes. Finally he walked through the field and, to get a better view, he climbed a knoll. Suddenly the "knoll" cried out in a shrill girl's voice.

Nina remembers that by the time the lessons were over the girls had developed a high rate of fire – five well-aimed rounds per minute. They learned how to get their bearings quickly on the ground, locate targets in a hurry and move to alternative positions without being noticed. Many of the girls got excellent marks and were awarded special diplomas. Some were awarded snipers' rifles with their names inscribed on them.

The knowledge imparted by exacting teachers was extremely useful in the girls' first engagements with the enemy in the Kalinin region, outside Moscow. Mostly the girls worked in pairs. Nina made friends with Vera Artamonova from Leningrad. They were always together, in ambush, in the forward trenches, in the dugout and at leisure times. Common grief had joined them together. Nina had lost her father early in the war, Vera her father and mother who died of hunger in besieged Leningrad.

Nina recalls the impatience with which she awaited and finally got an assignment to a firing position for the very first time. "At night we dug standing foxholes near the front-line and camouflaged them. At dawn we were already in them. We divided the enemy-held ground into observation sectors and worked out reference points. All we could see in front of us was a field, a few bushes, knolls, trees crippled by artillery fire. Not a single sign of life. We strained our eyes till they hurt. But we could see nothing at all. The next day was just the same. In fact there were no results for three days. The forward edge of the enemy position was imprinted in our minds like a photograph. I could close my eyes and see every bump on the horizon. On the fourth day we were in our foxholes before day-break. The first rays of the sun illuminated the enemy's forward position. At first we failed to notice any changes. But then after a careful look we noticed a mound of fresh clay. Then a helmet flashed before my eyes. I prepared to fire. I was afraid to miss. Finally I observed the target in the cross-hairs of the telescopic sight. My finger smoothly pulled the trigger. On that day Vera and I destroyed several of the enemy."

The other girls of the company also registered their first scores. Notes appeared in the snipers' notebooks. They would return from the front dead tired but in high spirits as they shared impressions of the day. In no way could they imagine the ordeal that lay ahead in the fighting towards Warsaw and Berlin. Nina calls them "landmarks" on the road to victory.

When the last major offensive began the women were divided into groups and attached to infantry units. But sometimes sharp-shooting skills took second place to other demands of the battlefield. Nina describes what happened during one battle that began in the morning of 21 October 1943 when German planes appeared over-head and hundreds of shells and bombs "turned the earth inside out". It seemed to Nina that no living creature could withstand such a barrage of fire.

"We were already near the state border, at a city called Nevel in Byelorussia [now Belarus]. We had not yet consolidated the trenches we had captured from the enemy and, suddenly, the Germans counter-attacked. During this battle," Nina says, "we women snipers fought shoulder to shoulder with men in rifle company formations. Our accurate shots silenced enemy soldiers forever. During the fighting we were amazed to see German soldiers walking at full height, in disorderly rows, shouting something we could not under-stand, and firing their submachine-guns all the time. When they got nearer we saw that many of the soldiers were drunk. We beat off twelve counter-attacks but our own casualties mounted." The girls who had fired so effectively at the enemy were now ordered to switch over to a new job – carrying wounded men from the field of battle. "I remember passing one of our disabled tanks and hearing groans. Vera and I crawled up to the tank and knocked on the armour. Having made sure who we were the tankmen opened the hatch. It turned out that the driver had been killed, the tank commander and gunlayer wounded. With great difficulty we pulled out the badly wounded tank commander and, having laid him on a sheet, we dragged him to our trenches. The gunlayer managed to follow us on his own. The way back seemed many times longer. You can imagine our joy when we reached cover safely. Inciden-tally, the tank commander lived."

Nina's personal archive includes a photograph of a company of women snipers, many of them teenagers, whom she led to the walls of Berlin in 1945. The women of Nina's company accounted for more than 3,000 enemy soldiers who were part of Hitler's invasion force. Nina herself accounted for eighty-nine.

CHAPTER 9

Rammers over Moscow

During the first hours of the invasion Russian pilots rammed a number of incoming German planes, sending them corkscrewing out of the sky. It was a high-risk tactic of air defence, each ram attack involving not only immense danger but exceptional courage and great skill. In his popular wartime novel, *The Living and the Dead*, the author, Konstantin Simonov, has a character say, after hearing that a Luftwaffe plane was rammed over Moscow: "Fancy smashing into another plane like that!" In reply, someone says the Luftwaffe have become less bold than previously; that the rammings had made the German pilots jittery.

There was some truth in this. On the opening day of invasion, six Russian pilots, having spent their ammunition, rammed Nazi planes, causing them to crash in flames. Hermann Goering's pilots might have been excused for feeling apprehensive at such news.

A terse radio broadcast from Moscow announced the first incident:

"At 0515 hours on 22 June 1941, about 200 miles inside Russian territory, Flight Leader Junior Lieutenant Leonid Butelin rammed a German Junkers-88 bomber, severing its tail with the propeller of his fighter. This is the first ramming of the war."

Rammings were supposed to be an expedient of last resort for Russian pilots. The Luftwaffe was all-powerful in the first weeks and months of the invasion and Russian air power was no match for it. German planes were generally superior and their pilots had the advantage of previous combat experience. But there was no shortage of Russian bravado. In the meantime, Russian pilots absorbed the

121

tactics of ramming and some of them not only survived but went up and rammed again.

Russian wartime directives actually spelled out when pilots *had to* ram enemy planes. For example, a Combat Directive issued to the pilots of the 6th Air Corps during the defence of Moscow said: "If machine-guns jam in the air, if cartridges are spent prematurely, if the enemy is out to destroy an important state object, go and destroy the enemy by ramming."

According to this Combat Directive, pilots were *not* being sent on suicide missions: "To ram the enemy is an act of the greatest heroism and bravery but is not an act of self-sacrifice." The Directive added the injunction: "You should know how to ram." There followed four pages on the techniques of ramming. Pilots who had rammed enemy aircraft early in the war and survived taught others this "act of total aggression" in the sky. The official reports said that ramming fatalities to Russian pilots were mainly the result of head-on collisions. Pilots survived, said the reports, if they were able to bale out or if they managed to land their damaged planes. Not mentioned was the detail that if and when both planes became uncontrollable after a ramming, their pilots were often doomed.

Here is how the Chief Marshal of the Soviet Air Force, A. A. Novikov, regarded the act of ramming: "Any technique of air combat demands valour, courage and skill by the pilot. But a ram attack makes incalculably greater demands on a pilot. Ramming means, first of all, a readiness for self-sacrifice; it is a test of loyalty to the people, to the ideals of the Motherland." Novikov went on to call ramming, "one of the highest forms of displaying a high morale that is inherent in the nation." But he also spoke of the importance of ramming in the purely tactical sense. Speaking after the war, he said: "The enemy pilots' fear of ramming gave our pilots advantages such as manoeuvring possibilities, and helped boost their growing superiority in air combat tactics."

The air ace Alexander Pokryshkin, who shot down fifty-nine Nazi planes, and became an air marshal after the war, gave this opinion of the wartime directives that imposed ramming as a duty: "Everything is correct; it was just like that. A strike by ramming is the weapon of fliers with iron nerves. In the defence of Moscow this method was rightly necessary." Pokryshkin added: "At short distances, behind the tail of an enemy bomber, our fighter was invulnerable. He got into the 'dead cone' of enemy fire, inched closer and cut off a section of tail, or a wing. One Nazi flier who bailed out after his bomber was rammed, said when interrogated: 'Rumors went around about rammings on the Eastern Front. But at first we did not believe in them. What a terrible thing it is!' "

Although the *Blitzkrieg* came as a surprise fighter pilots like Leonid Butelin saw action from the opening minutes of hostilities. And an increasing number of ram attacks was reported.

Seventeen pilots executed a ramming attack twice. Pilot Alexei Khlobystov used this terrifying technique three times, and Boris Kovzan four times. The records reveal that a woman pilot, Yekaterina Zelenko, destroyed a Luftwaffe fighter by ramming.

Apparently, ramming predates the Second World War. It is claimed that during the First World War a Russian pilot, Pyotr Nikolayevich Nesterov, was the first man in history to ram an enemy aircraft. This happened on 8 September 1914 during a dogfight with a German two-seater reconnaissance plane. But Nesterov was killed in the attack. According to Air Force Colonel Vladimir Amelchenko, a military writer, the ramming by Nesterov served during the Patriotic War as "a symbol of selflessness, courage and valour" for Russian pilots.

There is this story of a "Russian Rambo" that was confirmed by British pilots. Flying in northern skies, a Russian pilot had got into a dogfight with two German aircraft. He shot down one of them but, running out of ammunition, he rammed the second plane, sending it crashing to the ground. By chance his parachute landed near the downed two-seater German plane that he had engaged minutes earlier. Now the three aircrew faced each other across frozen wastes on a part of the earth so desolate that you could walk for days without seeing another human being. Quickly the Russian dispatched one of his opponents with his revolver. But a boxer dog that the German crew had, for some reason, brought with them, leaped at him and he was forced to shoot the dog. Then, grappling with the other pilot, the Russian's face was slashed with a knife from forehead to chin and some of his teeth were knocked out. The contest ended when he fired a flare at the enemy's head from his Very pistol at point-blank range. The survivor then walked four days and nights in the snow with frost-bitten feet and with his face hanging open until he reached a hospital. A couple of British military men who knew the pilot visited him in a hospital and were able to authenticate the story. In its toughness and determination, it represented to British eyes "something near the heroic".

Moscow, as expected, became the main target for enemy air attack. Hitler's intention to level Moscow required hundreds of bombing planes. For this purpose the Luftwaffe formed a special group of 1,600 aircraft made up of the best squadrons. The leaders of this air fleet, which provided support for the Wehrmacht's Army Group Centre, chose bombers of the newest types, including the Heinkel-111 with high altitude engines, the Junkers-88, and the Dornier-215. Pilots in these raids were picked from famous squadrons, including the "Condor" which had bombed Spanish cities including the Basque town of Guernica during the civil war, and others that had menaced the skies over London, Liverpool and Birmingham, or operated over Poland, Yugoslavia and Greece.

Moscow is an old city and its main thoroughfares are arranged in concentric circles – easily identifiable to unfriendly aircraft. To counter this, architects and artists altered Moscow's appearance. Roofs of houses were painted so they looked like a continuation of streets; many squares "disappeared". Rivers on starry or moonlit nights can be easily recognized from the air. To alter the landscape, when darkness set in, barges with camouflage nets were moored at specific points on the Moscow River. "New bridges" appeared and old bridges "disappeared" under smokescreens and other means of subterfuge.

In the first month of war the Luftwaffe made nearly 100 attempts to penetrate the skies over Moscow, clandestinely, one at a time, at a height of 26,000 feet. Only a few planes got through. Between July-December 1941 there were approximately 120 raids against Moscow comprising over 7,000 Luftwaffe planes. Of this number only about 200 German aircraft succeeded in getting close to the capital. The rest were shot down or chose less forbidding targets. In the July-August period nine enemy bombers were lost due to ramming. Moscow's air defence proved to be of a high order.

Of course, ramming was only one of the means to keep enemy bombers from penetrating Moscow skies. Significant in the city's defence were nearly 1,000 anti-aircraft guns, 200 large-calibre anti-aircraft machine-guns, 1,000 searchlights and hundreds of barrage balloons.

On 2 July, something unexpected happened. A Heinkel-111, equipped with a high-altitude engine, flew towards Moscow on an intelligence-gathering mission. On board was a colonel from the German General Staff who carried with him important documents including operational maps and codes. His aircraft was met by a YAK-1 piloted by Lieutenant Sergei Goshko. The YAK-1 was a wooden-winged plane with a top speed of over 279 mph which could outmanoeuvre some of the Luftwaffe's faster planes. Suddenly, after an indecisive aerial battle the Russian pilot struck off the tail of the Heinkel with the wing of his fighter, sending the intruder spinning to earth. For his exploit, Goshko was decorated with the highest combat medal, the gold hero's medal. Goshko brought down six more German aircraft by conventional means, making his last flight over a defeated Berlin on 8 May 1945.

To safeguard Moscow as well as other cities, Russian pilots rammed Luftwaffe planes on at least 300 occasions during the war. Many of these rammings took place on the approaches to the capital.

On the night of 22 July 1941 Hitler launched his first massive air strike against Moscow, 220 bombers taking part. Marshal Zhukov says that only a small percent of the enemy bombers reached the capital, most of the others being stopped by the Moscow Anti-Aircraft Defence System. About two dozen bombers were shot down outside the capital. This became the first of a series of aerial battles for command of Moscow's skies.

That same day over Mozhaisk, about 75 miles west of Moscow, a single aircraft, a YAK-1, engaged an incoming squadron of German Junkers-88 bombers. The Soviet pilot, Boris Vasiliev, an air ace from the Georgian Republic, used his propeller to saw off the tail of the bomber closest to him.

Erskine Caldwell, the American author of *Tobacco Road*, was in Moscow during the first month of the war and witnessed a series of air raids. This is what he said about the night of 23/24 July 1941: "I am unable to compare Moscow's air defence with that of London and Berlin; but judging from reports, if the Moscow defence is not superior it certainly must be every bit as effective in beating back air attacks as any air defence anywhere." After watching repeated air raids, Caldwell said that in five nights of raiding Moscow the intruders "have accomplished little more than the entire Swiss Navy accomplished in the First World War."

At the beginning of August 1941 Russians crowded around a German aircraft that had been shot down not far from the capital. Near the charred metal was a wooden signboard with the words: "Tail of a Nazi bomber downed by Senior Lt Yevgeni Yeremeyev." The pilot, who worked at a research institute of the Air Force, was a pioneer in night-flying. On the night of the first enemy raid on Moscow, Yeremeyev had shot down a German bomber with machine-gun fire.

"When I saw a report about night-time dogfights at the end of July 1941, I did not believe it," says General Yevgeni Klimov, then Commander of the 6th Air Corps. "I called up Yeremeyev and he told me how it happened, and I recommended this hero of night-ramming to be decorated with the highest award." The general adds: "We were soon holding discussions in all units about Yeremeyev's exploits at night." But the hero-pilot had only two more months to live. His life ended over Moscow when he was shot down by a Messerschmitt.

However, among those who attended the discussions was Viktor

Talalikhin, a twenty-three-year-old pilot, who was described by friends as "short, unassuming with clever brown eyes".

The Talalikhin saga began at 22 hours 55 minutes on the moonlit night of 6 August 1941, when enemy planes were trying to break through Moscow's air defences.

On that night his regiment was gathered at the edge of a forest where fighter planes were concealed. Everyone was absorbed in his own thoughts. Mechanics were getting the planes ready for night flying. The war was only two months old and night fighters were few at that time; the regiment was just learning the rudiments of combat flying at night. To complicate matters, the regiment was short of experts to train pilots for night duty. After a briefing from the regimental commander, the pilots were ready to take off. Suddenly the quiet was disturbed by the dull crackling of anti-aircraft guns that covered the approaches to Moscow. Shells flashed in the sky high above the outskirts of the city. They burst sporadically, sowing splinters over wide areas. Searchlight beams probed the skies, intersecting in twos and threes and parting to pick out intruding planes and harass them across the sky.

The pilots leaped into their cockpits and began taking off into the darkness with orders to intercept the enemy. Talalikhin was airborne within three minutes.

Flying at 14,000 feet the young pilot saw the moonlight reflected on the fuselage of a hostile aircraft heading towards Moscow. Without further ado he pushed the throttle wide open to overtake the plane. The distance between them rapidly dwindled and Talalikhin banked sharply to approach from the rear. Then he saw a swastika on the tail of the aircraft and he recognized it as a twin-engine Heinkel-111 bomber. "You will not escape me," he thought. He held his breath until the Heinkel was centered in his sights and then pressed the firing button. The burst of machine-gun fire entered the starboard engine which immediately caught fire. The Heinkel did not answer and tried to escape. Its pilot increased speed, turned and dived to put out the flames. Talalikhin banked to starboard and fired another burst. But the Heinkel zigzagged, sharply changed course and began losing altitude.

The pilot evidently hoped to evade Talalikhin's fighter at low altitude, a manoeuvre with which the Russian was familiar. He followed the Luftwaffe plane, closing in on its tail. Falling to 8,000 feet, he pressed the button again. After another turn he closed to within 50 feet intending to fire a point-blank burst.

Sensing the end, the German plane opened desperate return fire. As the enemy pilot was experienced, the pursuit went on, the pilot deftly manoeuvring towards hoped-for safety in the darkness. But Talalikhin doggedly followed. After a long burst his machine-guns went dead – he was out of ammunition. His silence possibly gave hope to the crew of the fleeing plane. But Talalikhin was becoming agitated as he realized the enemy might escape. "No, you shall not!" he said to himself. He was almost sitting on the enemy's tail. "Now is the time!" he thought. "He must not get away!" His decision was made: "Ram him!"

Talalikhin's movements became more confident as he closed on the Heinkel's tail. The enemy gunner suddenly opened fire with a machine-gun and bullets whistled on Viktor's right, some of them searing his arm. In response to the pain, Talalikhin pushed the throttle further open. His plane jerked up. There was a crash. The Heinkel burst into flames and plunged toward the ground. Talalikhin's plane also became uncontrollable. Releasing himself from the cockpit, he rolled overboard, dropping like a stone. He had to worry now about drifting out of the way of the falling planes. After a free fall of 3,200 feet he pulled the ring of his parachute. It paid out of the pack but he soon noticed that he was being carried towards a dense forest. Tugging at the lines he changed direction and landed in a shallow lake. Farmers who had gathered on the ground helped the pilot and took him back to his regiment.

The first night ramming attack by Talalikhin won him the gold hero medal. Meanwhile, his attack was written up in all the major newspapers. During the first four months of the war Talalikhin accounted for twenty-seven German planes. But Talalikhin's luck ended on 27 October 1941 when he perished with his aircraft in a duel with three Messerschmitts.

The first high-altitude ramming was also recorded during the Battle of Moscow. On 21 August Lieutenant Alexei Katrich (later promoted to general), pilot of a MIG-3 fighter, received an order to destroy a reconnaissance plane, a Dornier-217. Katrich climbed into the cockpit and took off.

A silvery trail showed up sharply against the bright blue sky. The "trail" was heading for Moscow. Katrich's plane gained altitude, rising to 16,300 feet. It was cold in the cabin and it became difficult to breathe. He put on his oxygen mask. He was now at 22,800 feet and still climbing. He approached the enemy plane from the rear and opened fire. The aircraft's gunner returned fire, but the crew decided to escape by turning westward. After a second attack Alexei saw flames from the port engine of the plane. He pressed the button to fire again but there were no bullets left. He decided to ram despite the high altitude. At full speed Alexei reached the tail of the bomber and cut its stabilizer and rudder with his propeller. Disintegrating in the air, the Dornier fell swiftly. Although Katrich's plane was also damaged, he remained in control and, taking advantage of the high altitude, glided to his airfield where he made a skilful landing. The engagement had taken place at 26,000 feet.

In the defence of Moscow pilot Mikhail Rodionov made a "double ramming". Seeing an enemy JU-88, he opened fire. One of the engines of the Junkers became silent but the plane kept flying. Rodionov repeated the attack, not knowing that it was a special aircraft with strengthened armour. Suddenly the Junkers started to dive from a height of 9,800 feet. He gave chase. Only at 163 feet above ground did the YAK fighter catch up. With his propeller, Rodionov put a deep gash on the right wing of the Junkers bomber. But still the enemy aircraft stayed aloft. Rodionov now came from the other side and delivered the *coup de grace*, striking the bomber's wing with his own. For his feat, Rodionov was awarded the gold star hero medal.

The archives of the Defence Ministry disclose another "double ramming" which occurred when two Russian fighters were in hot pursuit of an enemy reconnaissance plane.

The 124th Fighter Air Regiment reported:

"After several attacks the machine-guns of flight commander Boris Pirozhkov jammed. He closed to ram, slicing off the right half of the enemy's stabilizer. The Junkers-88 lost altitude but did not fall. Then Lieutenant Viktor Dovgii, who was alongside, made a decision to ram it from above. At a height of only 3,200 feet he struck off the tail of the Junkers."

As the front line moved closer to the capital enemy aircraft became more active and during October over 2,000 sorties were made; few bombers, however, got through to the city centre or the Kremlin. But General S. M. Shtemenko, at that time a member of the General Staff, remembers that on the night of 28 October a high-explosive bomb landed in the yard of the General Staff building. ("The building was shaken as if by an earthquake.") Several vehicles were destroyed; three drivers were killed and fifteen officers wounded, some of them seriously. A. M. Vasilevsky, one of the highest ranking officers in the Army was injured by flying glass, although he was able to go on working.

Some of the aerial battles staggered belief. The 606th Air Regiment had wooden and canvas biplanes that were no match for metal aircraft. On 7 October 1941 Lieutenant Ivan Denisov, flying one of these biplanes, an R-5, crashed head-on with a Henschel-129. The twisted metal of the Henschel fell to earth. The biplane broke up, too, but the pilot parachuted to safety.

The last ram attack in defence of Moscow occurred on 2 June 1943. A Junkers-88 was flying at a height of 26,000 feet. From a nearby airfield a MIG-3 piloted by Lieutenant Gennady Sirishikov went up to meet it. During the first attack the Russian fired two bursts which brought no results. The archive report says the pilot, "refused to leave the field of battle without winning". He closed on the invader and, with his propeller, sawed off the tail of the hapless Junkers.

Some remarkable rammings took place in Arctic skies. Pilot Alexei Khlobystov rammed three German planes in the far north and survived. His aerial exploits began in 1942 when the Arctic spring had set in. Heading for the northern port of Murmansk were twenty-eight Luftwaffe planes. Khlobystov, a veteran pilot, took off with his squadron and saw one Messerschmitt crash. He now manoeuvred to help his less experienced colleagues. Suddenly he saw below him a two-seater Messerschmitt 110. He swooped down and closed in. Flying over the edge of a forest, he saw a hill looming up ahead and he decided to ram the enemy plane with his wing. The impact was strong and his own plane bounced around but the intruder plane crashed. However, something wasn't right with Khlobystov's plane as it climbed jerkily. When he turned his head he saw that his starboard wing was a foot shorter than the port. Control of his plane was causing a problem although he could still fly. Suddenly he saw two enemy planes heading right for him. But now his fuel was running low so Khlobystov decided to ram a second time, thinking he'd be very lucky if he came out alive. As soon as one opponent veered aside, he struck at the other's tail, using his shorter, damaged wing. Again his fighter bounced dizzily and he temporarily lost control. Meantime, the foe had crashed. To Khlobystov's amazement his own plane was still navigable and he was able to land despite a partially sawed-off wing.

A short time later Khlobystov rammed a third enemy plane. But this time his opponent succeeded in hitting the engine of Khlobystov's fighter and he himself received two wounds. Thinking it was impossible to return to the airfield, he put on speed and rammed a Messerschmitt 109, which was sliced in half by the impact. Khlobystov's fighter was also smashed but he parachuted to safely. In his hospital bed he was decorated for bravery and exceptional flying skill.

Officially the orders on ramming were taken off the books in September 1944. By that time Russian pilots dominated the skies and few Luftwaffe planes flew over Russian territory. But the evidence shows that many years after the war commanding officers could still order a pilot to initiate a ram attack. The most notorious case occurred in May 1960 when a high-altitude American U-2 spy plane was detected over Siberia. In response, a Soviet Air Force major was ordered to take off and ram the intruder. The pilot became airborne but never made contact with the U-2 which no doubt saved his life. Hit by a missile, the US plane crashed, its pilot, Francis Gary Powers, parachuting safely. The 1960 order to ram the intruding plane was not made public until thirty years after the event.

CHAPTER 10

The Cossacks

German troops heard the swish of the Cossack★ sword from the early days of invasion and often it was too late for them to prevent the Cossack cavalry from overrunning their encampments. These fierce engagements increased in the second year of war when there was a large influx of Kuban Cossacks of the older generation into the Red Army. Far back in the past, the Cossacks had spread over the mighty rivers of the south, such as the Dnieper, Don, Kuban and Terek. Now, greybeards wearing the Cross of St George, awarded for distinguished service in the tsarist wars, gathered to volunteer; and there was the unusual spectacle of fathers joining up as privates while, increasingly, their sons had already become officers.

Hitler's advancing troops desired to win Cossack sympathizers; they hoped the Cossacks "would rise to a man" to help the Wehrmacht. There is some evidence that dissident Cossack troops were used sporadically by the Nazi Command on the Eastern Front from the summer of 1941. The Nazi officers told the Cossacks: "We have come to dissolve the collectives, redistribute the land, get rid of atheists and Jews and drive the Communists into Asia. When this is done there will be security and every man can work for himself." To the simple-minded these words sounded like deliverance.

★ Although I've visited Cossack country (the Don Cossacks), for some of the material in this chapter I've relied on the works of Maurice Hindus, who spent much time in Russia before and during the Second World War and travelled widely among the Cossacks. But the best source for discovering the wild and robust heritage of the Cossacks is Gogol's classic novel, *Taras Bulba*.

But there had been a noticeable transformation among the Cossacks, especially of the younger generation. True, their fathers had entered the twentieth century as instruments of suppression under the last tsars; as haters of Bolsheviks and the makers of pogroms; as warriors against "infidels" – that is, anyone outside the Orthodox religion, including Catholics and Muslims. Over a hundred years earlier Napoleon had spoken contemptuously of the Cossacks as "the disgrace of the human race," but the Cossacks of whom Pushkin, Gogol, Tolstoy and Sholokhov had written, often with exquisite sympathy, were historically a swashbuckling breed, wildly patriotic, sometimes driven to drunken excess as they flaunted danger.★ They had once made a powerful impression on Russia's political development. But adaptations and conversions were rife in the opening decades of the twentieth century.

By the time German armies appeared in some of their villages, the petty prejudices and antagonisms of the Cossacks had largely faded into the past so that the way had opened even for Jews and Gypsies who lived in Cossack neighbourhoods to call themselves Cossacks; while brilliant Cossack generals were serving in the Red Army. Some observers believe that the portrayals of the Cossacks in a more positive light in the new literature and the movies had hastened this transformation, so that the Cossacks no longer displayed the past riotous behaviour and unpredictability but held on to the more enviable Russian traits – in the first place loyalty and reliability.

An example is the Cossack General Nikolai Kirichenko. Much-admired by his men, this officer possessed a robust nature and the considerable skills of an experienced cavalryman. But – a signpost of the new breed – he combined these skills with the curiosity and intelligence of a budding scholar. A group of visiting foreign journalists who met him in 1942 (he was then forty-nine years old) were astonished at his enjoyment of literature; his home library in the Kuban district contained a thousand volumes, many of them recent

★ Nobel Prize-winning author Mikhail Sholokhov was himself a Cossack. During the war he was a front line correspondent. When I visited his home shortly before his death in 1984, I was shown where Hitler's bombs had fallen on his mother's home near the River Don, killing her and destroying his library.

novels signed by contemporary Russian authors. He also had works of modern British and American fiction. Here was the "new Cossack", a man who could discuss not only the art of warfare but poetry, novels, music as well as the theatre of Russia, America and other countries. He knew the Russian classics but had also read Shakespeare, Dickens, Shaw, Mark Twain and Jack London. This military man whose cavalry a few days earlier had wrought havoc among the enemy on the battlefield, now told the journalists, when the discussion turned from "the bastard art of war" to *belles-lettres*: "Without books a man withers away."

But the general had just been decorated and the bulk of his talk with the journalists was about his recent clash with the enemy. He and his cavalry had slipped through German lines to the tiny village of Kushtshevskaya. With his main force well camouflaged, hidden in a nearby valley and under the command of one of his generals, Kirichenko employed a successful ruse. He sent out a small detachment which caught the attention of the enemy; the detachment feigned a fast retreat. When the enemy advanced in pursuit, Kirichenko ordered his hidden force into action. Cries rent the air as the Cossacks flashed sabres, pouncing on the panicked Germans in an engagement which lasted nearly four hours. Kirichenko's summing up gives an idea of the sanguinary battlefield: "It took the Germans eight days to bury their dead."

Those foreign guests interested in "the art of the sabre" found a willing instructor in Kirichenko. With the coolness of a scientist he explained how to use the sabre in killing an enemy. Each stroke of the sabre and its effectiveness against the body depended on the physique of the enemy. There were, he informed in precise detail – as if lecturing acolytes – even different strokes depending on the *personality* of the enemy. He told which strokes, if executed well, would be *guaranteed fatal*. For example, between the shoulder blades or across the spine . . . "But these are only some of the strokes we use in battle."

Laying the edge of his hand on the side of his neck, Kirichenko was about to explain how a skilled Cossack cavalryman . . . But the general, seeing that his remarks were beginning to chafe, made it plain that his grim discourse must be understood in the context of war with an implacable enemy. The enemy, he reminded, came to kill and plunder; had burst into sleepy Cossack villages on the Sea of Azov and the River Don pillaging and burning these and other regions and carrying off as many able-bodied captives as possible.

Despite the general's uniform, his deep chest and carefully combed hair, to his guests he appeared more the headmaster in a private school than an army commander. They noticed his patience towards his men, how he took pains to clarify complex problems. He also possessed no military swagger but had an appealing modesty. His guests learned that he would in fact shortly take up duties in a classroom, military-style, that is. Formerly Kirichenko had commanded an army; now he had a little while ago been appointed head of a military academy and would soon depart for his new post.

The foreign journalists learned more about Kirichenko from his adjutants. While the stereotype of a Cossack cavalry officer was that of a flamboyant and profane individual, the general was actually "simple and straightforward", even "humble". They said the general was a "real hero", that although he had a breastful of decorations he refused to wear them on his uniform except at parades. He was different in another way: Cossack officers were notorious for their rich fund of obscenities. But this cultivated general had a "chaste vocabulary".

Asked if he had a family, General Kirichenko answered good-humouredly: "Of course I have a family. I am a Russian, and a Russian always has a family." With that, he drew a photograph from a leather wallet. "My daughter," he said. "Splendid girl. She is a college student in Moscow." On the back of the photograph were five words written in big letters: "To my darling 'little' father."

When the war broke out, there had already been a re-education campaign among the Cossacks, many of whom had formerly waged war with the regime that had ousted their beloved tsar. Sir Peter Ustinov, in his book *My Russia*, refers to the old-time Cossacks as frontiersmen who rode in posses, became adventurers, sometimes mercenaries, but never ceased being independence-addicts, similar to the pioneers of America's Wild West. Also – another similarity – just as Yankee pioneers blazed a trail to the West, so the Cossacks opened up the East, including Siberia, reaching the Pacific Ocean in the seventeenth century. Now – against Hitler's armies – separate Cossack divisions had been permitted in the Red Army. This showed the regime's confidence in Cossack loyalty. At the outset of war, Cossack esteem in Russia which had formerly not been high, was now in the ascendant.*

Wisely, the Red Army restored some Cossack privileges, for example, wearing their colourful Astrakhan cloaks and jaunty hats. They were also allowed to design their own dazzling uniforms.

The Cossack general was often a breed apart. For instance, General Selianov, Commander in the North Caucasus, was a lusty cavalryman, cool under fire, who had recently been decorated with a medal named after the commander who defeated Napoleon: Marshal Kutuzov. The story is told that when the enemy was approaching Vladikavkas, close to Grozny, when the enemy's tanks were counterattacking, Selianov's men were frightened and began to run towards the rear. The general dismounted and started walking in the direction of the Germans, carrying a small whip in his hands. "Where are you going, Cossack?" he shouted above the din of battle to each man he met. "Remember, these tanks are only machines made by men. What man has made man can destroy." Seeing their fearless commander, the troops turned around and a rout was prevented.

As soon as war came to Russia, the Cossacks began holding training courses in sabre fighting and, naturally, many of the instructors were men of the older generation. One Cossack, Nikifor Notluk, whose two sons were army commanders, proposed that young Cossacks should be taught the sabre-cutting style of the famous Zaporozhye Cossacks. His language sheds light on the pitiless encounters that were in store for the enemy.

* After the war, tens of thousands of Cossacks, who had been held prisoner by the Germans, were returned by British forces – a certain proportion of them against their will – to the Soviet Union, where an undetermined number landed in the gulag or suffered a worse fate. Some historians have questioned the wisdom of British compliance with the Kremlin demands for their return.

"The invader must be cleft from the shoulder to the groin," said Notluk. "Anyone can cut off a head or slice off an arm, but a Cossack must wield his sabre as his great-grandfathers did." Another instructor was Trofim Negoduko. It is recorded that his grandfather crossed the Balkans with the famed General Gurko and saw the minarets of Stamboul and the hills of San Stefano; that his father had fought in Manchuria with Colonel Samsonov's detachment. In the First World War Trofim joined his father to fight in (now) General Samsonov's army which broke into East Prussia, thereby helping save Paris from the Kaiser. In the civil war, Trofim fought the Germans in the south of Russia and defended Tsaritsyn (later Stalingrad, still later Volgograd) under the legendary commander, Semyon Budenny.

A daring exploit by the Cossacks was described in the *Illustrated War News* (of London) in 1914: "A patrol of ten Cossacks came upon a squadron of German cavalry who dismounted and opened fire to avoid a hand-to-hand encounter. The Cossacks, as they attacked, swung themselves beneath their horses' girths in their favourite style. The trick deceived the Germans, who mounted to ride after what they supposed to be riderless horses. Thereupon the Cossacks suddenly reappeared in the saddle and cut them to pieces."

Trofim, at fifty-four years of age, was now a senior sergeant. At the end of 1941 he rode with the "sharpened sabres" of General Dovator when his cavalry struck suddenly behind German lines before Moscow. A man of few words, Trofim said simply in reply to a question about his skill: "I do a Cossack's job well." And what, he was asked, was expected of a Cossack? His answer: "Fierceness. They expect him to deal heavy strokes. Well, I deal such strokes. A good stroke is never forgotten. It lives forever."

The sabres of Trofim's grandfather and father had captured the newspaper headlines of former days. His grandfather hewed through an enemy horseman from shoulder to waist before General Skobelev's face. In 1914, meeting enemy infantry, his father reportedly cut up a soldier in six parts with two blows of the sword. This was described as the "criss-cross" blow, and its fame attracted young officers to study with its practitioner. Trofim's father, Alexander, showed students how to cut in two a piece of cloth tossed into the air.

With pride, Trofim still used a silver-hilted sword with an Arabic inscription on the blade: "I serve the eagle-hearted." The hilt was now covered with 131 copper dots resembling freckles. That was Trofim's score against the Wehrmacht. But Trofim said eight dots were missing, that they'd been accidentally rubbed off. One of his deadly sabre blows he had dedicated to a forebear. "Even Grandfather Petro would have approved of it," he said. With a single blow he had dispatched an enemy officer – this was near Rostov – in three parts: head and shoulders, half the body and an arm, and the rest of the body. Armed with this battlefield gore, Trofim was now teaching young Cossacks "The Advanced Art of the Sword."

"Use your imagination," he told them. "Pretend that the invader is very broad and you're cutting him up like a cake. Don't hurry. Take it easy, and everything will turn out well." Then Trofim said mockingly: "Of course psychology plays a part, too. But it's none of our business if an enemy squeals. If the invaders don't like it they should have stayed at home. But once they've broken into our house, crying won't help them."

Discussing the Cossack as warrior and his role in the war on the Eastern Front, General Kirichenko said the following:

> Hitler laughed at us. He and his claque said they would blow us off the face of the earth with their planes, tanks and high-powered artillery. They did their best to scare us. Some of the boys fresh from the steppe were, on first sighting the enemy tanks, uneasy; all the more so because the machines made terrifying noises – screaming, wailing, shrieking until the men's ears nearly split. The enemy was expert in attaching noise-making gadgets to their weapons.

But, said the versatile general, the enemy's best weapons failed to intimidate the defenders.

Kirichenko later told about the recapture of the city of Taganrog on the Sea of Azov early in 1943. In this campaign the Cossacks are credited with having played the decisive role. "That," said the general, "was one of our magnificent campaigns. For almost two years the enemy had fortified Taganrog. They had built a chain of fortifications everywhere which bristled with firepower. A frontal attack was forbidden: we would've been slaughtered. So cocksure was the enemy that in the pamphlets which they dropped on our lines they said that if we came within range of their big guns they'd tear us to pieces with their shells. But the Cossacks weren't scared of their pamphlets or firepower."

The general explained the tactics of the Cossacks. "After the infantry blazed a passage for us, we plunged ahead at night into the enemy's rear. We found their staffs and annihilated them. We destroyed supplies and communications. We repeated the procedure the next night, going even deeper into the enemy's rear. The enemy's 'cards' were so badly mixed they didn't know how to play them. From our position we were pulling Hitler's entire army at Taganrog backwards, towards us. That's what we wanted. So they became more confused. Then our infantry and other units cut loose. The Cossacks joined with the infantry and we surrounded the enemy armies and eliminated almost all of them."

Next, this spellbinding general described the recapture of Rostov, a major city on the River Don. One detail of his account in particular stands out – how the Cossack cavalry crossed a frozen, slippery Don at night when the ice was phosphorescent. The Cossacks started to make their way across but the ice was so slippery the horses were sliding and falling. The men were in a desperate hurry; every minute was precious. They needed the darkness to plunge into the enemy rear; the more havoc they could create the better. But what to do? An elderly Cossack officer came to the rescue. He said the men must take the *burkas* (long black sleeveless cloaks) off their backs and spread them over the Don. In minutes hundreds of *burkas* flew off and were quickly spread over the ice from one bank to the other. And over this "black carpet" the Cossack regiments made their way across the river.

The general concluded: "We then galloped for a distance of

22 miles, tore up rails, blew up bridges, laid waste to everything of use to the enemy. We captured eighteen carloads of ammunition. We disorganized, confused and terrorized the enemy. Enemy tank crews jumped out of their tanks and fled. We jumped into the tanks and fired at the fleeing men. We were hitting them with all kinds of weapons. We slashed at them with our sabres and fired our guns. We fought on land that was holy to us – the land of our forefathers. We never fought any better. We wanted to teach the enemy a lesson which their great-great-great-grandchildren would remember."

It is common knowledge that cavalry charges on the Eastern Front sometimes failed dismally. The general addressed the question of the risk involved in sending mounted Cossacks (as happened early in the war) against powerful mechanized forces, with many men and horses destroyed. "Yes, those attacks were enormously risky," he said. Then he added: "But in war, risk is a noble principle . . ."

The general had described many Cossack campaigns in glowing terms. But did he – a man with a penchant for the humanities, who loved literature – not agree on the horror and wastefulness of war? He gave this answer: "All war is terrible. I, a Cossack general, say so. Our Kuban Cossacks were peaceful citizens. No longer were they professional fighting men like their ancestors. They were tilling their lands, white-washing their cottages, pruning their fruit trees, building nurseries, new schools, new cow stables, jam-making factories. Fighting was no longer, as in the past, their primary aim in life. They were toiling to bring joy and prosperity to their villages, their homes, themselves. The last thing they wanted was to drop their spades and hammers for rifles and sabres. But what could they do when an enemy filled with hate and primed for murder set out to conquer the world?"

Not to be forgotten was Kirichenko's belief in the connection of heroism with the stylish Cossack uniforms of the Kuban. The Kuban is a large area of fertile farmland near the Sea of Azov. (To be fair, other Cossacks have stately uniforms too, such as those from the Don region.) "Have you seen our uniforms?" asked the general. "There is a good reason why red is the colour of our Kuban Cossacks: red-topped astrakhan hats, red bands on our trousers, red-lined hoods on our back, red breast pieces in our cloaks. Red is the symbol of our invincibility, of indifference to blood, of defiance of death."

The coda of this Cossack recital was exquisite: "When blood courses down our breast the red front piece absorbs it. We don't see it and we keep on fighting."

CHAPTER 11

The Siberians

Hitler had arrived, flushed with initial victories, in the Belorussian town of Borisov on 4 August 1941. This was the first time since the beginning of the invasion in June that he had stood on hated Bolshevik soil. Moscow, the capital, was less than 500 miles distant. The Führer's armies were moving fast, increasingly devouring Russian real estate, although more slowly than at the beginning of the *Blitzkrieg*. Nevertheless, Hitler was so confident of his capture of Moscow that General Erich von dem Bach-Zelewski, one of Himmler's closest associates, was appointed future commander of the SS troops who would enter the defeated capital.

One trifle did not spoil Hitler's jubilation; if some members of Hitler's staff thought about it they also didn't think it worth worrying about. Some of the Nazi predictions for achieving a quick victory over Russia were already out of date. (One example: "In three weeks Russia's house of cards will collapse" – General Alfred Jodl, Chief of Operations, Armed Forces High Command.) The war had now lasted more than six weeks and Russian resistance rather than diminishing showed signs of stiffening. Another matter, perhaps trivial, needed readjustment: Hitler's plans for an August parade in Moscow (a parade leader had been named) did not look promising as it was already August and his generals were no longer talking about entering Moscow in the near future.

Fabian von Schlabrendorf, aide-de-camp to the chief of the operations division of Field Marshal Fedor von Bock's staff, preserved a record of the conversation in Borisov between Hitler and von Bock. He wrote: "Hitler discussed his plan for the capture of Moscow . . . Moscow was to be surrounded so that neither the Russian soldiers nor the civilians should be able to leave. Measures were to be taken to flood Moscow and its environs. The territory covered by Moscow was to become a large lake which was to hide the capital of the Russian people forever."*

Despite the fact that the Wehrmacht's advance was slowing down, the danger that loomed for Moscow was increasing. And the most critical time was yet to come, in October and November. But Moscow overcame the danger hanging over it. Some historians say that a key role, if not *the* key role, in alleviating the danger to Moscow was played by the Siberians . . .

Afanasy Pavlantevich Beloborodov (when the author met him in 1985 he found it easier to address him as "General . . .") was the commander of the 78th Infantry Division from Siberia whose actions in front of Moscow, including a victorious counter-offensive, won high praise from the General Staff and Supreme Headquarters. Beloborodov, himself a Siberian, was alerted on 14 October 1941 when his elite division was in the Far East, bivouacked 6,000 miles from the front line. His orders were to entrain immediately with his division for Moscow.

Beloborodov, buoyant and pink-cheeked, was thirty-eight years of age when he arrived in Moscow with his men. He had seen action in the civil war and then in China in the late 1920s. Throughout the Second World War he would fight in major campaigns against Germany and, later, against Japan. In the Battle of Moscow he was regarded as one of the outstanding divisional commanders. At the end of the war his uniform would show ten rows of campaign ribbons, and Moscow's Victory Museum would honour him with a life-sized portrait. (He is the only general so honoured; all the rest of the portraits are of the wartime marshals.)

---

* The parade in Moscow would of course have taken place in advance of Hitler's grotesque plan to flood the city, creating a big lake in its place.

Beloborodov's division arrived in Moscow when the city was under its greatest pressure from the enemy and was sent straight to the front. His men were soon to be in the thick of the fighting. But first they were visited by the commander of the Sixteenth Army, General Konstantin Rokossovsky (sometimes called "the soldiers' general" because of his popularity), who asked a few questions and then spoke about the enemy's "favourite tactics". Rokossovsky was "calm and charming, spoke unhurriedly and showed his implicit faith in our troops," says Beloborodov. But the Siberian frankly admits that he himself was nervous.

"I was very anxious about our debut in combat," he says. "We were about to fight a strong and experienced enemy, yet we were being committed to action for the first time. We realized that the first setbacks – and they were inevitable – might put the men off their stroke. I meditated upon the impending engagement while still on the way to the front." Meanwhile, political officers kindled in the men what Beloborodov calls a "sacred hate" for the enemy, discussing with them the execution of a sixteen-year-old partisan, Alexander Chekalin, in the Tula region south of Moscow. At the end of November the torture and hanging near Moscow of the partisan, eighteen-year-old Zoya Kosmodemyanskaya was also widely discussed by the men.

Beloborodov needn't have worried. His troops performed like the elite and well-trained unit they were; so well, in fact, that plaudits for their valour and stamina came from Rokossovsky and other generals. Later, Beloborodov sized up his own men in action: "They showed the best traits of the Russian character: selfless bravery, good administrative ability, inventiveness, coolness and inexhaustible optimism."

One of the very first actions of the 78th was to launch a surprise attack. Usually such assaults are preceded by a devastating artillery barrage, but this was cancelled so as not to give the enemy advance warning of an impending attack. It was a gamble but, says Beloborodov, "We did the right thing." Surprise was achieved, and when the Nazi soldiers began to run from their shelters to their weapon emplacements, they came under Beloborodov's artillery fire so that his men swiftly captured the enemy's forward defence line. After three weeks of engagement, the enemy showed respect for the fighting qualities of his men. Many round-the-clock skirmishes on snow-covered fields were settled by the bayonet, the hand grenade and the pistol. Beloborodov says the enemy was "mortally afraid of hand-to-hand fighting." He says with aplomb: "Our fighting men stood to the death." They had done all that was asked of them. On 14 November the Military Council of the Western Front had appealed to all soldiers, officers and political workers to "defend Moscow to the last drop of blood".

A natural barrier, the River Ozerna, had to be overcome by Beloborodov's men. The water was almost frozen over and the soldiers hesitated. In the meantime the enemy launched a counter-attack with almost a regiment of infantry supported by tanks and six artillery battalions. Beloborodov's attack was in danger of failing. But, he recalls, a young lieutenant named Igor Ivanov, commander of the 7th infantry Company, plunged with a loud "hooray" into the ice-cold water and was followed by the rest of his men. His company quickly crossed over and swiftly attacked the enemy flank. Other units followed and in savage fighting repelled a Nazi counter-attack.

In the difficult wintry conditions outside Moscow, Beloborodov's men were now given orders to stop the enemy who was advancing on the capital from the direction of Istra, 100 miles to the north-west. The fighting grew more intense with each passing hour.

The telephone that connected Beloborodov with the Sixteenth Army Headquarters, of which his division was a part, rang constantly.

"Where is the enemy?"

"Where are our units?"

"Do you have communications with your neighbours? Are you in close cooperation with them?"

The Front HQ was obviously worried.

Then, an alarming situation developed when Beloborodov's division found itself half encircled by the enemy which included the 10th Panzer and the SS "Reich" Motorized Division which had advanced up to 32 miles on their flanks. Worse, the enemy had superior forces.

It was necessary to withdraw to a new defence line. But such a step was impermissible without instructions from the Army Commander. In the nick of time, orders came to withdraw. "I cannot tell what would have happened if we had not received those orders," Beloborodov says.

In a brief memoir Beloborodov says that in those hard days and weeks, the courage of his men never flagged. He says that often equipment failed; tanks broke down and went out of service; horses dropped from exhaustion; German planes bombed their positions incessantly. Meantime, the cold was increasing and hoarfrost settled on the men's hats and collars. Many strongpoints in the division's sector changed hands several times.

The fierceness of the action can be seen in the fact that nearly every enemy attack ended in hand-to-hand fighting. But the men, says Beloborodov, stood to the death. "Our soldiers and officers performed miracles of heroism."

At the height of the fighting the division was visited by Generals (later Marshals) Georgi Zhukov, the Front Commander, and Rokossovsky. Beloborodov had had two sleepless nights and was taking a short nap when these officers arrived. Before Beloborodov could give a report, Zhukov asked calmly: "How are things?" Beloborodov explained the situation in detail and gave him a report on the casualties of the last few days. The two visitors were saddened and Zhukov said: "It's the same picture everywhere. Too many losses, especially from German aircraft. It's time we put a stop to it."★

On 25 November Beloborodov's division was ordered to withdraw to the River Istra line. The German forces along the Volokolamsk-Istra Highway hoped to prevent the 78th from reaching the eastern bank of the Istra but under cover of strong rearguards it succeeded in

★ The strain from the Battle of Moscow also affected Marshal Zhukov. Between 18 November and 8 December 1941 he managed to get no more than two or three hours of sleep a day. To keep going and be able to work he resorted to brief but frequent physical exercise, drank strong coffee and once in a while took a 15-minute work-out on skis. When a turning point in the battle was achieved, he fell so fast asleep that nobody could wake him. Stalin phoned twice and was told, "Zhukov is sleeping and we can't wake him."

reaching this line by the morning of 26 November where it took up defences.

The following day Beloborodov's men were attacked by the 10th Panzer, SS "Reich" Motorized and 252nd Infantry Divisions. Enemy planes appeared and dozens of tanks were approaching. Piercing the morning haze, Russian artillery shells flew in the direction of the tanks. Direct-fire artillery also went into action. The attack was repulsed and few panzers managed to escape.

Later that day Beloborodov's division received cheerful news. Supreme Headquarters in Moscow bestowed on it a new name: the 9th Guards Infantry Division. Meanwhile a message of congratulations came from Sixteenth Army Headquarters, saying: "To be called Guards during this bitter encounter with the enemy is the highest honour." It added: "You are selflessly fulfilling your duty to the last drop of blood in order that your beloved Motherland may live."

In their memoirs, eminent generals like Rokossovsky bestow high praise on the Siberian divisions that fought on the Eastern Front. Some of the generals speak of "these marvellous Siberians".

Three days later the Wehrmacht tried to break through to Moscow concentrating its main efforts in the zone of the newly designated 9th Guards. Beloborodov's men were joined by a neighbouring division and did not allow the enemy to pass.

The Germans persisted in their attacks, pounding the Russian defence lines with shells and bombs, throwing infantry into action and storming the line with panzers. It was clear that the belligerents were wearied by the virtual non-stop fighting and deafened by shell and bomb explosions. Losses were heavy on both sides but the Russians won time that was needed to concentrate fresh reserves required for a counter-offensive.

The village of Istra was again a hotly contested position. Unexpectedly there were ambushes by German submachine-gunners hidden in the thick tops of fir and pine trees. Artillery fire wouldn't shake them. Then Beloborodov was approached by one of his colonels who suggested using the skills of some Siberian hunters he had in his regiment. "They know how to stalk squirrels and sables," he said, adding: "I'm sure, general, they will have no trouble with these cuckoos in soldiers' clothing."

"Go ahead," said Beloborodov.

The hunters were dressed in white robes and disappeared unnoticed. A few minutes later the men heard the rat-tat-tat of machine-guns, and then everything died down. Red and white flares were seen over the forest. This meant the way was clear. As the columns now advanced, two hunters came out of the forest escorting three prisoners from the SS "Reich" Division. One of the machine-gunners reported that they had silenced fifteen enemy soldiers.

Meanwhile, the furious fighting for Istra went on day and night. One the morning of 11 December Beloborodov's men broke into the village and by the end of the day it was cleared of the enemy. Wrecked vehicles, weapons, corpses, piles of loot, documents, diaries and letters were scattered in the streets, squares and backyards.

In a letter to his wife, a soldier of the SS "Reich" Division, Hans Nalteis, wrote: "The fighting here is more than savage and very, very heavy. We are fighting for every inch of land, and the Russian snow soaks up the blood of the last SS soldiers. The sacrifices are very great and staggering."

The whole village of Istra was now on fire. Its historical monuments, famous monastery, libraries and schools lay in ruins. As Beloborodov noted, the age-old culture of the town had been reduced to ashes.

Now the River Istra had to be crossed. On the hills above the western bank of the Istra the German Command had mounted guns, mortars and machine-guns in pillboxes and other concrete emplacements. They also laid minefields. Thus Beloborodov's men had to attack under continuous fire. The first attempt to force the icy Istra failed. A main problem was that the battalion ordered to force the river lacked the necessary crossing equipment. Something had to be done to figure out a way to cross to the enemy bank suddenly and without heavy losses.

Innovation saved the day for the Red Army. An observer of the assault, General Rokossovsky, was astonished to see Beloborodov's men forge across the roaring River Istra under enemy fire. To accomplish this difficult action the soldiers used a makeshift flotilla of logs, small boats, and straw rafts. In this way Beloborodov's troops completely routed the enemy. But it took a whole night to cover 218 yards. Beloborodov admits to having paid a big price for those 218 yards. His medical corpsmen removed many wounded in hand-drawn sledges. He does not give specific casualty figures but admits that Russian losses for the month of December were heavy.

Meanwhile, Hitler demanded that his troops should hold their ground with "fanatic stubbornness". In his order of 3 January 1942 he stated: "You will resist to the last man and will cling to every inhabited locality; if you are ordered by your superiors to surrender it everything here must be reduced to ashes."

But by the end of January the Russian forces had advanced up to 93 miles and inflicted heavy losses on the Germans. The towns and villages in the environs of Moscow were now once again Soviet territory. The defeat and heavy losses of crack German units at Moscow gave rise to a pessimistic mood even among the leadership of the Nazi High Command and later revealed sharp differences in the assessments both for the reasons for the setback and the future methods of waging war on the Eastern Front.

The Battle of Moscow has naturally been overshadowed by the mighty Battle of Stalingrad. Yet some knowledgeable sources say categorically that the Battle of Moscow was as much a "turning point of the war" as the victory at Stalingrad; that the former had an enormous influence on the subsequent course of hostilities. Dr Valentin Falin, a Russian historian who was a high party official, has called Moscow, "the most important battle of World War II" Falin says that after the battle the "qualitative parameters" that Hitler's armies had enjoyed before the invasion were never restored; that the tactics of *Blitzkrieg* were over and done with. After this, he contends, Nazi Germany waged war "to save its skin" – not to dominate Russia.

There is some German support for this view. General Gunther Blumentritt, Chief of Staff of the German Fourth Army, has written that the campaign in Russia, "especially its turning point, the Battle of

Moscow, delivered the first powerful political and military blow at Germany." At the postwar Nuremberg Trials, one of Germany's senior commanders, Field Marshal Wilhelm Keitel, asked when he began to realize that Plan *Barbarossa* was failing, uttered one word: "Moscow".

In Beloborodov's opinion, the events of those days in the fields near Moscow were in scope, involvement of forces and consequences, "unequaled in the history of wars". He calls it one of the greatest exploits in the history of Russia.

After the victory at Moscow the world lost its belief in the invincibility of Hitler's armies.

At the end of 1942 Beloborodov was appointed commander of a rifle corps. Two years later he was promoted again, this time being made commander of the Forty-third Army. In this role he took part in Operation *Bagration*, also known as the Belorussian Operation because it took place on the territory of what is now the Republic of Belarus. The wiry, energetic, Siberian general told me in an interview that in this offensive more than fifteen enemy divisions were completely destroyed while some fifty other Nazi divisions lost upwards of 50 per cent of their personnel. This, said Beloborodov, weakened enemy forces on other sectors of the broad front and made Operation *Overlord*, the giant Anglo-American offensive in France, easier. On 17 July 1944, said Beloborodov, as a result of Russian success in *Bagration* and in other engagements, more than 50,000 German prisoners were paraded through the streets of Moscow.

Beloborodov's next major assignment was the command of an army against Japanese forces in the Far East. During the years that Russia was fighting Hitler there had been an uneasy truce between the USSR and Japan. Thus, in 1944, Moscow accused Japan of violating the Soviet Far Eastern border more than 100 times. Despite the existence of a non-aggression treaty between the two countries, the Japanese Navy sank a number of Russian transport ships. Between 1941–4 the Japanese reportedly detained scores of Soviet merchant ships.

There had been other signs too, that Japan had "designs" on Siberia. As far back as 1927 a secret memorandum purportedly written by the then Prime Minister, Baron Tanaka – and widely known after publication in the British and American press as the "Tanaka Memorial" – included these words: "We have to admit the inevitability of war with Russia . . . Railways [in northern China and Mongolia] will provide a base for our advance upon Siberia." In January 1942 an official organ of the Soviet Union – the newspaper *Pravda* – gave a warning to Japan after the Japanese press published diagrams that included Siberia (and Australia!) as being among Japan's future possessions. Three months later Moscow again protested, this time in stronger terms.

On 9 August 1945 a large Soviet army entered the war against Japan, launching several offensive operations simultaneously: in North-east China, North Korea, South Sakhalin and the Kurile Islands. Over a short period of time, the Russian armies with naval support cleared the Japanese forces from vast expanses of East Asia, leaving no alternative to Hitler's Far Eastern ally. Between 9 August and 20 August about 80,000 men of the Kwangtung Army – Japan's strongest – were killed and 600,000 taken prisoner. Approximate Russian losses were 8,000 dead and 22,000 wounded. Twenty-two Japanese divisions were routed.

"Our task," says Beloborodov, "had been to rout Japan's most powerful forces, the Kwangtung Army, and we are convinced it was this that predetermined the surrender of Japan."

Japan's leaders at first declined an invitation to surrender unconditionally. Then the US Army* Air Force dropped an atomic bomb on Hiroshima (6 August) and one on Nagasaki (9 August). Still, Japan waited five days before capitulating. Beloborodov's view is similar to the Kremlin's: that Tokyo's leaders saw the impossibility of continuing the war only after Russia declared war on Japan. He points out that on the same day (9 August) that Russia entered the war in the Far East, Prime Minister Kantaro Suzuki said: "The entry into the war of the Soviet Union this morning puts us in an utterly hopeless situation and makes further continuation of the war impossible."

* US Air Force not founded until 1947.

In Beloborodov's opinion – and some Western historians are inclined to accept this view – Japan would have surrendered even without the atomic bombings. One US expert, Admiral William D. Leahy, who was an adviser to President Roosevelt, wrote: "It is my opinion that the use of this barbarous weapon at Hiroshima and Nagasaki was of no material assistance in our war against Japan." In any case, five months prior to the use of the "revolutionary weapon", Japanese cities were being flattened by conventional bombs. On the night of 9 March, for instance, hundreds of B-29 bombers raided Tokyo, killing 97,000 people, wounding 125,000 and leaving about a million people homeless.

Reflecting on these statistics, Beloborodov says: "It's hard to understand what was in the minds of those Americans who said that Japan might have to be invaded."

Beloborodov recalls a dialogue he had with Lieutenant General Noritsumi Shimizu who at first refused to surrender. "I questioned him when he was captured and we had quite an interesting talk. First I asked him to tell me how many soldiers there had been in his army. He said 85,000. Then I asked him how many he had left. He said about 45,000."

Beloborodov: Then your army is crushed.

Shimizu: No, it is not crushed.

Beloborodov: Where is the other half of your army, the other 40,000?

Shimizu: The answer is that some were killed, some of them were wounded and some deserted.

Beloborodov: Do you confirm that your army is crushed? You must understand that as a military man you do not have enough men to attack the enemy.

Shimizu: [Thinking for some time] Yes, I agree, my army is crushed.

Beloborodov: Then, OK, accept the terms of unconditional surrender.

Shimizu: In the Japanese language there is no such word as surrender.

Beloborodov: You are sitting in front of me. You are captured. My men have taken prisoner another five Japanese generals. Your troops are throwing away their rifles. In Russian we call it surrender.

Shimizu: The word does not exist in the Japanese language.

Beloborodov: Why do you personally surrender then?

Shimizu: That was the order from the Emperor.

Beloborodov: What did the Emperor order you to do?

Shimizu: He ordered us to surrender our arms.

Beloborodov: That is unconditional surrender, what you are doing, whether you have the word for it or not. If you didn't have the word before in the language, now you'll have to add it.

General Shimizu was sent to a POW camp in Khabarovsk, north of Vladivostok. In the fighting in the Far East, a total of nearly 150 Japanese generals were taken prisoner.

The Japanese Army did not set foot in Siberia. In the end, Japanese representatives signed an act of unconditional surrender on the battleship USS *Missouri* anchored in Tokyo Bay on 2 September. General Afanasy Pavlantevich Beloborodov, the cool, plucky general from Siberia had fulfilled his duty and he and his men could share in victories on two continents.

CHAPTER 12

A Hundred Jewish Generals

After the traumatic setbacks in the summer of 1941, Russian generals gradually began to come into their own. Some of the commanders were former privates and non-commissioned officers of the tsarist army, such as Georgi Zhukov, Konstantin Rokossovsky and Ivan Konev; there was an old colonel of noble birth, Boris Sapozhnikov; and a priest's son and former tsarist captain Alexander Vasilevsky. All five became marshals of the Soviet Union. Younger military leaders such as Admiral Arseni Golovko, chief of the Northern Fleet, L. A. Govorov, who led armies on the Leningrad front; Sergei Rudenko, commander of the Sixteenth Air Army; and Afanasy Beloborodov, one of the "bright lights" in the Battle of Moscow, all joined the Army or Navy after the 1917 revolution.

How the early Bolsheviks regarded the tsarist generals and other ranks is revealing. A year after assuming power, V.I. Lenin, the founder of the Soviet state, made the following remark in November 1918; "Most of the old officers were the spoiled and depraved darling sons of capitalists, who had nothing in common with the private soldier. So in building our new army now, we must draw our officers solely from among the people. Only such officers will have any respect among the soldiers and be able to strengthen . . . our army so that it will become invincible." But in the beginning this rule was broken scores of times to permit ex-tsarist officers to serve in the new "people's army". However, almost all of the new generals were of peasant stock and of diverse nationalities, including Russians, Ukrainians, Belorussians, Armenians, Georgians and Uzbeks. Out of the minority peoples of Russia came such renowned generals as the Armenian Ivan Bagramyan and the Uzbek Sabir Rakhimov.

In addition to these, and virtually hidden under a cloak of anonymity, was the existence of a fraternity of Jewish generals, many of them in the thick of fighting on the Eastern Front. Several of these officers were awarded medals for leadership and valour. Fraternity in this instance does not signify an actual brotherhood, nor does it imply assertive ethnicity. Rather, these generals were indistinguishable from the majority of other general officers.*

The military rosters of the war years contain such names as Dovator, Goldberger, Rubinchik, Rabinovich, Cutlar, Dragunsky, Sapozhnikov, Khasin, Kreizer, Skvirsky, Vainrub, Weitsman. Colonel General David Dragunsky, twice awarded the gold hero medal (the highest combat decoration), told the author that there were at least 100 Jewish generals in the Red Army during the Second World War. This figure is also mentioned in an official booklet, published in Moscow, on minorities in Russia. (In the 1970s there were approximately 2 million Jews in the Soviet Union. With emigration, the number has now fallen sharply; there are probably only half that number now in Russia.)

Major General Lev Mikhailovich Dovator was an outstanding cavalry commander and, incidentally, a man of peasant Jewish stock. He had another distinction: he was known in some quarters as a Cossack-Jewish general. Many of the men who rode with him were from Cossack country. At the beginning of the war, when the Red Army was retreating, being thrashed by the strongest invasion force in history, Dovator's cavalry often dealt punishing blows to the advancing German troops. Dovator's daring raids behind enemy lines, combined with dogged resistance by Russian armies before Moscow,

---

* When Maurice Hindus, author of many books on Russia, toured the Crimea shortly before the war, he encountered many Jewish farming communities. These communities he noted were self-differentiated from their Cossack and other Russian neighbours "not by a hair's breadth". In Lenin's and Stalin's Russia, it was held that Jewry as a racial or religious fact was in the process of disintegrating, which made interested groups in the West uneasy. The handful of Jewish generals I spoke to had Russian or Ukrainian wives. A few of them declined my request for an interview on the grounds (this was the reason given) that to be interviewed on the basis of ancestry amounted in their eyes to flaunting an accident of birth.

forced delays in Hitler's *Blitzkrieg* timetable to the advantage of Moscow's defenders.

So effective were the Dovator raids that GHQ in Moscow included summaries of them in its "Documents on the Use of War Experience." One of these documents is entitled: "The Use of Large Cavalry Formations in the Enemy Rear." In addition, a summary of early cavalry operations, based in part on Dovator's exploits, is cited in Directive 005698 of the Supreme Commander in Chief, dated 14 December 1941.

Dovator graduated from a cavalry school in 1926 and, in 1939, attended the Frunze Military Academy, named after civil war hero Mikhail Frunze. After his initial thrusts against the enemy, Dovator's generalship stood out again late in 1941, when his troops held their ground, absorbing some of the heaviest blows that Hitler's armies could inflict in their attempt to seize Moscow at all costs.

One of Dovator's "textbook" raids against the enemy took place at dawn on 28 August 1941, near Smolensk, 200 miles west of Moscow. His cavalry group consisting of 3,000 sabres was hidden in the forests. Attacking swiftly the cavalry routed two regiments and broke through the German front, destroying garrison trains and storage depots, and also disrupting communications. Flushed with previously easy victories, the German 430th and 450th Infantry Regiments were taken completely by surprise. The raid also caused panic in the headquarters of the nearby German Sixth Army whose staff fled as rumours about the penetration of "one hundred thousand Red Cossacks" spread through the German rear.

The results of this cavalry raid have been recorded. Killed: over 2,500 German soldiers and officers. Destroyed: two regimental headquarters and the topographic department of the Sixth Army Headquarters. Captured: 200 motor vehicles, 2 tanks, 4 armoured vehicles, 4 guns, 6 mortars, and 130 machine-guns. In addition, Dovator's men seized more than 1,500 rifles and automatic weapons and a large quantity of ammunition which they turned over to a partisan detachment operating in the German rear.

Shaken by these raids, the German High Command held up the

advance of some of its units, even withdrawing some troops opposite the defending Sixteenth Army. But before the year was out, Dovator, only thirty-eight, was killed in action. His death, said Marshal Georgi Zhukov in his memoirs, was a "grievous loss".

General Yakov Grigorevich Kreizer was another extraordinary member of the so-called Jewish fraternity. Kreizer graduated from an infantry school in 1925 and later headed the Borisov Tank School. When war broke out he commanded the 1st Motorized and 1st Tank Divisions from June to August 1941 and succeeded in holding up the German Army's reinforced 18th Panzer Division for several days. At that time this was of considerable importance, says Marshal Zhukov, who adds that in the fighting Kreizer "proved himself a magnificent commander". Kreizer helped grind down the advancing German armies. In the memoirs of other marshals such as A. M. Vasilevsky and K. K. Rokossovsky, the names of Dovator and Kreizer are cited for military excellence.

Like many volunteers from minority groups, David Abramovich Dragunsky achieved an impressive war record. His beginnings were typical of millions of Russian Jews born in tsarist years in or near the Pale; that is, the restricted area in which Jews were allowed to live. Dragunsky's native village was Svyatsk which was close to but outside the Pale. Dragunsky recalls only warm feelings between Jews and their neighbours in Svyatsk.

Speaking about the position of Jews in Russia, the Russian-Jewish novelist and war correspondent Ilya Ehrenburg said in Moscow in August 1942: "As a boy, I saw a pogrom which was engineered by the Tsarist police and a gang of hooligans. But the Russian people gave shelter to the Jews. I remember how my father brought home Leo Tolstoy's letter, 'I cannot keep silent', copied on a scrap of paper. When he read Tolstoy's denunciation of the pogroms, my mother wept . . . I never once heard a Jew say anything bitter against the Russian people. I grew up in a Russian city; Russian is my native language and I am a Russian writer . . . I am [also] a Jew and am proud of the fact."

Dragunsky joined the Army when Hitler's rampant anti-Semitism became well known in Russia, not to mention the Nazi persecutions inside Germany. For years Soviet citizens had been propagandized against the Nazi regime. Incidentally, after Hitler's invasion of Russia, nearly half a million Soviet-Germans, who since the days of Catherine II (Empress of Russia, 1762–96) had lived on the eastern banks of the Volga, were exiled by Stalin to Siberia simply because of their ethnicity.

About his childhood, Dragunsky recalls: "There were, as they used to say at the time, twelve 'souls', or children in our family. We saw how our father, the village tailor, worked day and night and how our mother kept house. Neither of our parents had much education, and so they strove to give us as much education as possible. The 'ideal profession', according to my mother, was that of our neighbour, who worked as an accountant at the village shop. However, I failed at that. I went to Moscow to do construction work. But I didn't want to make that my life's work, so I entered the armoured forces academy and, later, studied at the Frunze Academy, which is the highest military educational establishment. My studies were interrupted in 1941 on the day Germany invaded our country."

Dragunsky's battlefield debut had come three years earlier, in 1938, when Japanese soldiers invaded Russian territory at Lake Khasan, near Vladivostok. At that time the short 5 foot 5 inch, genial, muscular officer commanded a tank company. In the Second World War as brigade commander, Dragunsky participated in many of the major tank battles with the Wehrmacht. Three times his tank received a direct hit and burst into flames. Each time he escaped. Severely wounded in the Battle of Kursk in 1943, Dragunsky was rushed to a field hospital where surgeons extracted from his liver "a large piece of German shrapnel" ("The doctors beat the odds and saved my life", he says.) Dragunsky belongs to a select group of soldiers who were twice awarded the Gold Star Medal for bravery.

"I got my first Gold Star for the battles at the Sandomierz bridgehead in August 1944", he says. "That summer was hot in more ways than one. Our troops were holding on to their sector on the left of the Vistula [in Poland] and managed to stand their ground, even though they had to repulse six and sometimes eight massive attacks a day of superior enemy forces. The second Gold Star was given to me for the assault on Berlin in April 1945. We went towards our goal amidst the heaviest imaginable fighting. Many of our friends with whom we marched to victory died but we won in the end."

Dragunsky said he remembered "quite a few" battles but the one he remembered best occurred on 23 July 1941. "The Nazis were attacking to try to cut off the Leningrad–Moscow highway. We were being hard-pressed, but we gave back as much as we received. That day, my men destroyed three Fascist tanks. When I saw them burn I realized that we could and that we would overcome."

In his memoir, *A Soldier's Life*, Dragunsky recalls a bucolic day in May 1941, a few weeks before the invasion, when there was a joyful gathering of the Dragunsky clan in Svyatsk. Many Jewish families lived in this village but Svyatsk was unlucky in its geography, being situated right on the border.

Looking back on that day – it was the last time he would see many members of his family alive – Dragunsky says that he and his two brothers were especially attentive to their mother. "She came up to us repeatedly and spoke especially tender words to each of us." But the parting was solemn, he says, because "in her heart she could feel the impending disaster". Events during the first days of the war developed so swiftly that Dragunsky's family did not have time to leave Svyatsk before the arrival of Nazi troops. For a year neighbours hid Dragunsky's mother at the risk of their own lives, but the invaders found her out because they were always staging raids in search of Jews. They took the small, grey-haired, enfeebled woman out to the square where other inhabitants of Svyatsk were herded and shot her and dozens of other Dragunskys, including the general's sister. In that same year (1942) Dragunsky's two brothers fell at Stalingrad.

"Learning of the tragedy of my mother's death was," says Dragunsky, "the most difficult moment in my life."

On the front lines, Dragunsky waged war with renewed fury. As commanding officer of an armoured brigade, Dragunsky fought at Kursk, forced the River Dnieper, liberated Prague and stormed

Berlin. Although he was sidelined with one wound after another, he returned to active duty as fast as he could recuperate or was able to rise from his hospital bed.

At Kursk, the venue for the greatest clash of tanks in history, Dragunsky's commanding officer was General Semyon Krivoshein. Dragunsky had only recently been discharged from the hospital and was eager to see action once more. But he now lacked a command. In desperation he appealed for help to the veteran tank general who passed a note to a subordinate, saying, "I'm sending you Lieutenant Colonel D. A. Dragunsky. He's a brave officer, but is rather hot-headed. He fights well. He will make a useful tank brigade commander. Try him – you won't regret it. Semyon."

Dragunsky got his tank command and was soon confronting enemy panzers.

In the closing weeks of war in April–May 1945, Dragunsky was part of the huge Berlin Operation. He says: "I was proud that the main ring of encirclement within Berlin had been closed by General Krivoshein's troops and by my 55th Tank Brigade. My teacher had met his pupil in the capital of the Nazis."

With the war's end Dragunsky figured his army career was over. "I was naive and felt that the profession of soldiering would no longer be needed in a world at peace." But as he was fond of swimming and fishing, he looked forward to a civilian's life. At one time he even contemplated a writing career: "I had often thought of myself as a future literary person or journalist." Instead, as Cold War shadows appeared on the horizon, he stayed in uniform but relinquished command of the 55th Guards Tank Brigade. He was shortly appointed head of a higher infantry officers' school.

Dragunsky recalled how, despite the fact that he was short of stature, he was able to take part in the famous Victory Parade of 14 June 1945, the biggest parade on Red Square in the twentieth century.

"At first my two close friends, Zaitsev and Demidov, and I were excluded from marching in the parade at the head of the Combined Regiment of the 1st Ukrainian Front, which was led by Marshal Ivan

Konev. The reason: the three of us were all rather short. True enough, we did seem to be lost among the other senior officers, all tall, hefty men. Then, before the parade, Konev approached us and I introduced those tankmen who would be taking part in the parade. Konev looked at me, and at Zaitsev and Demidov who stood next to me, with a smile and said to other generals nearby, 'Let's leave Dragunsky, Zaitsev and Demidov in command of the marching battalion. After all, they don't have to stand in the ranks but will rather be marching out front. They are after all, heroes, all dapper fellows, and they're surely not to blame if they're not so tall. When the tank brigades they commanded rushed to attack the enemy we didn't measure their height'."

Dragunsky thus took part in the parade whose climax came when soldiers and officers unceremoniously hurled hundreds of Nazi banners in a heap in front of Lenin's Mausoleum.

When I met Dragunsky at the War Veteran's Committee in Moscow he mentioned the names of some of his "fraternity brothers", among them Major General Boris Sapozhnikov. Arriving later at the general's flat, I saw him poring over Chinese and Japanese texts. Sapozhnikov was white-haired, slim, and scholarly-looking behind his black-rimmed glasses. But many years previously this scholar with a general's rank had fought at Stalingrad and, when his commanding officer was killed, took over the command of his rifle division. After Nazi Germany was defeated, Sapozhnikov made the long train journey to the Far East to join in the campaign against Japanese forces. Fluent in the Japanese language, at the end of the war he assisted in the interrogation of Japanese generals who were taken prisoner. He was now writing a book about China and Japan in the Second World War.

While still a youth, Sapozhnikov chose the Army as a career. He said with a smile: "My father would have been astonished to see his son in a general's uniform. I think he probably would have wanted me to be a Talmudic scholar. But I had early in life decided to join the Army because I thought one member of our family must help defend the country: me. In the Army I could acquire a technical skill; and I chose signal communications."

With war raging on the Northern front with its long frigid winters and heavy snowfalls, Major General Lev Solomonovich Skvirsky would often ski to his command post despite an old leg injury from a Japanese grenade. In the summer of 1939, he had fought under General Zhukov against Japanese troops who crossed into Mongolia, a landlocked country bound to Russia by a military pact. When Hitler invaded Russia, Skvirsky was Chief of Staff of the Fourteenth Army headquartered at Murmansk. Try as they might, German troops were never able to capture this strategic Russian port above the Arctic Circle where lend-lease supplies carried by Allied convoys from the United States and Britain arrived. Skvirsky fought on what was called the "Karelian Front" for almost the entire war, his men keeping the enemy, including battalions of Tyrolese Alpine troops, at bay.

Often, Skvirsky was on the phone to Stalin, the Supreme Commander in Chief, who demanded daily contact with those in command of major units. In Skvirsky's words, "Stalin didn't like beating around the bush; he had no patience with palaver. I saw right away that he expected no varnishing of facts. I also noted that he favoured commanders who applied themselves and carried out their assignments well."

Nearly 6 feet 5 inches tall, Skvirsky joined the Army when he was only fourteen years old. "I was big for my age and passed for seventeen." He adds: "I liked military life, especially its discipline." When he first entered the Army he was the only person in his unit who could read and write. "Therefore, I had to write all the personal letters for my fellow soldiers." Showing an aptitude for learning, Skvirsky was sent to one military school after another.

Each of these generals faulted the tsarist regime under which it would have been next to impossible for Jews to attain the rank of general unless they converted to Orthodox Christianity. Asked if they had ever encountered anti-Semitism in the Army, to a man they said no. "Men in the Army were impervious to prejudice," Skvirsky said. In Dragunsky's words, the political teachings in the Army had "weeded out the old prejudices" which he said included anti-Semitism. He told the following anecdote: "After we completed the Berlin Operation in 1945 only a handful of army men were awarded the country's highest decoration – the Gold Star Medal. I was one of those few. I was informed that Stalin himself approved the order, knowing that I was a Jew." Dragunsky (like many others he carved his name on the walls of the Reichstag in May 1945) was polemical: "Our army saved peoples from the horrors of Nazism and the Jews from total extermination."

General Sapozhnikov: "I'm a Jew. I never concealed it. And everybody knows it." Pointing to snapshots of his children, he said: "My daughter Ada has a Jewish husband, my son Grisha has a Russian wife." He said the fact that he was a general, and had many high-ranking army friends of Jewish origin, showed that a minority people could rise to the top in the Army. He also mentioned, in addition to Jews, examples of other minorities who had reached the top in the military, in particular Georgian and Armenian generals and admirals who had distinguished themselves in the Second World War.

General Krivoshein who led a tank corps in the war was unequivocal: "I never felt discrimination during my career, during my life, actually. I always tried to do the best I could in the service and I was rewarded with a general's rank." Krivoshein, a former cavalry commander, furnished a homily: "People of all nationalities may be divided into two groups, those who work hard and those who are lazy. People who work hard rarely feel any kind of discrimination. But Jews who are lazy, sometimes when they get reproached, they blame it on anti-Semitism, instead of trying to work better to avoid criticism."

Krivoshein's own career was kaleidoscopic. Here in brief is his chronological saga told in his own words:

"In the early 1930s, we cavalrymen switched over to armour when many European armies were doing the same. Stalin himself approved plans to train thousands of young officers in tank warfare, and I was one of them. Wars of the future, we felt, would be decided by masses of tanks and aircraft. On the other hand, we loved the cavalry and it wasn't easy for us to part with our scarlet and blue trousers and the long sabre for the khaki of the tankman. However, orders were orders and we swapped our horses for tanks."

In October 1936 civil war had engulfed Spain and one morning Krivoshein found himself sailing on a Russian transport ship to the Spanish harbour of Cartagena with eighty volunteer tankmen and dozens of T-26 tanks. The T-26 was then the Red Army's standard tank. "Our primary job," says Krivoshein, "was to train Spaniards in order to form Republican tank units. But the alarming situation at the front demanded that the tanks be used in combat against the insurgents; and as it turned out, we volunteers joined in the defence of Madrid before the Spanish tank crews had been trained.

"In Spain we were in constant combat, most of the time without the support of infantry. From dawn to dusk we drove the enemy away from the approaches to the capital, spent the night repairing the tanks, and returned to battle the following morning. But after a month, as a result of intensive fighting, most of our tanks were out of action and in need of basic repairs. Incidentally, our worst enemy at that time was not the German and Italian-supplied tanks but enemy artillery."

In speaking of Spain, Krivoshein cited the participation of his T-26 tanks at the Battle of Jarama about which the American novelist Ernest Hemingway wrote a much-quoted poem in honour of the fallen foreign – mainly American and British – dead. Says Krivoshein: "Our tankmen saved the day on several occasions, rolling back and destroying columns of General Franco's soldiers who were advancing on the Madrid–Valencia highway. Our tanks took part in all the major battles from the autumn of 1936 to the spring of 1938."

Five years later German and Russian armies and armour were getting ready to clash near the "Kursk Bulge", one of history's epic battles. Krivoshein's corps was bivouacked at the edge of a pine forest, his tanks smartly camouflaged. German historian Paul Carrell (in *Scorched Earth: The Russian-German War, 1943–1944*), writes that Krivoshein's corps was "magnificently equipped" and that huge Russian reserves, including a whole tank army, had been moved up from the rear, ready for action.

Krivoshein had busied himself with details about the probable tactics of his chief adversary, von Manstein, a Wehrmacht general with whom he had clinked glasses of vodka a few years earlier in

Poland. Finally the hour of reckoning came. At dawn on 12 July, 1943 endless formations of Russian and German tanks and self-propelled guns closed on each other in a blaze of fire and smoke near Prokhorovka, south of Kursk. Marshal of Armoured Troops Pavel Rotmistrov, who was on the scene, has given a bird's-eye-view of the action:

"The fighting in the Prokhorovka area was exceptionally bitter. It was hard to make out who was attacking and who was defending. Hundreds of tanks were moving in the battle. There was no room for manoeuvring. The tankmen had to fire at point-blank range. Built-up areas and dominating hills passed from hand to hand several times. The losses suffered by both sides were considerable and practically equal. But the German advance was halted and the counterblow by our army's major forces was successful. At the close of battle, the Tiger tanks and Panther tank-destroyers – they were the pride of the Wehrmacht – were turned into heaps of twisted metal."

The best units that Hitler could put into the field had been defeated. Field Marshal von Manstein's intention to punch his way north towards Kursk had come to nought, and, for his performance in this battle, Krivoshein was awarded the Gold Star Hero medal.

Gruelling months of additional struggle lay ahead for Krivoshein and his tank corps, including fierce battles on the approaches to Berlin. But by this time the general's long and arduous career that had begun as a cavalryman in the civil war began to take a toll on his health. Not long after Victory Day, on the advice of doctors, he retired from the Army. But unable to remain inactive the general took up new pursuits, one of them being folk dancing. Another general, who knew Krivoshein for many years, told me that Krivoshein even became a "virtuoso" in Russian and Cossack dances. "Semyon won't tell you this himself but he won many prizes in these dances."

In addition, this son of an impoverished tailor who had risen to become one of Russia's leading tank commanders, embarked on a second career: as an author of non-fiction books. In the space of a few years Krivoshein turned out four books about the battles and campaigns in which he had fought, including two volumes on the Red

Cavalry. Like many of his fellow tank officers, he retained a nostalgia for those early years as a mounted cavalryman.

Two or three generals spoke about radical changes made over the years not only in the daily occupations of Russian Jews but in their consciousness: for example, the appearance of Jewish pig-farmers. It was mentioned, that in the prewar period some Russians sneered at Jews because they detested pigs and refused to eat pork. The generals pointed out that this had changed; now Jews on Russian farms were sometimes cited in the press for raising the best pigs.

But the subject of anti-Semitism is slippery territory. Russian historian Roy Medvedev has published a seminal work, asserting among other things that during the war "many Jewish political officers" were discharged from the armed forces. Medvedev also said that a number of nominees for the editorship of Army newspapers were rejected, supposedly on the grounds that they were Jews. On the other hand, many popular Russian war correspondents were Jews, including Ilya Ehrenburg and Vasily Grossman. Moreover, the managing editor of the leading military newspaper, *Krasnaya Zvezda* (Red Star), Major General David Ortenberg, was a Jew.

It is a fact that some of the high-ranking Party members and generals shot during the prewar Great Purges were Jews. Nevertheless, the verdict of many historians acquainted with the Stalin era is that anybody at any time was liable to be exiled or receive a bullet.*

---

* High-ranking Jews in the armed forces who were accused of treason before the war included I. E. Yakir, Y. B. Gamarnik and B. M. Feldman. Gamarnik committed suicide; the others were executed. Another Jew, General G. M. Shtern, met his demise, for reasons unknown, shortly before the war, and Air Force commander Y. V. Smushkevich was also a victim, apparently four months into the war.

CHAPTER 13

Cabbage Soup in Hell

The opening shots of the Volga Battle ("The Battle of Stalingrad") were sounded on the Chir River on 17 July 1942. This was the beginning of one of the leviathan clashes of the war which spread over a vast area between the Don and Volga rivers.

The adversaries knew the strategic worth of Stalingrad: its importance as a hub of industry and also its communications links to the Caucasian oil fields in the south. The German High Command counted on crossing the Volga, thus setting the stage for capturing and holding the Caucasus. The Russians spared no effort in the struggle to hold onto the city.★

On 23 July, supported by 150 tanks, German troops attacked the main line of resistance of the 33rd Guards Rifle Division near the village of Kletskaya, and heavy fighting ensued. Joining their German allies in the march on Stalingrad were Italian and Romanian armies. The enemy managed to break through the Guards' lines and drive a wedge into their defence. The German advance continued and a month later Nazi forces broke through to the Volga north of Stalingrad on 23 August, presenting the city with a crisis. A "state of siege" was proclaimed and civilians were called on to help defend the city "to the last". Joining the ranks of the soldier-defenders were 75,000 men and women from offices, factories and farms.

★ For a blow-by-blow account of one of the great battles of all time, Antony Beevor's *Stalingrad* and John Erickson's *The Road to Stalingrad: Stalin's War With Germany* are recommended.

Despite heavy losses Hitler's armies succeeded in obtaining a toehold in the city by the middle of September. Heavy fighting broke out in the area of Mamayev Hill and the Central Railway Station, which changed hands at least a dozen times. Stubborn defensive action and bold counter-attacks by the Russians frustrated the enemy's offensive and pinned down fifty or more German divisions in the Stalingrad area.

On 21 August under heavy pressure the Russian forces withdrew from the outer ring of defences to the inner ring in the city. On 23 August the Luftwaffe sent several hundred planes to bomb the city and its civilian population. Marshal A. I. Eremenko has described what he calls the "monstrous hurricane" that had fallen on the city, claiming civilians as its victims. "The mind would not suffer the thought that it was impossible to prevent the pain of hundreds of peaceful people, especially the children."

On 13 September the fighting shifted inside the city and Hitler hastened to announce its fall. But such optimism was unsound. The embattled city would not surrender.

Displays of courage and gallantry were numerous. Near Kletskaya, four Russian soldiers belonging to the Sixty-second Army who had two anti-tank guns between them faced thirty German tanks. They destroyed fifteen of them in one day. On another sector sixteen soldiers led by Junior Lieutenant V. V. Kochetkov beat back five consecutive attacks by a company of Nazis supported by twelve tanks on 16 August. They put six tanks out of action causing the enemy to roll back. But the soldiers were killed one after another. Finally only four were left. Holding bundles of hand grenades, they prepared for a fresh enemy attack and fought till their strength gave out. They then threw themselves under the tracks of enemy tanks, damaging several more. The men were decorated posthumously – they became known as "The Feat of Sixteen" – a symbol of valour at Stalingrad.

At first, the soldiers had called Stalingrad a pocket edition of Hell. Now they changed this metaphor and began calling Hell a pocket edition of Stalingrad . . . Almost miraculously, despite hundreds of thousands having been evacuated to the rear, a crowd of civilians, mainly women and children, remained in Stalingrad during the battle, cowering in shell holes and gullies that intersected the city.

On Lenin Street the Russian trench-mortar positions ran through the upper floor of Building No. 36. The Germans held a basement on the opposite side of the road. Between these two buildings every square foot of space was under fire. No one could survive in this no-man's-land and, except for fighting men, almost everyone else had fled the city. It is said that even the bats had abandoned the buildings.

But on this particular street one person remained: a civilian. At dusk, a wraith-like creature would lift the lid of a manhole right in the middle of the street, almost exactly between the two firing lines. Her elderly hand would toss out bits and pieces of rubbish, then lower the lid and return to her underground home. She was living (perhaps existing is a truer word) in a cast-iron drainpipe in the city's subterranean belly. Russian soldiers remembered that she wore an old-fashioned winter coat with a frayed fox collar. The soldiers had become increasingly fond of her because she would creep across the street in the blackness of a moonless evening, when relative quiet reigned, climb the half-ruined charred staircase, bringing the smoke-begrimed gunners freshly washed foot cloths, or a newly darned shirt or trousers, or warm porridge.

In her underground home she had a small kerosene stove which hummed away quietly amid the thunder of battle.

Soap was a luxury but the woman – Maria Gavrilovna – would produce a small bar when the men needed it. When the battery commander complained of an awful toothache one day, she gave him a hot potion of some kind to ease the pain. Gradually the soldiers began to address her as "Mother".

One morning Maria Gavrilovna told her "sons" that today she would give them a feast – hot cabbage soup. Where she managed to find a head of cabbage nobody knows. But the cabbage soup in combination with tinned beef promised to be a special treat for the men. At dusk, when the firing slackened, the well-known figure lifted the manhole cover, climbed out and waddled across the street, carrying a piping pot of cabbage soup.

All of a sudden the men heard the deadly crackle of enemy rifle fire; but they saw Maria Gavrilovna continue to walk calmly, not hurrying, so as not to spill the soup. The Russians returned the fire in order to defend their much-treasured visitor. But when she climbed the stairs, without spilling a drop of soup, the men noticed blood forming beneath her kerchief. Putting down the pot of soup she sank to the floor without saying a word. She never regained consciousness. The soldiers buried her that night in the enclosed courtyard of House No. 36.

On her grave they wrote:

"Here lies Maria Gavrilovna Timofeyeva, Mother of the 12th Trench Mortar Battalion."

As the world watched the fight for the city, the defenders of Stalingrad took an oath, "Not a step back!" Every street and house was fought for, almost every inch of ground. Discipline was harsh for those who faltered or displayed cowardice. An official report says 13,500 Red Army soldiers were executed for desertion. After four months of fighting, the Germans were forced to assume the defensive. Without losing their momentum, the Russians prepared for a counter-attack.

The following paragraph written by General (later Marshal) Vasili Chuikov, who commanded the Sixty-second Army at Stalingrad, depicts the horror of the battlefield. Chuikov speaks of a German attack in force and calls it "the worst day of the war":

At the end of that attack the enemy had advanced only a mile. They made their gains not because we retreated but because our men were killed faster than they could be replaced. The Germans advanced only over our dead. But we prevented him from breaking through to the Volga. The Germans lost tens of thousands of dead in a half mile of soil and they couldn't keep it up. Before they could renew their ranks with fresh reserves the Russians launched a general offensive.

Chuikov himself was often in the thick of danger. On the day he speaks of, when the Wehmacht attacked in force, sixty-one members of his staff were killed and one of his officers was struck down while Chuikov was talking to him. Headquarters was only 200 yards from the front line.

On 19 November the defenders launched a counter-offensive and in a short time encircled enemy troops near the town of Kalach from the north-west and south-east. Large groupings of enemy forces were crushed. German General Alfred Jodl told the Nuremburg Trial: "We were entirely in the dark about the concentration of large Russian forces on the flanks of the Sixth Army. We had no idea of Russian strength in this sector. Nothing had been here before and suddenly a blow of tremendous force and crucial significance was delivered there."

In less than a week the Russian forces were able to break though the German defences and close a giant ring around almost two dozen divisions, numbering some 330,000 men. Fighting went on for two months and attempts to break out of the encirclement were foiled. On 2 February German Field Marshal Friedrich Paulus surrendered. Over 90,000 troops, 24 generals and 2,500 officers were taken prisoner. It was the end of the Wehrmacht's Sixth Army which had marched triumphantly through Belgium, France and into the heart of Russia.

Throughout Germany there was mourning. "It was," said German historian Walter Gorlitz, "the greatest defeat the German Army had ever experienced."

Understandably, Russians historians criticize those who dilute the importance of the battle or say that success was due to numerical superiority. Russian scholars point to remarks by General Fernand Gambiez, a member of the French Academy of Sciences, who told the newspaper, *Le Figaro*: "There were about a million troops and over a thousand aircraft engaged on each side in that gigantic operation." The French general said the victory was won because "the morale of the Russian Army was unquestionably much higher than that of the troops of the German Reich and its satellites."

After the end of the fighting on the Volga which lasted six and a half months, some historians began to refer to Stalingrad as "the greatest battle of all time".

CHAPTER 14

Endurance

Death Mask

Vera Mukhina, the well-known sculptor, was awakened one night and summoned to the Central Military Hospital for a special assignment. It was the autumn following the invasion when Hitler's armies were so close to Moscow that German officers could see the onion domes of the city's Orthodox churches through their field glasses. The defenders were putting up a fierce resistance but casualties were mounting. Tens of thousands of Russian soldiers lay wounded on stretchers along open train stations in Moscow's environs, waiting for removal to hospitals in the rear. At the Central Military Hospital Vera Mukhina was instructed to make death masks of outstanding front-line heroes who now lay dying or were already dead.

The next morning when Vera returned home she sat for a long time examining some of the fresh plaster of Paris death masks. One of them was of a well-known colonel who had been gravely wounded near Moscow. She had looked at his service record: the officer had had a distinguished career, had seen action in the civil war and had been wounded eleven times, including twice in the present war. He'd also been shell-shocked eight times and, in the civil war years, been sentenced to death by drumhead court martial. His last wound, received near the capital, was very grave and therefore the doctors did not think he would last until dawn. The wounded colonel, Ivan Khizhnyak, was still alive when the layer of plaster hardened on his hollow, bloodless cheeks, jutting chin and lined forehead.

The mask (it is today on display at Moscow's Tretyakov Art Gallery) show's the hero's iron-hard expression and, curiously, preserves a barely perceptible smile. It seemed, according to Mukhina, that the dying man had smiled at the last thought that flashed through his mind.

When war broke out in June 1941 Colonel Khizhnyak's 117th Infantry Division was in the thick of the fighting as city after city fell to the invaders: Bobruisk, Zhlobin, Rogachev. Men of the 117th were being battered but despite their fatigue they held out. The archives contain numerous messages passing between division and headquarters, and also congratulatory words about the courage displayed by the officers and men who on some days had to repel up to twelve enemy assaults. The name Khizhnyak also appears often in the official documents, cited for awards and decorations. One of the operations messages (among hundreds received) says: "The Division is ordered to destroy the supply depots in the village of Yashchitsky near the town of Zhlobin. They must be destroyed so that not a single shell and not a single litre of petrol falls into enemy hands."

Ivan Khizhnyak disagreed with this particular order. He consulted his subordinates and together they decided to risk trying to save the supplies. The result is noted in an official report: "Without weakening the division's resistance and inflicting blows on the enemy the colonel organized the evacuation of the huge depots. Several thousand men were detailed to this job and they were assisted by workers from the factories of nearby towns and villages. The columns of loaders were headed by army men; the general direction of this operation was assumed by the divisional commander. The work went forward quickly, the men acting as in combat. Trains arrived and were loaded despite the nearness of the enemy. Soon several thousand railway cars filled with cartridges, shells and food were speeding towards the rear."

Meanwhile the situation at the front worsened. Khizhnyak's division lost contact with its neighbours and – the worst possible predicament – found itself completely surrounded. The enemy was pressing hard, attacking even at night. Each morning the trenches were strewn with enemy leaflets that promised those who surrendered a "good life" in captivity. But as Khizhnyak recalls, "We had neither cowards nor traitors in the 117th. Instead, our men fought like lions."

When finally the battle became less intense, Khizhnyak made the decision to fight his way out of the German ring. While his deputy took command of the vanguard, the colonel and a hundred men brought up the rear. To break out of an encirclement requires exceptional military talent, not to mention stamina and iron discipline. Without this there is little hope of success. Khizhnyak did not want to risk his men unnecessarily and therefore laid his plans carefully. His men advanced in small groups using the forest as cover. They hid in depressions and struck back when called for. Thus the division slowly made its way out of the enemy encirclement. But difficulties were far from over. The covering group in the rear, including the colonel, needed only one mile to go when the enemy suddenly set up a machine-gun ambush. Khizhnyak ordered a bayonet charge. His booming voice, it is said, echoed in the forest, putting heart into his men.

The ambush was crushed in a matter of minutes but in the struggle Khizhnyak slumped to the ground after being hit by a burst of machine-gun fire. Blood soaked his uniform and his face became deathly pale. But he continued to give commands and he led his men to safety as two of them carried him on a stretcher that was hastily put together with rifles and overcoats. When they reached friendly lines the colonel was put on a small PO-2 plane to fly him to a hospital. But – again there was bad luck – the plane was machine-gunned by two Luftwaffe fighters and fresh wounds were added to those already received by Khizhnyak.

This was the grave condition in which sculptor Vera Mukhina found him when she was summoned to the hospital to perpetuate in plaster the image of this heroic soldier. It was only years later that the sculptor was informed that Ivan Khizhnyak was alive. He had survived and was engaged in writing his memoirs, entitled *Years of War*.

Upon his recovery from death's door, Ivan Khizhnyak was promoted to the rank of general and given command of the 11th Guards

Infantry Corps. But despite his rank he remained close to his troops and, as might be expected from his record, was a model of high courage. Often he would rally his men personally; and often Khizhnyak would be in the firing lines of the infantry, visiting the artillery observation posts in addition to the trenches, sometimes to thank his men when they especially distinguished themselves On one occasion he was told that a group of new recruits were nervous before going into combat for the first time. The soldiers were sure they would be seriously wounded or even killed. Khizhnyak gathered them together beside a stream and told them of his experiences in the civil war. Then, suddenly, he stripped to the waist. "Look at the scars from all the wounds I've got. But I'm still alive and strong."

This had the desired effect on the young soldiers who went into battle in high spirits, seeking to oust the enemy from the Kuban area, not far from the Black Sea.

Corps Commander Khizhnyak won additional honours in this battle. His men were part of a large force assembled to break through the enemy's "Blue Line" that stretched from the Kuban to the Black Sea and gave cover to Nazi units in the Crimea. The "Blue Line" consisted of numerous trenches and pillboxes as well as minefields and anti-tank ditches. Khizhnyak's corps was given the task of breaching this line.

The Wehrmacht clung to every square foot of land and every foxhole, ignoring the heavy toll in casualties. But, finally, the onslaught of the Russian corps and the full weight of aircraft, artillery and tanks persuaded the enemy to leave their positions and surrender. After the "Blue Line" was pierced special mention was made of the corps led by Khizhnyak and he himself was given the Order of Suvarov, a medal reserved for outstanding troop commanders.

"The Mother of the Human Race"

Yepistimiya Stepanova outlived all her nine sons who happened to be of military age when Hitler unleashed his war on Russia. Patriotism permeated the Stepanov household, and all of her sons were quick to enlist in the Army. The Stepanovs came from the small village of Timashevsk, situated near the River Kuban, not far from the Black Sea. When the mother died at the age of ninety-two, someone read a poem at the funeral service about a mother's grief. Written by the nineteenth century poet, Nikolai Nekrasov, the poem contains these words: "She could no more forget her children than a weeping willow can lift its branches."

A church choir sang a verse at the service which was attended by thousands of people from all over the country. The verse was from a poem by Rasul Gamzatov, a contemporary poet from Dagestan: "Sometimes it seems to me that the soldiers who did not return from the blood-soaked fields were not buried in common graves but were turned into snow-white cranes." The ceremony came to an end when nine girls in snow-white dresses covered the grave with handfuls of earth brought from all the places in Russia and abroad where the sons of Yepistimiya had fallen. Many who attended the service could not hold back their tears.

The memory of the Stepanov family is preserved in a one-room brick and glass museum in Timashevsk and contains many photographs of the nine brothers, first as small boys, then as students and finally as soldiers. Their father had died while they were still very young. There are pictures of Yepistimiya who time after time took her black mourning shawl out of her trunk. The kerosene lamp never died out in front of the icon in the corner where she prayed endlessly for her martyred sons.

Of Yepistimiya Stepanova's nine sons: Alexander Senior lived 17 years, Alexander Junior-20, Pavel-22, Nikolai-24, Ilya-26, Fyodor-27, Ivan-28, Vasily-35, Filipp-36.

22 June 1941 – invasion day. The very next day, Lieutenant Pavel Stepanov died fighting at the border near the Brest Fortress. On the same day his older brother Ivan, a machine-gunner, was severely wounded. Taken prisoner, he escaped; but was recaptured and executed.

Two other brothers – Alexander Senior and Fyodor – had fallen in other wars. At seventeen, Alexander lost his life in the civil war. Fyodor, a junior lieutenant, died helping Mongolian troops repel a Japanese incursion into that country in the summer of 1939.

In his last letter from the front in 1943, Vasily Stepanov wrote that by chance he had met his brother Filipp. It was the only time in the war that any of the Stepanov brothers got together. Shortly afterward, Vasily, while fighting with a partisan detachment, was ambushed and killed by Gestapo troops.

Filipp was by then a POW, dying in a German concentration camp. He lived until three months before Victory Day.

The year 1943 was the most tragic one for the Stepanov family. A few weeks before the death of Vasily, his younger brother Alexander Junior (named after his brother who was killed in the civil war) met a violent death on the bank of the River Dnieper. Alexander, who was a company commander, captured a bridgehead with his men; then they were counter-attacked and all were killed except himself. His bullets spent, but not wishing to be captured alive, he ended his life with a grenade.

Only a few weeks earlier, Captain Ilya Stepanov, commander of a tank company, fell at Kursk. Nikolai, the sole surviving brother, was unharmed until just a few days before victory, in May 1945, when he was severely wounded and hospitalized. Doctors, knowing they could not save his life, allowed Nikolai to go home, where he died in his mother's arms.

After Yepistimiya died the name of the Stepanov family disappeared. Nothing was left as a reminder of the heroic family except the small museum in Timashevsk where visitors learn about the lives of the nine brothers who had once been the pride of their village. In the visitor's book at the museum there is an entry by Igor Ignatenko, a teacher of English: "When I was two years old the war robbed me of my father. But how can my sorrow be compared with that of this woman, Yepistimiya – the Mother of the Human Race! Low and eternal bows to you, Mother, from all the sons of the Earth."

Out of a huge rock on the outskirts of the Ossetian village of Dzuarikao, near the Caucasian Mountains, stands a monument with seven bronze cranes, their long necks gently curved. The cranes have been expertly attached to each other by the sculptor and seem to rise up into the sky. At the foot of the rock-base is the carved stone figure of an aged woman who looks in the direction that the cranes are "flying" – that is, to the west, where the sun sets. In the twilight the woman is wrapped in a crimson glow. Local people say the scene is a constant reminder of the grief of the war years. Nazi divisions managed to push their way into the Transcaucasus area but were stopped in fierce fighting around Dzuarikao.

It was in Dzuarikao that Tazo and Asakhmet Gazdanov raised seven sons. The Gazdanovs were people of few words who put the highest value on family togetherness and had a deep love of the soil. The eldest of the brothers, Magomet, worked as a tractor driver. Makharbek became a teacher and gave language lessons to children in the local school. Dzarakhmet became a member of the village council but he also had a reputation as a brilliant horseman who could snatch a coin off the ground while riding at full gallop. Khajismel followed his older brother's example and became a tractor driver. Sazyriko was in his last year of a commercial school in the town of Orjonikidze, while the two youngest brothers had yet to finish school when the war broke out. Each Gazdanov brother left, one after the other, for the front line. Not one of them returned home.

Makharbek was killed in the defence of Moscow. Magomet and Khajismel fell in the siege of Sevastopol. Sazyriko died in the battle for Kiev. Dzarakhmet lost his life at Novorossiisk. Khasanbek fell near Minsk, during the liberation of Byelorussia.★ Shamil, the youngest, lived through the long march towards Berlin but was mortally wounded and died just four days before final victory.

Today, streets in Ossetia are named in honour of the seven Gadzdanov brothers; and the school where they studied is now part museum. Seven Circasian coats for the seven brothers, with cartridge

---

★ After the war ten cities were honoured with the title of "Hero City". The brothers Stepanov and Gazdanov fell defending some of them. The ten "Hero Cities" are: Moscow, Minsk, Sevastopol, Odessa, Novorossisk, Leningrad (St Petersburg), Kerch, Kiev, Tula, Volgograd (Stalingrad). In addition, the frontier fortress of Brest has been designated a "Hero-Fortress".

belts around the waistlines, are hung on the walls of the school in keeping with the tradition of this mountain people.★

Dead Man Walking

When you met Ivan Kotov after the war you immediately noticed that there was something child-like and innocent about him, a bull-necked man of middle height and compact build. After uttering two or three words, he would pause, stammer and, while staring at you, gurgle like a child beginning to speak.

"It's no use . . . I can't talk . . . I don't remember."

Another long pause and his face would light up; then he'd lift his hands in an expressive gesture and hiss out the remaining words that were on his tongue. It was clear that Ivan Kotov's powers of speech and memory were impaired. During an hour of conversation you could not wring from him more than fifty words.

But now and then Ivan managed a coherent sentence.

"Before . . . I was never like this . . . I was a carpenter . . . a wood-turner . . . Then I was chief of a housing unit . . . But now nobody can do anything for me . . . It's no use."

"What's no use? Why do you talk like this?" Specialists would try to elicit answers from him.

Ivan was about fifty years of age but looked younger. He had an oval face, a constant frown and dark eyes. Most of the time he rested his head in his hands and remained silent. He appeared bored and completely out of touch with the world. If you put a question to him, he did not answer directly but stared ahead as if wondering what he was supposed to say. You had to repeat your question again and again. Then he would say a few words but stop in mid-sentence. Something always cut off his power of speech. After a long pause he would repeat what he had already said, fidget with his broad fingers, then slap the top of his head as though fed up with himself.

★ But many other families lost their entire menfolk. Just two examples: There were the seven Shaklein brothers of Leningrad and the five Kupriyanov brothers of Belarus, all of whom fell in battle.

"It's no use . . ."

The doctors knew what his problem was. The war had made him an invalid.

Ivan Kotov had been thrown into a Nazi gas wagon – called in Russian a *dushegubka* – and was the only person to have survived. But he was marked for life. Afterwards the people in the southern town of Krasnodar spoke about him as, "the dead man who walked".

The enemy began using their new technology of death in the fall of 1942 not long after they occupied Krasnodar, located in Kuban Cossack country. At first when residents saw the unusual van going about the city, they couldn't figure out what it was – it looked so ordinary. Some people thought it was a refrigerated vehicle for transporting food or pharmaceuticals that had to be kept at a freezing temperature. But it didn't take long to learn its true purpose; then the people recoiled at the sight of it.

This death wagon – a "pocket version" of the gas chambers at Auschwitz – was a diesel-powered seven-ton truck. Inside there were no seats or windows. Only one large door was opened from the rear. On the floor was a grating and under it a tube that was attached to the exhaust pipe of the engine. When the engine was turned on, carbon monoxide gas was carried into the van's interior. The door, being slammed shut, tightly sealed the car. Quickly the gas was bottled up and grew thicker; in a few minutes those inside died of asphyxiation.

Ivan Kotov had been shut inside this portable execution chamber and lived. The following details were coaxed out of this unfortunate man.

Late one afternoon during the second year of the war, in 1942, Ivan Kotov went to a city clinic to obtain an official paper confirming that he had received some minor medical treatment. The doctor was busy and he waited two hours before he received the paper. It was already twilight when he left the building but he noticed that in the yard there was a large grey van and that men and women patients in hospital pyjamas were being herded inside it. He kept looking but couldn't figure out what was going on; then, as he walked past a Nazi officer, he was seized by the coat collar and, without a word, shoved inside the van that was already packed with men, women and several small children. He couldn't move at all since everyone was pressed tightly together. Shrieks and wails filled the van. But with the roar of the motor no one could hear the screams on the outside and therefore no one thought there was anything out of the ordinary. Then, suddenly, a half dozen more people were flung inside. When the heavy door slammed again, Ivan felt like an animal in a windowless pen.

He heard the truck's engine start and the van began to move. Immediately Ivan felt as if he was going to choke but, instantly, he understood he and the other occupants were being gassed. He reacted instinctively for he had fought in the First World War and learned what to do in case of a poison gas attack. Also, as building manager in Krasnodar, he had attended lectures on how to survive if an enemy initiated chemical warfare. In case of emergency the first thing to do, he remembered, was to moisten a cloth and cover the nose and mouth with it. But where was he to obtain water in the murder van? What could he do when a mass of people was pressed together, gasping and screaming while toxic carbon monoxide gas poured in from the floor grating.

With no time to waste, he wet his shirt with his urine. He then tore off a piece of the cloth and put it over his nose and mouth. But after a few minutes he too lost consciousness like the others.

Waking up later he found himself in a ditch among corpses. Some were covered with a thin layer of earth while others were exposed to the elements. He was unable to tell how long he'd been in the van or how long he'd been lying in the ditch. But he understood what had happened and knew he had to remove himself from this gory site. Looking around to see if he was alone, he managed to rise to his feet. But he had a terrific headache, was wobbly and felt nauseated. Remaining out of sight behind trees and bushes, he groped his way to the city.

While the enemy stayed in Krasnodar, Ivan Kotov remained in hiding, not appearing in the streets until the town was liberated. Afterwards he was treated by experts in neurology and psychiatry. But the specialists were not hopeful. When people met him on the street, they were reminded of the hell under the occupation. They would listen patiently as Ivan repeated a few words: "Doctors can't help . . . I'm no good anymore . . . It's no use . . ."

CHAPTER 15

The Pilot who Crawled

The Story of a Real Man by Boris Polevoi was published some years ago in Moscow. It is about pilot Alexei Petrovich Maresyev who flew almost one hundred combat missions and was shot down only once. But that one incident turned him into a folk hero. Alexei told me what happened as he sat in his comfortable secretary's chair in the building of the Russian Veterans' Committee in the heart of Moscow. On the wall behind him was a large green map of the Russian Federation.

Alexei was twenty years old when he entered a flying club in the Far Eastern region of the country. The following year, in 1937, he was recruited into the Army. Three years later he graduated from a special Air Force school at Bataisk, near Rostov. When war broke out, Alexei piloted an E-16, a plane he describes as having "a big nose, small wings, and four machine-guns and a top speed of 250 mph." In the beginning these planes were used to attack land forces and did not engage in dogfights. But later, in March 1942, the Air Force received new planes: the YAK-1 and LA-5 fighters which had a cannon in addition to machine-guns.

Looking back, Alexei says it was a "pity" that at the beginning of the war the Russians had good pilots but "their planes were inferior" to those of the Luftwaffe. He has "painful memories" of those first months of the war when Nazi pilots shot down hundreds of Soviet planes. One German general has referred to these early Russian losses as being analogous to "wholesale infanticide".

At the time of his calamity, Alexei was attached to the 1st Baltic

Front near Leningrad. It was the beginning of April but the weather was still freezing at night, the mercury often plunging to minus fifteen or sixteen degrees below zero Celsius.

"It was noon and I and my companions were flying four YAK-1 fighters when we encountered twelve Messerschmitts. Two of them attacked me at once. My altitude was only 1,300 feet. I turned my plane over to avoid being hit, but when I did this a third Luftwaffe plane shot up my engine, breaking the oil system and damaging the engine. So I was forced to make an emergency landing. But it was difficult to find a place to land because below was a sprawling forest. I manoeuvred the plane, trying as hard as I could to avoid the trees. But my wings touched the tips of the trees and my plane turned upside down, throwing me out of the cockpit. I had hit some thick branches and both my legs were broken. All around me was desolation but I told myself I must reach a friendly area despite my injuries; and since my arms were OK, I began to crawl on the snowy ground."

Alexei's feet had in fact been badly crushed when his aircraft slammed into the trees. And his situation worsened.

"I was wearing special fur-lined air force boots. But the trouble is, I was moving worm-like on my stomach so that the snow entered my boots. During the day the snow melted because of my activity; but at night the moisture turned to ice."

During the day he was plagued by hunger but there was little he could do about it. He says that because of the frost the silver birch trees had no "juice" under the bark, so he could get no nourishment from the trees.★

Poking beneath the snow he found some wild berries and moss, which he chewed. Once he encountered a huge ant-hill "almost as big as a haystack". The ants were inactive, "probably asleep," says Alexei. He put his hands into the soft mass and when he withdrew

★ During the war trees helped sustain children from Leningrad. Artist Anna Grubina says in her reminiscences: "In 1942 our whole school was evacuated from Leningrad to the town of Karpinsk in the Urals. As soon as we got there we were rushed to the park – not to walk amidst the trees but to eat them. It was the larches we relished most; their soft fragrant needles were really delicious. That year the people in the Urals were starving, too."

them the ants were clinging to his skin. He began eating the insects with great relish, feeling the tart taste of formic acid in his dry, cracked mouth. He grabbed more handfuls of ants until he had disturbed the whole ant-hill. His hands, lips and tongue were stung by the ants and they got under his flying suit and stung his body. But the burning sensation and spicy taste acted as a tonic. And the best part of it was that the ants provided the energy for him to go on crawling.

When he felt thirsty he put some snow into his mouth. Once, after almost two weeks, he suddenly saw a puddle of brownish water and put his head down to drink but recoiled when he saw his reflection in the water. He saw a skeletonized skull covered with dark skin and overgrown with straggly hair. The eyes, wild and shiny, stared back at him from deep sockets. He was greatly shocked. "That can't be me!" Alexei told himself. But he was afraid to take another look into the water. Now, crawling became increasingly hard. His arms trembled and were unable to pull the weight of his body.

When asked how he ever managed his superhuman feat, Alexei said: "I'm a strong man; I come from the Volga region." It seemed clear, given the fact that Alexei is an example of human endurance, that the Volga region must be a good breeder of robust sons and daughters.

"How old do you think I am?" Alexei suddenly asked. With his thick black hair with no grey to be seen and fine oval face, he appeared to be in his late fifties or early sixties. Actually I knew his age, but gave him a chance to beam with pleasure. Was he, perhaps, sixty or sixty-five?

"Eighty-two," he said, with unaffected relish. (The year was 1999.)

Often – he continued his narrative – he would fall asleep as he crawled. Crawling steadily, rolling over and over when his arms tired, he was probably in a continual state of oblivion, or close to it; but he went on crawling and rolling, struggling to pull his damaged legs along, until he would collide with a bush or tree, or his face hit the snow. He would then pause to rest. When he moved again it was pretty much an automatic effort: Left arm left, right arm right . . . then wriggle, wriggle, wriggle . . . Alexei completely lost track of time.

Did he ever think he wouldn't make it?

"I didn't think I'd die. I made up my mind to reach our positions. But was I actually going the right way? I didn't know. My only idea of direction came from the sun. It rises in the east and so I crawled in that direction, hoping to reach friendly lines. Before crash-landing I was unable to contact my unit because there was no radio on the plane or any other special equipment."

Although it was the month of April, there were still some small frozen lakes in his path. Alexei kept moving, not in a straight line but zig-zagging, avoiding lakes, clumps of trees and other impediments.

Then an unexpected danger loomed. "One day I heard steps; somebody was walking nearby. I lay still. And out of nowhere a brown bear as big as life approached me, a 200-pounder at least. I held my breath as the bear came almost up to my face, sniffing at the dried blood on my legs. There was no time to lose; I pulled out my pistol and shot the animal eight times before he dropped to the ground. I'm sorry, but I had to do it."

After Alexei had crawled for eighteen days, peasants from a nearby village spotted him. They brought a cart to where he lay on the ground and took him to a hospital where doctors tried to save his legs. But they were frozen and it was impossible to mend the bones or save his legs. He was constantly sedated with pain killers and sleeping pills.

Alexei remembers the head surgeon coming to his ward and addressing him always with the words: "Well, crawler, how are things with you?"

"This was the beginning of the toughest period in my life," he says. "After ninety days, I was fitted out with artificial limbs, and I started taking lessons on how to walk on my new legs." His first steps were not encouraging. They resulted in bleeding corns on his maimed body and excruciating pain. However, he went on and trained himself to walk so that when people looked at him they would not think him an invalid.

But not everything went well with Alexei. He moped for a good deal of time before he was encouraged to walk again. The experts say that it is not at all rare for people in such circumstances to withdraw into themselves. For whole days Alexei did nothing but lie motionless on his back, his eyes following the long cracks in the ceiling. But while lying in bed, he listened to the war communiqués, catching news of aerial dogfights and ground offensives against the enemy. "Lucky fellows," he thought. "They are fighting and dying but I will never fly again." Yet for some reason he kept thinking of a line from the story *The Song of the Falcon* by Maxim Gorky:

"Those who are born to creep cannot fly."

One day a member of the hospital staff gave him an article about a Russian airman of the First World War. A picture accompanying the article showed a young officer with a moustache that turned up at the sides, who wore a cap with a white cockade. The officer had lost a foot when hit by a German dumdum bullet while flying over enemy lines. But, making himself an artificial foot, the officer had returned to his post and sometimes risked a combat flight in his fighter plane. For his gallantry he was awarded the St George Cross.

"It's natural to follow another's example, and from that moment on I began to believe that it was possible, through intensive training, to learn to fly a plane without feet." Now his former cheerful outlook on life returned and he was filled with the desire to get back into the air. He pursued this new object in his life with the same stubbornness he had demonstrated when, badly injured, he had saved himself by crawling several weeks until rescued.

"I applied for permission to fly again and persuaded my superiors that I was really a master flying instructor. But I had to begin all over again, having to pass flying tests to prove myself." Incidentally, while in the hospital, Alexei fell in love with Galina Viktorovna, a cartographer. They later married and had two sons.

Once, during the wintry month of February Alexei Petrovich took a flying lesson with an instructor who had not been told about his disability. The instructor asked if his feet, which were bootless, were not freezing. No, Alexei said. "These are not my feet." With a frown, the instructor said: "Let me see." Like a magician performing a trick, Alexei lifted his trousers to the other's astonishment.

Finally he was permitted to fly solo again. "In my service record it was stated that I was capable of flying all kinds of planes. But now they gave me slow, trainer-type aircraft. But I asked for permission to fly fighters. I wanted to fly the American Aerocobra. I said that if it looked too difficult I would not fly it. Actually, because of my condition, I was unable to handle this American plane and, instead, I flew the LA-5 when I was sent to various fronts."

In June 1943 Alexei arrived at a forward air unit. This was just before the Battle of the Kursk Bulge when the air war had intensified and combat missions began almost immediately. In dogfights near Orel, north of Kursk, Alexei brought down three enemy planes. After the victory at Kursk, Alexei was awarded the highest combat award, the Gold Hero Medal.

During the war Alexei flew ninety-two combat missions and destroyed eleven enemy planes, four before he was shot down and seven after he was released from the hospital. After the war Alexei became an inspector at a fighter pilot school in Moscow. He also went on lecture tours all over Russia and became active in veterans' affairs.

Lyubov Kosmodemyanskaya, herself the mother of a hero (the partisan girl, Zoya), said the following about Alexei Maresyev six years after the war: "He is the living embodiment of the Russian people, their courage and determination, their selfless bravery and endurance." She added that Alexei's feat had been "an expression of all the noble qualities of the people."★

★ There were others who emulated Alexei. Although they lost limbs in the war they returned to the front lines or did war-work in industry and agriculture. For example, Zakhar Sorokin piloted a fighter plane on the northern front, was severely wounded in action and, discharged from the hospital with both feet amputated, he returned to his regiment and brought down another twelve enemy planes, bringing his total to eighteen.

There also is a parallel story about the legendary British fighter pilot, Douglas Bader. After losing both legs in a prewar flying accident Bader, with a "pugnacious desire" to duel with the Luftwaffe, returned to the RAF at the beginning of the Second World War to lead a squadron of Spitfires during the Battle of Britain. He once said: "I have an engine in front of me, armour plate behind me, tin legs under me. How the devil can the enemy hurt me?" When he was shot down over Occupied France, his German captors had to take away his tin legs to prevent him from escaping.

CHAPTER 16

The Thirteenth Commandment

At dawn on 10 July 1943, Georgi Gubkin's infantry company sighted the advancing yellowish-green enemy tanks with their black painted crosses. As part of Hitler's huge operation to dislodge Russian armies from the Kursk Salient, the tanks were closing in relentlessly together with infantry. It seemed no force on earth could stop them. The Battle of the Kursk Salient was destined to be one of the turning points of the Second World War and the huge forces gathered by both sides occupied a vast area, 25,000 square miles, located 200 miles south of Moscow. But Gubkin was an experienced thirty-year-old combat officer who had fought fearlessly at Stalingrad and he was not daunted by impending danger. However, as he ordered his men to stand by he anxiously wondered what would happen if the German "Tiger" tanks with their 88 mm guns and the "Ferdinand" self-propelled artillery overran the anti-tank reserve.

Gubkin's men had one idea in mind: to stop the German advance at all costs.

Closer and closer came the rumble of engines and the roar of enemy artillery. The wind carried the smoke and smell of burning oil to the Russian trenches at the same time as the sounds of gnashing metal grew louder. The men watched as the armada of enemy tanks moved closer. They were now able to estimate that the interval between each tank was 25–30 yards. Following the "Tigers" were the "Ferdinand" assault guns 200 yards behind. The latter were followed by medium tanks, armoured personnel carriers and, finally, trucks carrying infantry. There seemed to be no end to the "wave of steel" as it came rolling towards the trenches.

In a number of places the flat-nosed yellow-green machines had already pierced the positions of the army anti-tank reserve and were approaching the trenches manned by Gubkin's company. The decisive moment for these men was close at hand.

It was the third summer of the war on the Eastern Front and it was common knowledge that the German High Command wanted a big victory to avenge the disastrous defeat at Stalingrad in February. Despite strict German secrecy, the outline of the new operation, called "Citadel", was known to the Russian General Staff. Their counter-plan, approved by the GHQ of the Supreme Command, was to bleed the enemy white in a defensive action and then quickly mount a counter-offensive.

The Russian 184th Infantry Division had arrived at the Voronezh Front late in June 1943, a month before the Battle of the Kursk Salient started. It took up defensive positions on the chalk hills, east of a giant government farm called Chapeyev. Reinforced with a six-gun anti-tank battery, Georgi Gubkin's 4th Infantry Company were ordered to dig a total of 3 miles of trenches and provide them with weapon emplacements.

The trench-digging got underway slowly. Because many of his men appeared phlegmatic in their digging, Gubkin reminded them of "the soldier's Thirteenth Commandment": "It is better to dig 10 metres of trenches than a 3-metre grave." But some of the men still worked at a casual pace, digging haphazardly. Gubkin responded by throwing off his sweat-soaked uniform and putting his own shoulder behind a shovel. Seeing this, the men began digging in real earnest.

A week had passed and the company had accomplished much. The engineering works had been completed and the men now awaited the enemy offensive. But it didn't come and a scarcity of information depressed the men. They were extremely tense.

On the night of 1 July General Nikolai Vatutin, Commander of the Voronezh Front, demanded frequent reports on the enemy's behaviour. A sheet of white paper – a directive signed by the Supreme Commander in Chief – lay on the table at Vatutin's headquarters. It said: "According to information on hand, the Germans may start the offensive on our front in the period July 3 to 6. The GHQ Supreme Command, hereby orders:

"To conduct more active reconnaissance and observation of the enemy to establish his intentions in time. The troops and air force are to be ready to repel any enemy attack."

On the German side, Hitler gave orders to his troops on the night of 4 July. The Fuhrer formulated the purpose of Operation *Citadel* as follows: The German armies were to take Kursk in three days and rout the Russian forces holding the Kursk Salient. Wehrmacht officers assured their men that this would not be difficult since German industry had provided them with very powerful tanks and self-propelled assault guns with armour that was invulnerable to ordinary anti-tank guns.

The Fuhrer's appeal to his men ended with these words:

"God be with you! His will shall be fulfilled by Tiger tanks."

But the Wehrmacht did not suspect what lay in store for them. Having established the time of the German offensive, the Russian Command decided to carry out a massive forestalling artillery and air preparation. In addition, new Russian anti-tank guns and high calibre anti-tank shells had been delivered to the troops to cope with the enemy's heavy tanks and assault guns.

At 0230 on 5 July the silence before dawn was suddenly broken by Russian salvoes. The roar of howitzers merged with the howl of *Katyusha* rockets. Tens of thousands of artillery and mortar shells hit German troops concentrated in the assault assembly areas. The air shook and the earth trembled as red-hot metal struck the ground. To foil the start of Operation *Citadel* the Russian artillery emptied over 300 rail cars of artillery and mortar shells. The German Army was compelled to delay the hour of its assault, thereby losing the advantage of surprise.

At daybreak the telephone rang sharply and Gubkin picked up the receiver. His battalion commander, Melnichenko, shouted in a hoarse voice: "The Germans have pierced the defence positions of the forward echelon. Have you got that? They may be here any moment now. I want you to know and to tell everybody that the security of the entire regiment depends on the steadfastness of your men. Your company's position must be impregnable."

Fighting was now raging only 2 miles west of the chalk hills. A German panzer division began to attack the weak points of two Russian infantry divisions and grey clouds of smoke hung over the battlefield. Sudden red flashes indicated the shell and bomb bursts on the ground. To eye-witnesses, it seemed as if the sky itself was being torn to shreds.

The intensity of the battle continued to grow, the firing not stopping for a single moment. Concentrated along a narrow front, hundreds of artillery pieces were firing from both sides. The Germans had committed everything they had to this battle. Although the forward echelons of Russia's Voronezh Front were putting up stiff resistance, they were slowly withdrawing to prearranged positions.

Gubkin assessed the danger. Covered by the "Tiger" tanks, the Germans appeared capable of crushing any obstacles in their way. Gubkin looked at each of his men, now silent and tense, and his eye fell on the teenager, Nasreddinov. The boy was standing in the trench as if hypnotized. He gradually sank down on his right knee, his dark eyes round with terror. He had laid his carbine down on the breastwork of the trench as if it were a useless toy. His hands unconsciously gripped lumps of clay.

A distance of only several hundred yards now separated the advancing tanks from the trenches. Muffled sounds reached the men as they watched red flares soar into the air. At that moment a hail of artillery fire from closed positions struck at the German attack formation. One "Tiger" tank after another ground to a halt as smoke and flames enveloped their hulls. The sight of the burning tanks lifted the spirits of Gubkin's men. Someone exclaimed:

"Say, these 'invulnerable' Tigers burn like ordinary tanks."

When the smoke dispersed, the men saw that on their left flank nine tanks had turned directly onto the positions their company was holding. They were followed by dense skirmish lines of German infantry. Though the "Tigers" were now what Gubkin deemed dangerously close, he saw with surprise that one of his men, a middle-aged artilleryman, was calmly sitting by the side of his gun smoking a hand-rolled cigarette. Turning to the battery commander, Makhmudov, Gubkin raised his voice:

"Azim! What are you waiting for?"

Without taking his eyes away from his field glasses, Makhmudov answered:

"For them to close in. We'll begin when they're right up close!"

Gubkin put his reliance on Makhmudov's men. But he cast an anxious glance at the new men who had recently joined the company. He knew that fear paralyzed new men before their first battle and that a man had to conquer this fear before he could become a "real soldier". Quite a few of Gubkin's men were from peoples in Siberia or Central Asia. Most of them made excellent soldiers and had previously received high combat decorations.

The German tanks were now closer. Their turrets were slowly turning from side to side as if sniffing for something before opening fire. "It's time to begin," Gubkin thought and he fired a green flare which was the signal to the anti-tank riflemen. At almost the same moment an anti-tank gun opened up. The forward German tank disappeared in smoke and flames. Gubkin thought:

"That was Makhmudov for sure. Good aim, Azim!"

A second later, a "Ferdinand" assault gun fired two rounds, straddling the position of Makhmudov's gun. In reply a heavy gun opened fire. The turret of the leading tank was knocked off and landed on the ground several yards away. Gubkin telephoned to Makhmudov's battery and was overjoyed to hear that Azim was alive and unharmed; that he had rolled his gun away to safety seconds before. The shells from the enemy assault gun had exploded on empty ground.

Soon Makhmudov scored a hit on another "Tiger" tank, knocking off one of its tracks. As one of the men said, the tank began to spin "like a beetle stung by a hornet".

Gubkin's company strongpoint was now attacked by over 200 German infantrymen who followed the "Tigers". Now it was Makhmudov's turn to wonder why the machine-gunners were not firing. He rushed up to Gubkin and, short of breath, cried out:

"Are you blind? There are hundreds of them! Open fire! With the infantry on my firing positions I won't be able to do anything with the tanks."

"What are you worrying about, Azim? We mustn't advertise our firing positions too soon."

Finally, keeping his eyes on the cratered field in front of him, Gubkin signalled to the machine-gunners to cut the attacking infantry off from the tanks. But defying the heavy fusillade, the Germans forced their way ahead. Gubkin fired a red flare, a signal to open fire with small arms.

The Germans now stepped up their fire from six-barrelled mortars. Shell splinters and lumps of soil rained on the men in the trenches. Gubkin was half buried and felt sand in his eyes. Wiping them with a moist bandage, the company commander seized his field glasses. The new replacements of his 2nd platoon were holding their ground and had not budged at all. Through his glasses Gubkin identified more enemy tanks. Suddenly one of them raised a cloud of dust and smoke: it had hit a mine. In a few seconds five more tanks had been stopped. Then two panzers with anti-mine rollers took over the lead. The other tanks gave them cover with artillery and machine-gun fire, at first from stationary positions, then while on the move.

The enemy infantry was still being held by machine-gun fire and the anti-tank battery was maintaining a steady, rapid rate of fire. Makhmudov's boyish voice could be heard even over the din of battle.

"Vasili, the leading 'Tiger' has exposed its side. What are you waiting for?" Makhmudov shouted. He repeated the order to the 3rd platoon: "Fire at the lead tank!"

A voice in the receiver rasped: "The lieutenant has been seriously wounded. Sergeant Semarenko's in control."

One of the gun crews was manned by a father and his son. Vasili

Semarenko, the son, was the gun crew commander and Nikolai Davydovich Semarenko, the father, was breech operator. Semarenko's second round scored a direct hit on the "Tiger". The tank lost its starboard track, turning it into a wounded serpent.

By this time Makhmudov's battery had also suffered losses. The 1st platoon had only one gun intact and the platoon leader had been wounded. The 2nd platoon had lost all its guns and the leader had been killed. Both guns of the 3rd platoon were still in action.

Makhmudov continued to adjust the fire of his guns himself. The duel with the "Tigers" continued, the guns still firing rapidly.

Suddenly a messenger appeared out of breath.

"Sergeant Yefimov, gun crew commander, is seriously wounded. Two 'Tigers' are trying to outflank us along the ravine on our right!"

Makhmudov thought: "If the 'Tigers' force their way from the flank to the rear of our battery, we're done for." Without looking around, he made for the remaining gun of the 1st platoon which had lost its commander.

At this moment, four German tanks were rolling ahead. Gubkin ordered his men to get ready to fire their anti-tank grenades. On the right flank about thirty German machine-gunners had penetrated the first and second trench lines. Avoiding Makhmudov's battery to the north they approached it from the rear. Meanwhile, two "Tiger" tanks and up to 100 machine-gunners were advancing on Gubkin's strongpoint from the front. Two "Ferdinand" guns attacked Gubkin's neighbour on the left.

By now Gubkin had only about forty men left. Only one out of the three officers, Junior Lieutenant Zaitsev, was still in the trenches. The remnants of the 3rd platoon were divided between the 1st and 2nd platoons. Sergeant Zakabluk had temporarily taken over command of the 2nd platoon. The situation was critical.

Gubkin had to make a quick decision: either to use all the men he had left to repel the Wehrmacht assault or to detail a few men in an attempt to save Makhmudov's battery. Since the Germans enjoyed a tremendous numerical superiority, it was difficult for the company to hold its defence positions. But if the German submachine-gunners overran Makhmudov's battery Gubkin's strongpoint would cease to exist anyway without anti-tank artillery. It was a hard choice.

Gubkin decided to abandon the idea of concentrating his forces on the main effort. Taking twelve of Sergeant Zakabluk's men, he rushed along a trench to the flanking position in order to prevent enemy machine-gunners from reaching Makhmudov's battery. The Germans were now heading straight for him, but they still had to cover another 160 yards of open ground.

Gubkin was sure he would arrive before them. But just then somebody cried out in desperation:

"They're in the trench already!"

He cursed the fact that the Germans were grabbing the initiative. Just then, a hand grenade exploded at a bend in the trench and a man was wounded.

Without losing a second, Gubkin removed the safety pin from a hand grenade and hurled it around the corner at the intruders. Darting around the corner of the trench Sergeant Vavilov fired a burst from his submachine-gun at the Germans heading for him and jumped back quickly. The returning German fire missed him. Suddenly everything was drowned out in the rumble of shooting. It seemed that hostilities were now centred on this serpentine trench. Private Litvinov set his light machine-gun on the parapet and fired over the trench to prevent German machine-gunners from getting their bearings. Just then Litvinov's machine-gun was silenced; he had been hit in the head with a bullet. Gubkin seized the gun and jumped beyond the corner of the trench only to find that there was nobody there.

The Germans had retreated despite their numerical superiority, apparently unaware of the size of the opposing force. Gubkin signalled his men to advance.

He reached another corner in the trench. To his horror, Gubkin saw an enemy grenade with its long wooden handle fly over his head. Then, it fell. Taking a long jump, he landed on the bottom of the trench beyond the turn. He closed his eyes waiting for the grenade to explode. It did, but in front, not behind him as he had expected. The

In September 1941 a half-million civilians, mainly women, took part in digging trenches and building tank traps around Moscow.

Russian's engaging in street fighting amidst the ruins of Stalingrad.

Skeletonized buildings in Stalingrad are all that remain of much of the city after one of the most ferocious battles of the Second World War.

Russian tanks advance. On 12 July 1943 the biggest tank battle of all time was fought near the village of Prokhorovka, south of Kursk.

Victorious troops in Berlin hasten towards the bombed-out Reichstag.

The banner of victory is hoisted over the Reichstag by Russian soldiers on 30 April 1945.

A female orderly drags a wounded soldier away from the battlefield.

Victory Day at last. The face of jubilation.

Looking haggard, Field Marshal Paulus, commander of the German Sixth Army, walks towards his captors at the end of the Battle of Stalingrad in early February 1943.

Colonel-General David Dragunsky, in a meeting with the author in 1976, describes the 1943 Battle of the Kursk Salient where he was seriously wounded.

Lieutenant-General Semyon Krivoshein's tank corps in the summer of 1943 won a hard-fought battle against German panzers commanded by General Erich von Manstein at Kursk, south of Moscow. He was interviewed by the author in 1977.

Shot down in 1942, pilot Alexei Maresyev crawled for eighteen days in the snow with two broken legs (later amputated) before being rescued. He is shown in his office at the Veterans' Committee in Moscow at the start of the new millennium.

blast hit him and pungent smoke burnt his lungs. Wondering what had happened, he opened his eyes and saw one of his men, Obraztsov, in front of him.

"Where is it?" he asked.

Obraztsov was as white as a sheet and didn't answer. His hands were shaking. By some miracle he had managed to catch the German grenade and throw it aside. In this engagement which had lasted only a few minutes two of Gubkin's men had been killed and one wounded, but the others had held their ground. When the company commander arrived at his observation post he learned that Makhmudov had been wounded in the head. The wound was bleeding.

"What are you waiting for?" Gubkin shouted to the battery sergeant major. "Bandage his head and carry him to the first-aid station as fast as possible."

"But we've no more first-aid kits left because so many men have been wounded since morning," the sergeant major replied.

Obraztsov handed Gubkin his own first-aid kit. Gubkin was finishing bandaging Makhmudov's head when somebody cried out: "Tanks ahead!"

Gubkin ordered Junior Lieutenant Zaitsev to cut the infantry off from the tanks. Meanwhile Gubkin kept a close watch on the tanks which were heading straight for his trench. Makhmudov shouted to the battery:

"Use high calibre shells. Ready. Fire!"

The gun reports were deafening. The fourth shell hit the front of the leading "Tiger", causing a shower of sparks. But the tank continued to make headway, fitfully jerking the barrel of its gun. However, for some reason it changed course sharply. Although Sergeant Semarenko was out of earshot, Makhmudov shouted to him:

"You're always trying to hit the front of the tank. You should aim for the side."

Another round was fired and a cloud of smoke mushroomed over the "Tiger's" turret. But when the smoke cleared, the men saw that the tank was steering straight for the anti-tank gun as if nothing had happened. The German tankmen had fired a smoke pot to simulate a direct hit. Although Semarenko was an experienced gunner, he could not catch the tank in the crosswires of his sights. The panzer was artfully dodging the shells.

"Damn their souls!" Semarenko cried angrily and fired again. The blast of a shell exploding nearby hurled him to one side. When he got up, he feverishly felt to see if he was injured, and was glad to learn that he was unharmed, except for being stunned. But he saw with horror that his father was lying in a pool of blood near the wheel of the gun carriage. The son hastened to his wounded father, but the father weakly pointed to the tanks and ordered his son to return to the gun. Blinded by anger, his head aching, and feeling an attack of nausea, the young sergeant put his eye to the sights. The "Tigers" were crawling ahead one after another, halting briefly to fire. The distance was now less than 218 yards. Vasili realized that if he missed or if his gun misfired, this would be the end. Concentrating as hard as he could, he finally caught a tank in the crosswires and fired. The forward "Tiger" stopped abruptly, a flame bursting out from under its armour.

Vasili rushed to his father with his first-aid kit. Nikolai Davydovich was lying flat on the ground holding the wheel of the gun carriage with his left hand, his right lying in a pool of blood. Vasili lifted him in despair. Blood gushed out of the older man's mouth and he died in his son's arms.

At that moment Vasili thought the German tanks were almost on top of him: the roar of their engines filled the air around him. Laying his father carefully on the ground, he got to his feet. But his movements were unsteady. A slightly wounded gunner helped him load one of the guns. The defenders saw that as the enemy tanks approached the trenches they increased their speed. A "Ferdinand" was speeding towards the gun. Vasili fired point-blank and the assault gun burst into flames. This was the third German armoured vehicle Sergeant Semarenko had destroyed in the engagement.

A critical stage was now reached in the battle for the chalk hills. Disregarding heavy losses, the German Command committed another sixty tanks at a point where the flanks of two Russian divisions met.

The positions of Gubkin's company were under attack by three "Tigers" and four "Ferdinands". They tried to bypass Makhmudov's battery by advancing along the ravine so that now the last two anti-tank guns were being threatened.

By this time Gubkin's company was down to thirty men. Gubkin ordered Zaitsev to prevent the enemy from overrunning the positions from the front and to hold the ground to the last man and the last round. Taking two anti-tank rifle crews, he decided to block the way of the panzers advancing on Makhmudov's battery. He ordered Junior Sergeant Loginov, commander of the first anti-tank rifle crew, to destroy the tank approaching from the left. He ordered the other crew under Sergeant Vavilov to blast the "Ferdinand" that was heading for them with an anti-tank grenade. Taking Private Nasreddinov with him, Vavilov took up a firing position in the trench about 22 yards away. The panzers were firing incessantly and Vavilov was mortally wounded with a shell splinter.

When the nearest German tank was very close Nasreddinov jumped out of the trench and made straight for it with a grenade in his hand. He crawled flat on the ground. When the Germans finally spotted him about 55 yards away from the tank, they tried to stop him with machine-gun fire. But it was too late because he was too close. The tank then rushed at him. However, rising on one elbow, Nasreddinov just had time to hurl his anti-tank grenade and see the vehicle burst into flames and disappear behind a cloud of smoke. Breaking through the smoke a second tank that was following fired a machine-gun burst of tracer bullets at the soldier and appeared, still firing its gun, directly in front of the trench.

Viewing the scene, Gubkin figured the enemy tank would now start flattening the trenches. Then it would break through the lines, so it had to be stopped at all costs. When the tank reached the top of the hillock and exposed its side, Gubkin hurled an anti-tank grenade. But it exploded too far from the target and he swore hotly. He realized that if he raised his head above the trench the Germans would be sure to hit him. Acting almost entirely by instinct, feeling the scorching heat of metal and deafened by the roar of the tank's engine, he decided to explode his last anti-tank grenade underneath the "Tiger". At that moment he didn't care if he himself was destroyed along with the tank. As the seconds ticked away he thought it a pity that he hadn't finished writing his letter home . . .

Keeping his eye on the "Tiger," he saw that it was now moving slowly, wary of mines. The clanging of the tracks caused a pain in his head. Clenching his teeth, Gubkin grasped an anti-tank grenade and made up his mind not to miss his target.

Suddenly Gubkin saw the soil falling off the parapet. Holding the grenade in his hand he pressed his body flat on the floor of the trench. For a moment it was completely dark and he felt lumps of earth falling on his back. The smell of oil and exhaust fumes was stifling. Without raising his head, he knew the tank must have crossed over because the wall of the trench was again suffused in light. He jumped to his feet and hurled the grenade at the receding tank. Then he ducked behind the wall of the trench. A terrific explosion followed. The "Tiger" was out of the fight.

Makhmudov's battery finished off yet another "Tiger" tank. However, the remaining tanks managed to force their way through the first and second trenches. But now they ran into the army anti-tank reserve which had already been deployed and which finally beat off the German assault.

After the artillery stopped firing a deathly silence set in. Deafened by the din of battle, black with soot and dust, hardly able to stand on their feet, Gubkin and Makhmudov lost all sense of time. If the fighting had lasted another half hour they would have dropped from exhaustion. But the enemy's strength gave out first.

Now on the beaten earth that was torn with shells a warm July dusk descended. The ground was no longer shaking from explosions but it was still smoking in places . . .

On 12 July 1943 – two days after the nightmare of battle – Gubkin was dressed in a clean uniform and was decorated at command headquarters. He was also appointed senior adjutant of the 2nd Infantry Battalion and promoted to captain's rank. Gubkin would receive more medals and promotions right up to Victory Day. In early 1945 as commanding officer of the first battalion to fight its way to the frontier with Germany, Gubkin was honoured with a Cross of Valour and a certificate signed by US President Roosevelt.

A year and a half after Gubkin's exploits at Kursk, Gubkin's battalion was dug in on German territory. Snow was falling as Captain Lakizo, a portly Russian officer, jumped into the snow-filled trench where Georgi Gubkin was standing and reported: "There's a German officer in no-man's-land who demands to see you."

"You mean he wants to see me personally? Did he mention my name?"

"Yes. Last night the Nazis devoted a whole radio programme to our battalion. They know we were the first to reach the 1941 pre-invasion frontier of Germany. They are spreading fantastic stories about us. They also know that Roosevelt gave you a decoration. Their intelligence is really good!"

After a further exchange of words, Gubkin and Lakizo appeared on the forward edge of the trench and gazed in the direction of the German lines.

"Where's the officer?" Gubkin asked. Lakizo pointed to a tall pine along the roadside.

"Over there."

The intrepid German was about 200 yards away.

Gubkin peered at him through his fieldglasses.

Lakizo continued: "He says, 'Captain Gubkin, if you are a brave man, come out and meet me.' He says he is a Luftwaffe ace who shot down sixteen Russian aircraft, but now he's fighting on the ground. He wants to fight a duel with pistols with the man who was first to set foot on German soil."

Gubkin was not surprised that a pilot was fighting as an infantry-man. Only the day before he'd been told that Hitler was sending all those who had been born in East Prussia to fight in Army Group North, even if they had served in the Luftwaffe or Navy. After a short interval, during which he made sure his weapon was in working order, Gubkin walked slowly towards the Nazi officer and beckoned him to come nearer. He had already covered 55 yards, all the time watching the German's every move.

The distance between the two grew shorter. Gubkin could now hear the crunching of snow under the boots of his adversary. He saw at once that the German's holster was open and that it was swinging in time with his steps. But he did not notice any other weapons on him.

The two men were now separated only by a narrow strip of snow-covered land, a strip that would become fatal ground for one of them. Finally both stopped, their eyes fixed on each other. Gubkin was first to go for his gun, an extra pistol in his chest holster. He fired. The German was a fraction of a second late and fell onto the snow, wounded. Covered by fire from the Russian trenches, the German was dragged to Gubkin's lines where, after his wound was dressed, he was brought to Gubkin for interrogation before being sent to divisional headquarters.

With the information received from the prisoner and from his own scouts Gubkin decided to launch an attack without further delay, helped by a simultaneous artillery barrage. At 1100 hours Gubkin reported that his battalion had taken 700 prisoners including several senior officers. Only a handful of enemy staff officers managed to escape.

On the night of 21 January, Georgi Gubkin's battalion broke into the city of Insterburg in East Prussia. On the roadside were burnt-out hulks of Wehrmacht tanks and trucks. A message from Supreme Headquarters said Insterburg was "an important junction and a powerfully organized fortified area blocking the road to the city and port of Konigsberg. Hitler ordered his troops to fight to the last man. Those who suggested that continuation of the war was useless were put down as cowards and panic-mongers and were to be shot on the spot. Those who surrendered were sentenced to death in absentia. The Nazis told their men horror stories about Russian captivity, thereby encouraging every man to fight to the end.

In mid-February 1945 Gubkin's battalion had penetrated the outskirts of a village on the southern approaches to Konigsberg. The Germans in their stone houses were putting up stiff resistance.

Defying enemy mortar and artillery shells and machine-gun fire, Gubkin's men forged ahead. One of the soldiers described the scene as a "wilderness". Someone noticed a lonely stork hovering over a burnt-down house. But when a shot was fired from the debris on the opposite side of the street, the stork flew away.

At this moment Gubkin felt as if an iron rod had struck his wrist. The sharp pain made him stumble. At the same time a shell burst nearby and a splinter hit him in the chest. He felt sick. He tried to shout for help but instead heard himself wheeze. The pine trees began to revolve – and Gubkin fell to the ground unconscious.

The next morning a woman surgeon woke him up. Everything was ready for an operation. Gubkin received a local anaesthetic and the surgeon removed a bullet from his arm and dressed the wound. But it was decided not to risk operating on his thorax.

After the operation Gubkin fell asleep and dreamed that his mother was giving him an elixir of red berries that always restored his strength when he was sick. Gubkin and some of his army companions who were also seriously wounded were evacuated to a military hospital in Lithuania. It was not the first time he'd been a hospital patient, and he knew many of the doctors and nurses who were attached to his divisional medical station. He had fallen in love with one of the nurses, Muza Sobkova, during the fighting at Stalingrad when he was wounded for the first time. But then he had not shown his feelings, believing that the life of a soldier was too unpredictable.

But now he was on the operating table again. The chief surgeon, who recognized Gubkin, gave him an anaesthetic and started the operation. He opened his chest but could not find the splinter. When Gubkin recovered, the surgeon asked him: "Why are you getting in the way of shrapnel all the time?"

"Such is war," Gubkin said. "Doctor, please show me the splinter."

"Sorry, but it must be buried very deep. I couldn't find it."

Gubkin went into a cold sweat. After all the suffering, and now this . . .

It took more than ten days before he began to recover. The splinter in his chest did not trouble him and his hand was healing quickly. He could move his fingers and he was overjoyed. One day he opened a newspaper and saw his name in it. He had been awarded the title of "hero" of his country with its gold medal, the highest combat decoration. The entire hospital staff congratulated him and gave him an "official dinner". Asked whom he wanted to invite to the dinner, he mentioned nurse Muza Sobkova.

During the last few days Georgi had met her a number of times and he felt she had become very close to him. When a waltz was played after dinner, he asked Muza to dance with him.

Outside the hospital the city of Kaunas was sinking into peaceful slumber. After the dance, Gubkin took Muza's arm and they went for a stroll in a nearby park. They had become more than just friends and would remember this happy evening for many years to come after they were united in marriage.

CHAPTER 17

Tracking the *Tirpitz*

Fighting in the Arctic regions began somewhat later than in the other theatres of operation but the campaign in the far north was conducted in extreme meteorological conditions. In the Arctic, danger from the elements was a constant threat. But there was also occasional beauty: now and then the *aurora borealis* filled the sky with a display of cosmic lights. It was something that could be seen only in the high northern latitudes. But the war was on and there was little time to admire nature; man-made danger lurked on and beneath the waters. Hitler's navy used the great depths of the Arctic Ocean and the many winding fjords of Norway to good advantage, giving warships, including U-boats which attacked Anglo-American convoys, room for concealment and manoeuvre. Lend-lease supplies from the USA, Britain and Canada reached Russia mainly through the northern ports of Murmansk and Archangel; and this compelled the German Navy to increase its strength in that region.

Russia's Northern Fleet had few warships: eight or so destroyers and approximately a dozen submarines. The fleet lacked modern, well-equipped naval bases but it had no shortage of intrepid submarine crews.

Admiral Ivan Kolyshkin, himself a submariner, has described the agonies of the men who served in the Northern Fleet: "Our war was totally unlike the war that was being fought on land. We did not see blazing, smoke-blackened towns and villages, the ashes of houses or sobbing children and women. But the acrid smell of fires penetrated down to us, under water, and made our eyes smart. The winds driving across Russia brought us the smell of grey ash, which plucked at our hearts and called for revenge."

On their torpedoes the Russians traced the words "For the Motherland", "For Kiev", "For Minsk", "For Sevastopol". The latter were the names of cities that had surrendered after intense struggles to the Wehrmacht.

Sailors in the "cold and confined steel box" of submarines dreamed of an early end to the war. None, says Kolyshkin, supposed at the beginning that ahead of them were four years of bloody fighting, that the road to victory lay across gigantic struggles on the Volga, on the plains near Kursk, on the approaches to Berlin, and lastly inside the Nazi capital itself.

Hitler's strategists hoped by a quick thrust to capture the ice-free port and city of Murmansk, seize the Soviet Northern Fleet's main base at Polyarnoye, and sever the Murmansk–Leningrad railway. If this were done, the enemy would have cut off the Kola Peninsula, occupied Soviet Karelia, and established control over the White Sea as far south as Archangel. If at the same time the Germans succeeded in choking off the Arctic sea route – another Nazi strategic goal – by which the British and Americans were delivering military equipment and other supplies, the fortunes of Russians would have been poorer.

Initially the Nazi forces hoped to complete their task in a matter of a few weeks with the help of land forces and the Luftwaffe. Their optimism stemmed from a sizable superiority in manpower and equipment and from the element of surprise. Their Alpine units were trained for action in the North and had special weapons and equipment for operating in a frigid climate. But the blitz offensive against Murmansk got bogged down, checked by the Fourteenth Army under General Vasily Frolov, a veteran of the civil war, and the Northern Fleet under Admiral Arseni Golovko. Both men acted boldly and coordinated their actions, the fleet supplying fighting units for duty on land.

The failure to attain victory on the ground in the North combined with the running of Allied convoys in the Barents Sea compelled the

Nazi High Command to increase its naval strength in that region. Meanwhile, the weakness of Russia's Northern Fleet was manifest, at least in the beginning; in addition, the fleet's air arm had only about 100 aircraft, mostly obsolete types.

Arseni Golovko, who was one of Russia's most educated admirals, had been appointed to his post at the age of thirty-four. He deployed his submarines not for defensive action but for cruising in patrol zones close to Nazi bases in Norway. They searched for German transports and warships in the Barents Sea, attacking and sinking many of them. After Russian subs sank a dozen enemy transports, including several troopships, German General Dietl asked for reinforcements, above all, warships. Shortly afterward, the German High Command hastily transferred to Northern Norway the new battleship, *Tirpitz*, three heavy and one light cruiser, and a large number of destroyers and submarines.

By the middle of 1942 many of Hitler's capital ships, formerly based in Trondheim, Norway, began to appear often at a string of naval bases located along the coast of Norway north of Narvik. Some were moved to Alten Fjord, near Hammerfest, north of the Arctic Circle. Among these was the *Tirpitz*, which usually stood at the head of Alten Fjord behind booms and nets, concealed not only from the sea, but also from any Allied aircraft that might fly over at low level.

Tall cliffs overhanging the narrow roadstead made Alten Fjord an ideal hide-out. A labyrinth of rocky islands and several exits to the sea enabled the big warships to conceal their movements when setting out for operations or returning to their bases. Distance and weather were important factors for placing Germany's best warships north of Narvik. For instance, the distance between the northernmost British base, Scapa Flow, to Alten Fjord is 958 miles. This distance, doubled by the return flight, was a factor that British and American bombers had to reckon with. Moreover there was usually better flying weather in the Baltic area than over the northern fjords of Norway. Thus, keeping the ships in Alten Fjord was principally a means of removing them from the striking range of Allied aircraft.

*   *   *

The Soviet Northern Fleet had another important task: to protect the vital sea lane plied by Anglo-American convoys. As a strike force against these convoys the German High Command concentrated a large naval squadron and a sizable Luftwaffe force in northern Norway.

For the first dozen or so convoys the losses were not disastrous, but the fate of PQ-17, which had left an Icelandic port on 27 June 1942, was tragic and caused dissension among the Allies. The convoy consisted of thirty-five British and US merchant ships carrying $700 million worth of war materiel and other supplies. Its immediate escort comprised nearly twenty warships, including destroyers and submarines. There were also other covering forces consisting of a half dozen cruisers, two battleships, an aircraft carrier and ten destroyers.

The Royal Navy had by then accumulated a wealth of experience in convoy duties in the hazardous waters of the Atlantic and the Arctic. There previously had been minor losses; but in this case events took an unpredictable course. After a series of German attacks, the escort and covering forces were ordered by the Admiralty to abandon the convoy and proceed westward. The slow merchantmen were advised to disperse and proceed on their own to their Russian ports of destination. But this left the merchant ships as vulnerable as sitting ducks. As it was the month of July, the sun shone round the clock. Like tigers surrounding defenceless prey, German submarines and dive-bombers made short shrift of the convoy.

It appears that there was apprehension at the Admiralty over a secret report that the battleship *Tirpitz* was speeding towards the convoy with dozens of other warships. But the Russians claim that the German squadron never came within striking range of the Allied convoy. Also, the Russians argue, the combined covering force of PQ-17 was superior to the German squadron.

In any case, the Admiralty's orders put the Soviet Northern Fleet in a tight spot. Admiral Golovko didn't have a tenth of the strength of the British and American naval units that had abandoned the convoy. Golovko himself thought the decision of the British Admiralty was "unsound" because the German warships had not yet passed through the patrol zone that was guarded by a Russian submarine. However, the admiral reacted by ordering a handful of submarines that were available to engage the Nazi squadron. One of these, submarine K-21, seized the chance to attack the well-defended *Tirpitz*.

During four days of searching for the German naval squadron the K-21 sailed on the surface. It sighted more than fifty aircraft.

"We had to make forty-eight quick dives," recalls an officer, Sergei Lysov, who served on the K-21. "But the risk paid off. We found the *Tirpitz* before she saw us."

Although he risked discovery by Nazi aircraft combing the area, the sub's commander Captain Nikolai Lunin resorted to frequent re-connaissance. To increase the probability of a hit it was necessary to break through the screen of destroyers protecting the *Tirpitz* and dive under them. The German squadron was on a constant look-out for submarines and was doing everything to evade detection. Never-theless, Lunin raised the periscope fifteen times to adjust his course.

Sergei Lysov continues: "Several minutes before we reached torpedo range the enemy squadron, which had been zig-zagging on a submarine-evasion course, made a sharp 90 degree turn and we found ourselves encircled by enemy ships stuffed with depth charges."

Tension was at its peak aboard the K-21. No vessel belonging to Russia's Northern Fleet had yet forced her way through such a dense screen of ships as this or attempted to engage a warship as awe-inspiring as the *Tirpitz*. But now, new manoeuvres by the German squadron were complicating things for the Russian commander. He had to decide quickly on a correct position for his attack. Due to the circumstances, Lunin made up his mind to attack the battleship with his stern torpedoes. There were only four torpedoes in the stern compared to the six in the bow but there was no other choice.

"At last," continues Lysov, "came the command to fire." At 1801 hours the K-21 fired four torpedoes at the *Tirpitz* at intervals of four seconds. "Everyone's eyes were on their stopwatches. It was a dramatic moment that hardly any of us would likely experience again."

Without further delay Lunin dived and quickly withdrew. The

K-21's listening device could distinctly hear the screws of the destroyers churning the water overhead. In two minutes and fifteen seconds everyone on board the submarine heard two explosions. There were huge sighs of relief. Meanwhile, in the confusion the enemy screening ships failed to detect the K-21. When the sub surfaced at 1909 hours there were no ships on the horizon and Lunin ordered a message to be sent to headquarters about the attack on the *Tirpitz*.

Lysov says cheerfully, although he no doubt exaggerates the extent of the damage: "The *Tirpitz* was crippled. She turned tail and limped home."*

On the following day Russian reconnaissance planes spotted the German squadron off the Norwegian coast. It had apparently given up its intention of striking at the remaining vessels of the convoy and was returning to its base. Soon, according to intelligence reports, the *Tirpitz* was forced to enter the dock for repairs.

There is a British sequel to the attack by the K-21. Early in April 1944 ships of the Royal Navy carried out operations aimed at destroying the *Tirpitz* which had just completed repairs. British bombers protected by fighter planes which were based on aircraft carriers dealt massive blows at the German battleship. Though protected by anti-aircraft fire, the *Tirpitz* suffered several direct hits and was once more put out of action.

---

* There is some scepticism among Western experts about whether Lunin's sub actually scored a hit on the *Tirpitz*. But it is not open to question that his sub did get close to the heavily guarded battleship and got off its torpedoes.

CHAPTER 18

Cemetery under the Barents Sea

It was a frigid March day in 1942. Immediately upon leaving its northern port the Russian submarine P-421 was greeted by a murderous sea. The sub's home port was Polyarnoye, to the north of Murmansk and, now, entering the Barents Sea she was on patrol against German shipping. The submarine rolled violently, taking a list of 40 degrees. Calm rarely visits the Barents Sea in any case, and Captain Fyodor Vidayev's submarine had a long way to go, having been assigned to one of the most distant patrol areas.

This was a proud day for Vidayev as it was his first independent patrol. The idea that he, in command of his first submarine, would soon find himself helpless and vulnerable, to the point of nakedness in the face of the enemy never entered his head. He was self-confident and known to be calm when danger threatened. All of Vidayev's superiors had the highest opinion of this unassuming, tough, barrel-chested man. About him they used such phrases as "level-headed", "thoughtful", "easy to get on with" – but also "tenacious" and "courageous". A fellow officer summed up Vidayev and his men with this rousing image: "If nails were made of them, they'd be the toughest nails in the world."

On his maiden voyage as captain, Vidayev had an important passenger on board – Admiral Ivan Kolyshkin, the submarine division commander. Without much ado, the admiral began inspecting the submarine's compartments, talking to the crew and sizing them up. Men off duty were having their evening tea and the admiral was glad to note that only two of the fifty-man crew were seasick. The nucleus of the P-421 crew consisted of veterans of the Finnish War of late 1939 and early 1940. Bad weather had little effect on their capacity for work or their appetite, although the onset of heavy seas slowed them down. But stormy weather was common to the Arctic and members of the Northern Fleet were used to it.

A wireless message from headquarters was received early the next morning, 21 March, ordering P-421 to "Area N" to provide an Allied convoy with cover against an enemy naval force. Shortly before this patrol, the sub's crew had attended a party to which British sailors were invited. The overseas visitors said their mission in the Barents Sea was the most difficult they'd ever had. Kolyshkin was pleased with the frankness of the more experienced British crews who admitted they were having a rough time of it.

The Allied convoy in question was the PQ-13. As in previous cases submarines were diverted from their patrol areas to give the endangered convoys added protection. Hitler had considerable naval strength, including at this time some of the most modern warships, in Norwegian ports, and these ships, together with aircraft, could inflict frightful losses on the slow-moving convoys. The Russians therefore widened their area of operations to include not only their own sea lanes, where the enemy often lurked, but the enemy's own supply routes as well.

The P-421 was part of a screen for two days, during which no enemy ships were encountered. The convoy passed by without incident and the submarine was ordered to return to its assigned patrol area.

The days were now growing longer and this forced the sub to spend more time under water. But there were no other signs of spring as the weather remained stormy, with icy temperatures as before. Snowfalls were frequent.

The P-421 had not yet engaged the enemy, and Vidayev found it hard not to show his impatience. He and his crew were eager to see action, to fire their torpedoes in anger. According to Admiral Kolyshkin, who kept an eagle eye on Vidayev, a torpedo attack provided the "crucial test" for what he called "the moral right" to be the captain of a submarine. For Vidayev the test began at 1432 hours on 28 March near Porsanger Fjord, north of latitude 70 degrees. Vidayev, who was at the periscope, looked away for a moment, and then said, smiling:

"I think we've found our target."

Then, in a louder voice with a note of severity: "Stand by for a torpedo attack!"

An enemy transport and two patrol ships were following a zigzag course along the coast heading for the big fjord. Although the enemy was still miles away, the position of P-421 made it possible to initiate an attack. Minutes dragged by as Vidayev's submarine began to close in.

"We looked at the enemy transport in turn through the periscope," says Kolyshkin. "From time to time the hydrophone [an early-model sonar device] operator reported the transport's position, and Vidayev was handling the situation so calmly that it was unnecessary for me to interfere. I could see he had confidence in himself and in his men."

It was now urgent for the captain to give orders for his torpedo tubes to stand by. But as Vidayev raised the periscope he groaned with disappointment. Silently he stepped aside and let Kolyshkin look. The convoy had changed course sharply, and was now rounding the cape at the mouth of the fjord. Although the P-421 was now actually a stone's throw from the enemy, the change in course altered the angle to target making it impossible to fire. In this situation an attack was usually called off. But there was, the admiral thought, one possibility of still hitting the enemy, although not every submarine captain would see it. But Vidayev quickly saw it and gave the order.

"Helm to port, course 165! Coxswain, take her down to twenty metres." Turning to the others around him, Vidayev said: "I'm going to dive under the convoy for an aft salvo."

Kolyshkin recalls: "That was exactly what I had in mind. My opinion of Vidayev soared. He was displaying enviable tenacity."

The whirring of the enemy transport's propellers passed overhead. The P-421 rose to periscope depth and manoeuvred into position to attack.

"Aft tubes, stand by!"

But just then, as luck would have it, the convoy changed course again, falling out of the sub's angle of attack. The convoy's anti-submarine zigzags were unpredictable. Vidayev, however, with a commander's insight, saw through the convoy's intention.

"They've changed course again," he said. "We'll have to go into the mouth of the fjord and wait for them there."

The P-421 headed for that invisible point where the captain planned to strike. Through the periscope Vidayev watched the convoy now drawing near the submarine, now moving away, as though it knew danger was lurking and wanted to escape. Vidayev kept the submarine steadily on course. The attack had lasted nearly an hour, and he was covered with sweat. He took off his cap and padded jacket and rolled up his sleeves.

The enemy convoy finally completed its last turn and everything fell into place for the attacking sub. The convoy, unaware that it was being stalked, now seemed to have deliberately positioned itself for disaster. The P-421 steered an attack course.

"Aft tubes, stand by!"

Suddenly there was a muffled explosion under water – an anti-submarine depth charge. The time was 1528 hours. Why, the men wondered, had this depth charge been released? Was it only a precautionary step? Vidayev felt sure his sub had not been spotted. At 1534 hours there was a series of explosions. But the captain kept his submarine on its attack course.

After the command, "Fire!" the sub's crew felt four jolts one after another as the torpedoes left their tubes. Luckily for the P-421, it had a bubble-free firing system which did not give away its position.

Within fifty seconds there were two explosions. A look into the periscope showed that the transport was sinking. Vidayev now began a post-salvo manoeuvre. At 1545 hours the first of a series of depth charges aimed at the sub exploded. Vidayev took his vessel deeper. The depth charge attack continued for two hours, Vidayev counting forty-four of them. But they all exploded astern. Apparently a sudden snowfall had spoiled the enemy's accuracy. The P-421 got off lightly – only its gyrocompass failed for a short time.

There followed long, uneventful days and nights. The monotony was broken a week later, on 4 April, while the submarine was recharging its batteries. A radiogram from Fleet Headquarters said the P-421 had been given a high award – the Order of the Red Banner.

All day on 8 April the P-421 remained in the vicinity of Porsanger Fjord, where Vidayev had made his successful debut as submarine captain. But nothing else was sighted and the captain sailed a northerly course when it grew dark. But disaster wasn't long in coming.

The crew could never be indifferent to these dangerous waters. Nevertheless, in the wardroom the steward was laying the table for evening tea and the men off duty were resting, reading or getting ready for sleep. Suddenly, at 2058 hours, a terrific explosion rocked the submarine. It began to list. Bunks and possessions clattered to the floor. Water gurgled here and there. Some of the men in the sixth compartment were hurled into the fifth and the trim in the stern began to change.

When Vidayev and the admiral rushed to the control room, the officer in charge had already ordered the submarine to surface as the only way to keep it afloat. Had the officer hesitated, the water pouring into the aft compartment would most probably have made it impossible to bring the submarine to the surface. The captain gave the order to the aft compartment to secure the hatch and begin patching up the hole in the casing. The six men in the compartment instantly sealed themselves off from the rest of the submarine. By an iron-clad "law of the submarine" they had to remain in inky darkness, single-handed against invisible gaps in the casing, through which icy water was rushing. They knew that it might cost them their lives, but they would save the submarine. They also knew something else: that their only chance to remain alive was to save the vessel from sinking. If they once found themselves in the icy seas they could not survive longer than a few minutes.

On the horizon there was nothing but a blinding snowstorm,

actually a piece of luck for the men. Free from detection, the crew had time to take stock. It was certain the P-421 had touched off a mine although nobody had heard the mine-cable scratching against the side of the hull. A first inspection showed that the submarine had suffered great damage. The bridge hatch had been wrenched out of shape; the upper lid had been torn off and the only reason the compartment had not been flooded was that the lower lid had withstood the pressure of the water. In the control room the radio was knocked out of its place and seriously damaged. Also, the gyrocompass was broken.

The first thing everyone did was to pump water out of the seventh compartment where the men were desperately striving to keep the sea water out. The sailors found the holes, stuffing into them everything they could lay their hands on. Where nothing helped, they pressed themselves against holes until assistance came.

Vidayev's men had learned much from the experience of another sub, the D-3, that had faced a similar emergency during its patrol the previous month when a depth charge tore holes in its side. The submarine returned home only because the crew prevented the water from flooding all the compartments. The crew of the P-421 turned on the pressurized air to counter the pressure of the sea and stopped up the holes. Everyone did their bit which, together, saved the submarine from sinking. But everyone asked: how long could they survive? And another danger lurked, as terrible as the sea. The Norwegian cape, where the enemy had an observation post and an artillery battery, could be seen through the fast-falling snow. The P-421 was in no condition to dive and it was not even known if the sub was navigable. It was only a matter of time before the disabled vessel became a sitting duck for the shore batteries. And if the wireless radio defied all efforts at repair, there would be no way to signal for help.

But at least temporarily the snowstorm offered cover for the submarine and it continued unmolested until the onset of the short April night. However, the men's worst fears about being able to get underway were confirmed by 2300 hours. The submarine's propellers were missing! Unless help came, the chance for survival was nil.

However, the two wireless operators Rybin and Svinyin, repaired the wireless by 2320 hours and the captain sent the following message to the Fleet Commander in Chief: "Hit a mine. Unable to move or dive. Position . . .".

Meanwhile, another danger arose. The navigator reported that a slow current of about one and a half knots was steadily pushing the submarine shoreward. Now the outlook for P-421 was all black. Admiral Kolyshkin suggested a last-ditch solution: make a sail out of the rough canvas coverings in the engine room and use the periscope for a mast.

"We were thinking of it ourselves," Vidayev said. "We only need to put about ten miles between ourselves and the coast. Once we're safe, we can think of something else."

"All right, carry on," said the admiral.

It was impossible to tell what the outcome would be. Would the ersatz sail be strong enough to move the submarine against the current? Putting numbers on a sheet of paper would not help; only the trial itself could provide the answer.

The improvised sail was ready by 0100 hours and was fitted on the periscope with the help of a makeshift beam. A periscope and a sail! The sight of it provoked laughter. A highly modern optical instrument – the periscope – was now being used as a mast; and attached to it was a sheet of rough canvas, the crudest kind of sail, reminiscent of sails that had served small boats since time immemorial. But it worked. The sail filled and the submarine moved away from the coast, driven by a fair wind. It was slow going but the crew began counting the distance. The magnetic compass showed the submarine was on a course of 350 degrees. At 0600 hours a message arrived from Fleet Headquarters. It informed them that a sister submarine, the K-22, patrolling nearby, was coming to the rescue. Instantly, the men's spirits soared.

After an hour of this tension-filled journey the sail had to be hauled down. The wind had dropped, visibility had improved and the enemy-occupied coast at Nordkapp and Cape Helnes could be seen distinctly. If the sail was not lowered it would be spotted.

Soon another message was received from home base. It confirmed the previous one, saying: "K-22 is going to your assistance. If unable to save the submarine, save the men and destroy the submarine."

The men on P-421 again raised their sail at 0700 hours when it began to snow and a light wind blew up. At 0900 hours visibility returned and the sail was lowered again. To keep out of sight as much as possible Captain Vidayev filled the main ballast tank, so that the deck could hardly be seen above the water.

Meanwhile, the crew was kept busy. The electricians and men in the engine room recharged the batteries, the stokers refilled the pressurized air tanks and the compartments were tidied up. All of the usual routines were kept up to distract the men's thoughts. For there was still no telling how the crisis would end. If the sail ceased to work the current would carry the damaged sub towards the occupied coast at a speed of a mile and a half an hour. The men wondered: Would the K-22 captained by Viktor Kotelnikov reach the P-421 before it was detected and sunk by the Germans? In any case the men had to be prepared for the worst and, therefore, both of the submarine's deck guns were manned. For it was decided, if it came to that, to fire if fired upon. Preparations were also made to blast the magazine as surrender was out of the question. One officer had the job of blowing up the magazine, while another was ready to explode one of the aft torpedoes.

All of these preparations were made unobtrusively but the men quickly learned about them. Meanwhile, it was reported to the captain that the men were discussing the possibility of an encounter with the enemy. All of them, Vidayev told the admiral, were prepared to die rather than be taken prisoner. Later, the admiral learned that Vidayev had slipped the chief wireless officer a note, telling him: "Send this if and when you get the order from me." The message consisted of seven words: "We are under attack but not surrendering."

Meanwhile, the submarine continued to drift shorewards. The tidying up of the living compartment was completed. Vidayev now ordered the sailors to clean and polish the brass fittings.

Some distance away the K-22 was speeding to the rescue. She had left her base at Polyarnoye, six days after the P-421, and had twice been bombed heavily. On 3 April she had attacked a German convoy consisting of one transport and three patrol ships. The K-22 fired two torpedoes at the transport and, after quickly changing the angle of attack, fired another at one of the patrol ships. These were accurate "sniper shots" and all found their mark. The remaining patrol ships pursued the K-22, dropping twenty-two depth charges, but none caused substantial damage. Captain Kotelnikov shook off his pursuers and the next day revisited the area where he had attacked the convoy. He saw life-belts, pieces of wood, suitcases and a portrait of Adolf Hitler floating on the surface.

"Crap always floats," said one of the sailors.

Like the P-421, the K-22 had no enemy sightings during the next few days.

On the night of 9 April she arrived at her battery-recharging area. A pre-dawn frost was in the air. It was almost time for the submarine to dive: the enemy shore was comparatively close. At exactly 0500 hours the officer on watch woke the captain who was dozing and reported that the submarine was ready to dive. Kotelnikov inspected the battery compartment and climbed to the bridge. The shore was still enveloped in dense twilight. Prickly snow was falling. The captain made a crucial decision to postpone the dive to 0600 hours to give the batteries a chance to cool and be ventilated properly. Visibility was low enough to allow him this respite.

It was this one-hour delay that decided the fate of Captain Vidayev and his crew. At about 0600 hours, K-22's wireless operator received the message: "To the Captain. Submarine P-421 ran into a mine. Her engines are disabled. Proceed to her assistance. If she cannot be saved, take the crew off and sink the submarine. P-421's position is . . . Fleet Commander-in-Chief." If Kotelnikov had dived earlier he would not have received the message.

At 0845 hours K-22 arrived in the assigned area and began looking for the crippled P-421. The watch peered into the blue haze, thinking they might be too late. K-22 searched for more than an hour. At 1050 hours, Marinkin, the officer on watch in P-421, saw a dark spot in the north-western part of the horizon. He took his bearings; the spot was moving. He ordered the guns manned and inspected the spot through his binoculars. The minutes dragged. Finally, the officer lowered his binoculars and yelled for joy: "It's one of ours! A *Katyusha* sub!" The men cheered.

"It's Viktor at last," Captain Vidayev said, sighing with relief, as he ordered the signal flags to be hoisted. Soon the *Katyusha* (the "K" in K-22) could be seen with the naked eye; then the men on the bridge were recognized. Finally the K-22 stopped in the heavy swell some 16 yards away from the disabled sub.

Through a megaphone, Admiral Kolyshkin explained the situation. The captain of the K-22 communicated the orders of the Fleet Military Council; namely that K-22 would try to take the P-421 in tow and, if that failed, to take its crew on board and sink the submarine.

The tow lines were made fast at 1200 hours. The gun crews stood by and K-22 started moving. Five minutes after P-421 was taken in tow, a treacherous swell did its work: the lines snapped. The K-22 came alongside and tried to tow another way. But the swell prevented it. Next, the crew tried fixing the hawsers stern to bow, but they not only snapped but also tore out the *Katyusha*'s bitts.

It was decided to try the anchor chain. But before it could be tried a German reconnaissance aircraft appeared and fired several flares in the direction of the two submarines. It was 1320 hours and visibility was excellent. Now a ship appeared in a fjord some distance away. The situation was becoming desperate for there was the risk of losing both submarines. On the authority given him, the K-22's captain ordered Vidayev to abandon ship and take along all top-secret documents.

The two subs were touching each other as the crew of P-421 began jumping onto the other's deck. The P-421 was abandoned in the nick of time, for soon another enemy plane appeared and everyone knew an attack could be expected at any minute.

Before leaving the P-421, Kolyshkin and Vidayev inspected all compartments to make sure nobody was left in them. Then they climbed to the bridge and stopped at the wet, storm-frayed ensign. The silent farewell was a bitter pill to swallow. Meanwhile, Captain Kotelnikov's voice rang out:

"Hurry or we'll lose both ships!"

Vidayev had pressed himself to the ensign and there were tears in his eyes.

"Let's go," Kolyshkin shouted.

The officers of K-22 and P-421 shook hands and immediately the K-22 swung around and took up a position close to the disabled "Pike" submarine. A torpedo raced out of one of her stern tubes and ploughed swiftly through the water. The men bared their heads as an explosion erupted and a column of water wrapped in black smoke rose in the air. Ten seconds later all trace of P-421 had gone.

"Unidentified aircraft to starboard, aft," the lookout cried.

"Clear the deck! Emergency dive!" Kotelnikov ordered.

The K-22 entered home base at Polyarnoye at midday on 10 April. After firing two salutes she hoisted P-421's signal flags and then fired another salute in honour of her last victory. The Naval Brigade Commander came on board as soon as the gangplank was in position, shook hands all around, and said:

"Congratulations on your victory and on saving a ship's company."

War is merciless and it finally claimed Vidayev's life. It happened one year later when he was captain of another submarine, the P-422. Under his command the sub had sunk seven enemy transports in the Arctic waters. Late in June 1943, Vidayev told his friends with his customary optimism and shy smile: "I'll make just one more run and then go on leave. The Fleet Commander-in-Chief has promised to let me go. I must see my new-born son." On 1 July, the P-422 put to sea. When Vidayev's submarine was long overdue, his fellow officers hopefully recalled the previous year when his submarine was lost but everybody was saved. But now, as his colleagues put it, "the situation was a thousand times worse". There was nothing but silence; neither submarine nor crew ever returned. Nobody discovered what happened to them.

*   *   *

From newspapers of 24 August 2000: "Many of the 500 relatives of the 118 sailors lost when the Russian submarine *Kursk* sank in the Barents Sea on August 12th have gathered at the naval village of Vidayevo, north of Murmansk . . ." No mention was made by the media that this naval community was named in honour of Captain Fyodor Vidayev whose submarine disappeared in the Barents Sea almost sixty years before the *Kursk* tragedy.

CHAPTER 19

Waltzing with the Queen

As they shared the same dangers in the Barents Sea, the Russian and British sailors developed an understanding – even friendship – never achieved elsewhere by the two allies.

One summer the Northern Fleet received a complement of British seamen. The men and their submarines *Tigris* and *Trident* were given traditional Russian hospitality. Animated discussions took place despite the language barrier. Comparisons between their submarines were inevitable. British subs were newer, but Russian subs were tidier. Also, it was agreed that discipline was tighter on Russian subs, there being less informality, with the men frequently saluting each other. When the the *Tigris* and *Trident* scored hits they returned to port flying Nazi flags upside down and sounding their sirens to show how many ships they had sunk. The Russians would throng to the pier to congratulate the British who, in turn, reciprocated the courtesy.

Shore dinners featuring roast suckling pig were a welcome relief in the sailors' routine. But such wartime luxuries were reserved for victorious crews. As one might suspect, this custom became very popular and shore base personnel were at pains to keep a large enough pigsty. A full suckling pig was served even to the Russian crews of midget submarines – when they scored a hit against the enemy. But even if the sailors were few in number, nothing was left on the table after such gala dinners.

The British used the northern naval base at Polyarnoye, until 1943. In April 1944 Russia's Northern Fleet was suffering from an acute shortage of destroyers. In three years of war the Germans had sunk two destroyers of the Northern Fleet, leaving the Russians only five that were still seaworthy. With the surrender of Italy in 1944, a solution to the shortage seemed imminent as Russia's share of the Italian Navy, which was divided among the Allies, came to one-third. But since Moscow was unable to dispatch a single vessel to the Mediterranean to collect the Italian ships, they might – as someone said – have been a million miles away from Murmansk or Archangel.

Then, Prime Minister Churchill offered to lend Stalin eight British destroyers, one battleship and four submarines until the end of the war to offset the Italian vessels Moscow was unable to put its hands on. But in Russian eyes this was hardly an even swap. Churchill, a former First Lord of the Admiralty, knew his naval craft well; he'd ensured that the "deal" with Russia was weighted in Britain's favour. But Churchill was candid enough to admit that the British destroyers on loan, although battleworthy, were far from modern ones. On the advice of his naval minister, Admiral N. G. Kuznetsov, however, Stalin accepted the offer.

At the end of April 1944 3,000 Russian sailors joined a convoy at Murmansk bound for Britain to spend three months helping to outfit the destroyers.

Near Medvezhy (Bear) Island in the Barents Sea, a German Heinkel-111 reconnaissance plane suddenly came in sight, having taken off from its northern Norwegian base. A Hurricane fighter quickly scrambled from an aircraft carrier to intercept it and AA–guns on the escort ships opened fire. The Heinkel was soon hit and, leaving a trail of smoke, disappeared in the direction of the coast. But it had done its job by drawing enemy fire. Within fifteen minutes Hitler's "submarine admiral" Karl Doenitz doubtless had news of the Heinkel's destruction and, therefore, the route of Convoy RA-9 was now revealed to the enemy. A day later, on May Day, the convoy seemed to be out of danger. Konstantin Lyubimov, one of thirty men from the Russian destroyer *Rasumni* who were passengers on the American cargo ship, *Liberty*, has described how the crew of the *Liberty* gave the Russian guests a "holiday" chicken dinner with chocolates for dessert.

Out of ignorance, says Lyubimov, the Russians who saw chewing gum for the first time, swallowed that too. Then disaster struck one of the transports.

"We came out on deck and as we were lighting our cigarettes there was a thunderous roar and one of the transport ships split in two," says Lyubimov. "A huge pillar of water shot up above the masts. It had been torpedoed." Within only a couple of minutes the ship's bow plummeted to the bottom with all of its Canadian crew on board. The stern section, with men from the Soviet destroyer *Dostoini*, remained afloat.

From his viewpoint 500 yards away, Lyubimov clearly saw men jumping overboard, but knew his and other transport ships could not go to their aid. These vessels were under strict orders to get as far away from any torpedoed ship as quickly as they could, ignoring the cries of those who were floundering in the ice-cold water. From experience, a transport ship which defied this iron rule inevitably became the next victim.

It was the job of the warships to try and rescue the people in the water and therefore a frigate and a destroyer approached the scene. But forming an arc around the stern of the disabled Canadian transport, they first began dropping depth charges. Unfortunately the Russian sailors in the water were buffeted by the shock waves and fifty of them – a quarter of a destroyer's crew – were killed outright. Those who caught hold of the nets cast from the escort ships were bleeding from the ears: their eardrums had burst.

The convoy proceeded to head westwards but the British warships behind the transports took a long time scuttling the ill-fated ship to prevent her from falling into enemy hands. The Canadian vessel stubbornly refused to go under despite repeated attempts to sink her with torpedoes and gunfire.

Several days later the convoy reached Glasgow. Then, by overland journey, the Russians went on to Newcastle where the ships were to be handed over. Approaching the Albert Dock, Lyubimov saw a forest of masts – forty-six destroyers, eight of them intended for the Russians. But their hearts sank: the old ships had been built by the

Americans in 1916–7 and, as it turned out, had something of a chequered history. To counter unrestricted German submarine warfare during the First World war, the US had rushed into mass production a type of low-cost destroyer. But there was no time to prove their battleworthiness before the war ended; so they were moth-balled. Twenty-five years later the US Government under lend-lease made an exchange: the American destroyers for British naval bases in the Caribbean.

Crossing the ocean two of the "old tubs" sank naturally, as it were, while the fate of two more was revealed by British sailors. It seems they were packed to the gunwales with explosives, after which their steering wheels were made fast and they were directed towards the Dutch sea walls to demolish Nazi shore batteries. Anyway, these outdated destroyers were turned over to the Russians and Lyubimov says that he served aboard the *Deyatelni* whose previous American incarnation was the *Lincoln*, and whose British was the *Churchill*. She had two masts and just one gun. It was, admits Lyubimov stoically, Hobson's Choice: take it or leave it.

Says Lyubimov: "We decided to select those vessels least riddled with rust and cockroaches. After a great deal of hard work, helped by the former crew and British dockyard workers, we began to accustom ourselves to the equipment on board. Since we Russians knew barely any English and vice versa, we had to invent our own working language as we went along."

Stereotypes, he says, quickly fell by the wayside. For example, the British officers whom the Russians previously viewed as "mercenaries of imperialism" turned out to be "nice chaps who treated us wonderfully". And why not? he mused. After all, they both were sharing common convoys and fighting a common enemy. And, as Lyubimov phrased it, "We all stood an equal chance of finding an unmarked grave somewhere between Jan Mayen and Bear Islands."

It was true. Here is one tragic story I learned about from survivors. On 27 May 1942 the British ship *Empire Lawrence*, loaded with ammunition (but also planes and tanks) destined for Russia, exploded in the Barents Sea when it was hit by JU–88 dive-bombers 280 miles east of Bear Island. Many of its crewmembers were killed in the explosion. Eddie Grenfell and Neil Hulse were flung into the icy sea by the blast but luckily were rescued. After the war Hulse served for a time as Navigation Officer on the liner *Queen Mary*. Grenfell became a Royal Navy Commander before he retired. In 2001 he was President of the 1,700-member Russian Convoy Club.

Until it left for its new home base, the *Deyatelni* lay at anchor near a huge dock where British battleships were under construction. Every morning the sailors went on deck and, in full sight of the whole shipyard, lined up for PT – with Lyubimov as instructor. "Soon our exercises attracted the young women yard workers. The sight of Russian sailors stripped to the waist clearly made them feel cheerful. And they soon began to tease us by showing us their own none too modest version of PT. On my 'swing your legs' command, the girls pulled their skirts up to their thighs and began to dance the cancan. Of course our boys' eyes were glued to the girls, which only encouraged them even more. The appeal of shapely legs on our women-hungry men naturally did nothing to concentrate their minds on our PT programme."

During shore leave one of the Russian sailors "yielded to temptation" and went out with a local girl. The relationship soon grew "immensely intimate" and, back aboard ship, he announced to his curious shipmates: "They don't wear any stockings at all! They've drawn on their bare legs with what looks like coffee grounds."

"Myself," says Lyubimov – he was a ruggedly handsome sailor back in 1944 – "I never managed a close relationship with an English woman. But towards the end of my stay in Britain I did happen to dance with one who was far from ordinary. By that time we had satisfied ourselves that the destroyers were battleworthy and were only waiting for the official handover ceremony on 17 July. This was a formal occasion and both the British and Russian officers wore full-dress uniform. Bored with hanging around, our crews entertained themselves with boxing matches against the British. One of our lieutenants was outpointed by a red-haired Englishman; but in my fight, things looked like they were definitely going my way. Engaged in these fights we paid no attention to the approach of a long motorcade of Rolls Royces. But the referee cut my match short, announcing a draw. However, our audience had already forgotten all about us and assembled on the pier." Lyubimov dressed hurriedly and made himself as presentable as he could before joining the crowd.

Lyubimov remembers that a lady in a grey outfit and hat emerged from one of the automobiles. Immediately she was surrounded by her retinue, among whom the Russians recognized only the Mayor of Newcastle. The elegant lady waved her hand and to the strains of "Rule Britannia" the Union Jack was slowly lowered. Then the Soviet anthem was played and the naval flag was run up the flag pole. At this point the crews were invited to a farewell lunch. Lingering on the pier, Lyubimov suddenly found himself in the middle of the naval officers who were being introduced to the lady in grey. As the band struck up a waltz she was introduced to a Russian admiral named Fokin, but she declined his invitation to dance. "Maybe," jokes Lyubimov, "his name had an unpleasant sound to the English ear."

"Then," continues Lyubimov, "she noticed me – after all I had just handed out a thrashing to one of her sailors. For whatever reason, she turned away from the admiral, approached me and asked me to dance. She smiled and said she would like a farewell waltz with an ordinary Russian sailor. Overwhelmed, I gingerly took her hand and we whirled around the improvised dance floor on the pier. She was an excellent dancer, and as we circled the floor the sailors laughed and catcalled: 'Do you know who you're dancing with? You'll never get the chance again! Hug her a bit closer!'

"Then, as my partner was whisked off to the waiting Rolls, a British officer came up to me. Offering congratulations, he told me I'd been dancing with 'Her Majesty, Queen Elizabeth'."

Forty-five years later, when some British veterans of the Arctic convoys visited Russia to celebrate the anniversary of the anti-Hitler coalition, one of them agreed to send a letter written by Lyubimov, offering congratulations to the lady in grey – now the Queen Mother – on her 90th birthday. Eight days later, he received a letter on her behalf from her private secretary, expressing her pleasure at his remembrance of the impromptu quayside waltz.

The war was never far away and tragedy soon befell some of the destroyers. Historians say that the convoy JW-59 on which Lyubimov returned to Murmansk in the autumn of 1944 was one of the "classic" Allied operations of its kind during the Second World War. The ships had no alternative but to run the formidable gauntlet of air and U-boat attacks on their outbound voyage from Britain.

However, on this particular convoy the crews managed to keep the convoy intact with the loss of only two escort ships. The convoy ploughed through four seas: the North, Norwegian, Greenland and Barents, and en route the *Deyatelni* sank a Nazi submarine. The convoy, when it landed, was made up of thirty-three merchant vessels, eight destroyers, a battleship and eleven submarine hunters received from the United States. Soon hundreds of women in Murmansk were wearing white coats they made from the British blankets the Russians had received as a royal parting gift.

Thus reinforced, the Soviet Northern Fleet now ruled the waves and all officers and men sensed that victory was near. In October 1944 the forces of the Karelian Front under Marshal Kiril Meretskov went over to the offensive. They first made diversional landings from several dozen ships on enemy-held shores in northern Norway; then a sizeable ground force went into the attack. Despite a snowstorm and strong Nazi resistance, the offensive was a success due to its suddenness and speed. After two days of fierce fighting the Russian troops achieved their objective in the Pechenga area. The defending Germans were unable to stand up to hand-to-hand fighting and fled.

The war in the Arctic sector of the front had virtually ceased, except sadly for the *Deyatelni*.

On 16 January 1945 this destroyer accompanied the 78th Arctic convoy, practically the last one of the war. Between Archangel and Murmansk she was waylaid by a Nazi U-boat. It happened in the middle of the White Sea. An acoustic torpedo homed in on the noise of her propellers and completely wrecked her stern. The explosion blew away all her lifeboats and when the destroyer began to sink her captain, Konstantin Kravchenko, did not leave the bridge.

The crew followed suit, but not, asserts Lyubimov, out of heroism. In his phrase, going down with the ship was "infinitely preferable" to an agonizing death from hypothermia in the icy Arctic waters. According to the few survivors, the men who'd gone to the bottom on the *Deyatelni* had assembled in the boiler compartment and battened the hatches from the inside.

Among the victims, says a pensive Lyubimov, "was the lieutenant who had boxed in Newcastle and the sailor who'd strengthened Anglo-Russian ties in the bedroom".

CHAPTER 20

"The Wounded Won the War"

In the last few days of the war, in April 1945, near Berlin, Surgeon Doctor Boris Petrovsky examined the men of the Eighth Guards Army under General Vasily Chuikov. Many of them had been wounded five or six times but they had returned to the front and continued to fight. This decorated surgeon who began tending the wounded from the very first day of the war ("We snatched only two or three hours' rest a day.") says that throughout the conflict almost 75 per cent of the wounded and over 90 per cent of those who fell sick were returned to the army in the field. This is why, he says, one could truthfully utter the words: "We won the war with the wounded."

After the war Petrovsky calculated that "by the most conservative estimate" he had made over 800 extremely complicated operations on blood vessels at the front. "All the surgeons worked in the same way everywhere on the front." Stretcher-bearers also worked under difficult conditions, pulling the wounded to medical aid stations on improvised sledges, more often than not using an overcoat or stretcher, frequently being themselves wounded or killed.

Konstantin Kolesov, who combined soldiering and writing, has provided this pen-portrait of the wounded: "The shell fragments, large and small, and the bullets that had flattened out against our bones were plucked out in field hospitals from us, half dead, then we were sewn up or patched up with white threads (yes, they were white, I saw it myself) in field or other hospitals and many of us went back to the flames, to the battlefieds, covering that lethal road over and over again. Over and over again!" Kolesov, who was born in 1925, went to fight late in the war, relating his experiences for the first time nearly forty years later. After the war he made his home in Brest, a city famous for its fortress on the frontier with Poland.

The endless flow of Russian wounded often taxed the skill and stamina of the combat surgeons. Senior Surgeon V.V. Kovanov, who was attached to the Fifth Shock Army and who became one of the most skilled army surgeons of the war recalls often going without sleep for forty-eight hours at a time in order to attend to the wounded. He says he and the other medics supported themselves on strong tea. He remembers once "finding some 2,000 wounded on our hands" with only 5 doctors, 12 nurses, 8 orderlies and some lightly wounded soldiers to help out. Many of the wounded had more chest, abdominal and pelvic wounds than could reasonably be coped with, he says.

The "mistake" of the medics, said Kovanov, was failure to prepare for great influxes of wounded after savage fighting. "We had assumed our field hospital could receive and treat up to 200 wounded a day. If pressed we could cope with 300 or 400. But when 2,000 descended on us, we were swamped."

Towards the end of the war, Chief Surgeon V. V. Kovanov's medical department pitched camp at Blankenfeld, about 12 miles from Berlin. Close by was a German field hospital just taken by the Russians and Kovanov was detailed to make a tour of the German hospital and examine its wounded. "For all we know, some Nazis may have disguised themselves as patients," said Colonel Viktor Tarasenko, head of the Army Medical Department.

An expert in therapeutics, Roman Sharlai (who always kept a pistol under his white coat, "just in case"), decided to accompany Kovanov. Half an hour later they arrived at the German hospital to find a lonely sentry at the gate. There was not a soul around; the building appeared deserted. The sentry, however, said that a captain from Army Intelligence had just gone inside. As they walked up the porch steps they heard a pistol shot and dashed into the entranceway. The captain, white as a sheet, one of his arms hanging limp, leaped out of the front door.

As Kovanov applied a tourniquet made from a handkerchief, the captain muttered angrily, "The bastard. I should have finished him off there and then, of course. But I couldn't. His legs are torn off."

A few seconds later an elderly German in the uniform of a medical officer came running out. He was the head doctor who was shaking all over as he tried to explain in halting Russian that the wounded German soldiers were unaware that the hospital was in the zone overrun by the Russians; and that was why this tragic incident had occurred. When the legless SS officer saw a Russian captain he grabbed his Walter pistol from under his pillow and pulled the trigger. Fortunately for the captain, the bullet went clean through the soft tissues of his left shoulder without touching the bone. In the hospital's operating room Kovanov treated the wound and applied an antiseptic dressing.

The intelligence officer then spoke sternly to the German head doctor, telling him it was his duty to warn the personnel and patients of the "full consequences" that would follow any further provocation on their part. Later when Kovanov and some of the German staff went through the hospital, Kovanov forgot caution, but Sharlai kept a sharp lookout, his revolver at the ready. They went from ward to ward until satisfied that there was no one in the hospital who had no business being there.

A few weeks earlier Kovanov and his medical staff had reached Domnau, a small country town buried among green trees, the houses with peaked tiled roofs, looking warm and cozy. But behind the facade of coziness in the outskirts of the town was a concentration camp disguised as a hospital. Hundreds of POWs from France, Poland, Belgium, and Russia were languishing in captivity in the camp. Domnau left an indelible impression on Kovanov who later saw for himself what kind of experiments the Nazi "executioners in white coats" tried on the inmates of Auschwitz, Buchenwald and Dachau.

Kovanov faithfully recorded: "Hitler's doctors tried on the prisoners their latest psychotropic drugs designed to break down the patients psychologically, and also a variety of toxic agents and poisonous substances. Experiments were staged to find the effect of ice-cold water on the human body. People were put in ice-cold water and left there until they passed out. Most of them died when their body temperature was brought down to 25–26 degrees Centigrade. Those who survived this inhuman experiment were later used in testing the effectiveness of various methods of bringing them around. Nazi doctors also inoculated POWs with cultures of typhoid fever and exanthematous typhus. They were deliberately infected with malaria and used as guinea pigs in experiments designed to follow the successive stages of the disease and the circumstances ending in final death."

Kovanov, a handsome, compactly built man, went through almost the entire war without seeing his family. His wife, Klavdia Andreyevna, also a surgeon, was evacuated from Moscow with their three children to the small village of Buturlino, east of the capital, where she worked in the local hospital. When a military hospital was opened nearby, she was put in charge of its surgical unit. ("The flow of wounded soldiers there seemed endless," Kovanov's wife told him.)

Kovanov had already gone through many hectic days and had come close to losing his life from a German bomb. There was also the time when a wounded SS officer was brought in to one of his medical aid stations and Kovanov agreed to examine him but the SS officer tore off the bandages, produced a knife and lunged at the doctor. He escaped injury only because the German was too weak, lost consciousness at the last second and slumped to the floor.

The Russian Twenty-Eighth Army had engaged the enemy on the outskirts of Berlin and the medical aid stations were deployed close to the battle zone. A short distance behind them were a few field hospitals ready for action, with more waiting until the main body of the army made contact with the enemy. Hitler was throwing his last reserves into the fray and there were increasing numbers of young boys and elderly men – veterans of the First World War. There were few experienced or seasoned soldiers left among the German forces, such as had begun the war at Dunkirk and had later been transferred to the Eastern Front. Many had found their death on the limitless steppes of Russia. Now all resistance was being crushed and the roads along which Hitler's forces retreated were cluttered with masses of heavy equipment, crippled tanks, trucks and empty food vans. But it was impossible for all this to be moved to the rear areas since most of the escape routes into Germany had been cut off.

About a week earlier, in the Polish town of Slutsk, most members of Kovanov's staff were so tired they could barely stand. Kovanov decided to relieve one of the surgeons to give him a chance to get some sleep. Suddenly, a wounded soldier was carried into surgery with a shell splinter in his stomach. He was about eighteen years old, was in deep shock with no discernible pulse. The doctors who examined him believed he had a very slim chance to survive. But they did what they could. They made the soldier warm, gave him anti-shock injections and also a blood transfusion. He was then taken to the operating table.

Kovanov noted the man's face was pinched, that his eyes had bluish rings under them. He was semi-conscious. Kovanov decided to operate under a local anaesthetic, giving him general anaesthesia if the need arose. "When I opened the abdominal cavity I saw that the intestines were floating in their own contents. After I made a careful examination of the small and large intestines and was satisfied that they were not damaged extensively, I pulled out the damaged convolutions and had a good look inside the cavity to see if the liver or kidneys were damaged. Luckily they were not. To save my patient any additional pain, I injected an ample dose of Novocain solution into his abdominal membrane and also into the solar plexus, as my mentor Dr A. V. Vishnevsky, had recommended. I carefully dried the abdominal cavity and the pelvis and then stitched up the holes in the small intestine. I worked as quickly as I could. Simultaneously, 500 cc of fresh blood was given to the boy."

When the operation was over everybody heaved a sigh of relief. The soldier was transferred to the post-operative department where they could keep him under observation.

Kovanov barely had time to wash his hands and put on a fresh smock when another wounded man was placed on the table. His right shin had been mangled by a mine explosion. Actually, what was left of the shin was a mass of torn tissues dripping with blood. The shin bones were completely crushed. It was clear to Kovanov that it would be impossible to save the foot and that amputation was the only answer. But the soldier pleaded with the surgeon not to cut his foot off. It was with a heavy heart that Kovanov persuaded him that this was not physically possible.

After putting the man under local anaesthetic Kovanov began by cutting out a skin flap with which to cover the surface of the stump. He then made a deep incision through the muscles right to the bone. Then he sawed through the bones. That done, he covered the surface of the stump with the flap. Next he put well-spaced stitches on the skin, while around the edges of the flap, he inserted two small cotton tampons to absorb any secretions that might follow.

All this happened in the morning and afternoon. Later that evening German bombers appeared over the town dropping bombs on the houses, schools and the field hospital. Kovanov says: "I heard the sound of crushed glass and the lights went out. One of the bombs scored a direct hit on the barracks where a well-known Byelorussian surgeon was operating at that moment."

A few minutes later the wounded surgeon was brought in with part of his legs torn off; he was bleeding profusely. Before putting him on the operating table Kovanov put clamps on the bleeding vessels, joined them and gave him a blood transfusion. The blood would not flow, however, because of the drastic drop in the man's blood pressure. A nurse gave him a shot of morphine and caffeine. Now the time had come to start the surgical treatment of the wounds. But just then a bomb went off quite close to the operating room. Kovanov was knocked off his feet, hit his head on something hard and passed out for a few minutes. When he came around and got back on his feet he resumed the operation as if nothing had happened.

"But," says Kovanov, "I could see that it would be impossible to save my colleague's life. I had barely enough time to put on a fresh dressing and apply a splint when a new air raid began. It was followed by another and another at short intervals. The howling of diving

Junker bombers and the thundering explosions continued all through the night. At dawn the surgeon died. The funeral was attended by the whole population of Slutsk. During the German occupation the dead man had been doctor to the partisans and had saved many lives. These tough villagers, including hardened partisans, were so grief-stricken that they wept openly."

When Kovanov and his staff arrived in newly liberated areas, they were instructed to give urgent medical assistance to the population, especially in the city of Sedlec. Its local hospital was overcrowded and the three local doctors and a few nuns could not cope with the mass of patients. Food was also scarce. Most of the patients were victims of Luftwaffe air raids and former inmates of the local Nazi concentration camp. These suffered from a severe form of dystrophy. Especially heart-breaking was the sight of the wretched children. Kovanov's staff distributed equipment, surgical instruments and medicines and organized a sanitary screening service, including giving baths to the sick and cutting their hair. The sick and the wounded were separated. In three days the town hospital was transformed almost beyond recognition.

Kovanov remembered the Mother Superior telling him pointedly that although he was a "godless person", he and his staff were nevertheless acting in accordance with Christ's teaching.

"Coming from her that must have been the highest praise," he says.

By mid-April 1945 the Russian armies had taken up positions for the final attack on Berlin. Meanwhile pockets of resistance remained where panicky Wehrmacht troops desperately tried to break out of encirclement in the rear of the advancing Russian army. No one paid much attention to the scattered and demoralized groups of Nazi soldiers in the rear as their fate was sealed. Nonetheless they sometimes caused trouble, particularly when they came upon field hospitals, depots, stores, shops and post offices. Pockets of resistance in Elbing, Danzig and Graudents could not influence future events but they could cause problems.

One day, Kovanov remembers, they halted in a small country town. In the middle of the night they were roused by a battle alarm.

Still bleary from sleep, it took some time to realize what was afoot. It seemed that a large body of enemy troops complete with tanks and artillery which had burst out of encirclement was advancing on the medical facility.

Largely thanks to a staff member, Alexandra Dmitriyevna, the medical services broke camp with the least delay and started towards the army's first echelon. No sooner had the trucks left town than a bombardment began. "We had barely time to escape," says Kovanov. "Unfortunately some staff members were less lucky and paid with their lives for their tardiness."

Staff members like Alexandra Dmitriyevna were responsible for saving many lives during the war. The wife of General A. N. Tsybin, Chief of Logistic Sevices, she had gained war experience during her years with the armies in the field. On several occasions when she had found herself under shell fire and bombing, she had kept her head and acted quickly, issuing orders to remove wounded men to safety.

A college friend, the head of a field hospital in the eastern part of Germany, was happy to greet Kovanov although a tragic accident had just occurred at his hospital. The retreating enemy had apparently assumed that the town's hospital building would be used by the Russians as a field hospital and had therefore planted mines. Arriving there, the head doctor asked bomb disposal experts to take a good look at the place. They discovered several delayed-action mines, collected them and stacked them in the courtyard.

"While they were busy sorting out equipment, putting beds into the wards and making the usual preparations, the leader of the bomb disposal team, a lieutenant, kept warning the girls not to come anywhere near the mines. He reproached the head doctor for rushing things because, he said, 'If one of those things goes off, God forbid, the hospital would be blown to smithereens.' Finally a horse-drawn cart, driven by two sappers, arrived to take the mines away. The doctor said goodbye to the lieutenant and went into the building. As he left he heard him giving instructions to his men and cracking a joke. Seconds later a terrific explosion rocked the building to its foundations. The doctor was blown off his feet and fell to the ground, flying glass and pieces of plaster showering over him. When he recovered and climbed to his feet to look around he saw no sign of the lieutenant, his men, or the cart with the horse. Apparently one of the delayed action mines went off spontaneously.

"It was," says Kovanov, "an absurd and unfair death. How many of them there were during the war years!"

Colonel Grigory Yelisavetsky commanded the regiment that liberated the Auschwitz concentration camp. He describes what was done to save the lives of a few survivors:

> Our sixteenth Army pushed forward with utmost speed to take possession of the Auschwitz area. By this time we knew a great deal about the Nazi atrocities and the tragic position of the inmates of the concentration camps. But what we saw and what we heard from the prisoners who by some miracle had remained alive defies description.
>
> The unit under my command freed the Birkenau [Auschwitz] camp where the gas chambers and cremation furnaces were located. We found there several barracks occupied by Jews slated for extermination. All told, there were some 500 barracks on the territory of the camp. They were the visual embodiment of the monstrous Nazi plan of oppression and annihilation of peoples.
>
> We saw no sign of life. Everywhere in the snow lay the bodies of women, children, old people, all shot at pointblank range. In the semi-gloom of one of the barracks we saw emaciated, half-dead people lying on wooden shelves built in three tiers as in a warehouse. They were Jews from different countries.
>
> We knew immediate action had to be taken to save the physically and morally crippled people. It is impossible to describe how our doctors, nurses, officers and soldiers worked without sleep or food to attend to the unfortunates, how they fought for every life. Unfortunately, many were beyond help. At the cost of incredible effort our medical personnel managed to tear 2,819 persons from the jaws of death.

Lieutenant Colonel Natan Polyansky, a Russian doctor specializing in infectious diseases, took part "in an action I shall never forget". It happened in Gniewin, a village south of the Polish port of Gdansk. It was March 1945.

"On the grounds of a landed estate there stood a long wooden shed," relates Polyansky. "On the floor was a thick layer of straw and under it two rows of bodies reduced to skin and bones, packed tightly together, with the heads to the wall and the feet to the passage in the centre. All stark naked.

"Who were they? We repeated the question in English, German and French. But there was no answer. Swarms of insects covered the bodies which meant that they were still alive. (For parasites crawl away from the dead.) We quickly established that it was typhus. We got busy at once. We worked for three days and nights. We began by pulling the sick out of the straw, took them to the bathhouse, shaved their heads and showered them, and put them to bed. All told there were 210 women, alive but so weak that throughout the lengthy procedure they did not open their eyes, did not react to injections or answer questions."

After a few days Polyansky learned that they were all Jewish women from Hungary, Rumania, Czechoslovakia and Poland. Five or six weeks later these patients had recovered sufficiently to be sent to transshipment centres, and from there to their home countries.

CHAPTER 21

The High Cost of Victory

The Russian march from "Brest to Berlin" had been arduous. There was fierce fighting for 1,418 days and nights along a front stretching from 1,800 to 3,700 miles. When victory came after four years, the toll had been high: one life every five seconds of the war, 13 lives every minute, 791 lives every hour, 19,000 daily. In human terms every family lost one or more members, or close relatives, or friends.

The final major engagement on the Eastern Front – the storming of Berlin – began in the last days of April 1945. The Germans had fortified the city in advance, building three defence lines around it. Some of the 400 formidable reinforced concrete gun emplacements, pillboxes and bunkers reached a depth of 60 feet. Such a stronghold could house a whole regiment. All told, Berlin was defended by over 300,000 troops, including SS, Volkssturm, members of "Hitlerju-gend", in addition to 32,000 police. The Nazis did everything to prevent defeat.

The Berlin Operation alone cost the Red Army 300,000 killed and wounded.

There was a realistic maxim about Russian longevity on the Eastern Front. It said that a lieutenant and a platoon leader survived, on average, one attack and a half; a tankman one battle and a half; a pilot one and a half combat missions.

Of course nobody could tell when their luck would run out. Some soldiers fought the entire war in a reconnaissance unit, stepped on a booby-trap but lost only the heel of their boot, while others were blasted in a dive-bombing attack en route to the front. But fairly accurate data has been compiled on battle losses; and though there may be discrepancies, a few conclusions may been drawn.

One out of three Russian officers did not come home from the war. That is, about one million officers died, or some 35 per cent of all the officers in the armed forces. Every two weeks a platoon commander had to be replaced due to death or wounds. The mortality of general officers was high. Among the well-known generals to fall in action were Dovator, Vatutin and Chernyakhovsky. About 150 Russian generals died at the front. Hundreds more were wounded or suffered concussion.

Losses among the Russian ranks were heavier. Although they made up approximately 65 per cent of total Army strength, they accounted for almost 75 per cent of all casualties. The picture is especially grim for tankmen and pilots. At the start of 1942 the Army had about 8,000 tanks left intact. That year some 30,000 new tanks reached the front and of these 15,000 were destroyed in combat.

In the entire war about 43,000 Russian planes were shot down and 36,000 pilots did not return from their missions. Except for a few thousand, the majority of pilots were lost with their aircraft. In 1942 more than 5,000 airmen died, or one in every four. And the 1943 losses were higher – almost every other pilot was lost, or approximately 40 per cent of the total.

Various post-Soviet studies of Russian military losses have been compiled, including a notable study supervised by Colonel-General Grigori Krivosheyev. The grim statistics show that more than 11 million servicemen lost their lives during the war, including some 7 million killed in action or died of their wounds or were reported missing; and about 4 million who died in POW camps. Those wounded, shell-shocked, frost-bitten or suffering from burns or illness numbered above 15 million.

It has been said that the Germans were "overwhelmed by Russian cadavers". The Germans themselves lost approximately 8 million officers and men on the Eastern Front out of total losses of 13,448,000. From these figures it appears that the Russians lost 30 per cent more men than the Germans, and this greater loss occurred mainly in 1941.

According to Professor John Erickson, of Edinburgh University, who is one of the world's leading experts on Russian military affairs, Hitler's invasion accounted for not 25–27 million soldiers and civilians dead but over 40 million. Erickson (see his book, *Barbarossa, the Axis and the Allies*), calculates that the drastic fall in Russia's birth rate at war's end, resulting in population loss, was a direct consequence of the invasion and should, therefore, be added to the overall toll of the war. Belarus suffered exceptionally in this respect.

What is now the Republic of Belarus was under German occupation between September 1941 and July 1944. The war cost Belarus about half of its national wealth and resources. Material losses are estimated (in 1941 prices) at 75 billion rubles.

Of 270 cities and towns in Belarus, over 200 were destroyed, many of them burnt to the ground; over 9,000 villages were razed. In addition to the destruction of thousands of factories, farms, schools, libraries, theatres and hospitals, nearly all electric power plants were destroyed and over 400,000 farm houses demolished.

In human casualties, Belarus lost 2.2 million people, or one in every four of the population. In the town of Vitebsk, the death toll was higher: one in three. Virtually every family lost at least one member. The occupiers also drove 380,000 Belarussians into Germany as forced labour.

Although Belarus was totally occupied, many of its people fought back as members of partisan detachments. Belarus became known as "The Partisan Republic" inasmuch as 374,000 citizens took part in armed struggle against the invader. An estimated 400,000 people, although inactive, rendered assistance to the partisans when necessary. The damage to the enemy meted out by partisans was extensive. On Belarussian territory these detachments derailed more than 11,000 special trains, destroyed 29 railway stations, almost 1,000 Nazi garrisons, 5,500 bridges 1,355 tanks and armoured vehicles and 900 arsenals. They executed hundreds of thousands of the enemy, including collaborators. But in turn, the Nazis killed 44,791 partisans in Belarus or about one out of every eight activists.

Due to the heavy toll of human life in Belarus, the level of prewar population in the republic was reached only in the 1970s.

Even now some historians debate the question of whether the Russians paid too heavy a price for their final victory. Yes, says historian and biographer General Dmitri Volkogonov who, before his death in 1996, probably had greater access to more state archives than anyone else. (To write his biography of Lenin, he used 3,724 documents that he said had never before been published.) According to the general, the big Russian victories of Moscow, Stalingrad, Kursk and Berlin were far too costly. Russia, Volkogonov says flatly, "need not have paid so dearly". The nation need not have lost three men to every German casualty. The blame, he says, rests with Stalin because, Volkogonov told me, "had no professional military skills at all". Stalin had failed to alert his troops on the frontier or place them in ready-prepared battle position when the invasion began. "It is clear," he says, that if Stalin had "agreed to this simple measure the war need not have cost us so much". Volkogonov maintains that had border units been alerted in time, the German troops "would not have been able to advance farther than 100–200 miles" into Soviet territory.

There were also the disasters – Volkogonov calls them "tragedies" – at Vyazma, Kiev and Kharkov, to name three prominent setbacks. But, a careful historian, he admits that there exist some "blank spots" in determining the full reasons for these defeats.

In summing up, Volkogonov says that the painful blows of Hitler's invasion were "the colossal price paid for illusions, insidiousness and political intrigue."

Some generals do not agree.* For instance, General of the Army

* A number of officers at the Institute of Military History who had fought on the Eastern Front were critical of Volkogonov's writings on the war because he had never set foot on a battlefield. He was, they said, an "armchair-general". Volkogonov was eventually dismissed from the Institute. General Shavrov was Chief of Staff of a tank corps on a number of fronts between 1943–5.

Ivan Shavrov, who worked in the Defence Ministry's Institute of Military History, said in 1991: "If we had concentrated many more troops in the border areas – as Hitler wanted us to do – they could all have been destroyed then and there. We were short of anti-tank weapons and aircraft . . . and we could have had even more casualties at the border."

Another question is sometimes asked: Were Russian generals profligate in their use of troops particularly in the latter stages of the war?

Marshal Ivan Konev, a prominent commander in the Berlin Operation, gives this answer:

"I happened to hear arguments that the fighting in Berlin could be conducted with less fury, fierceness and haste, and therefore with fewer casualties. There is outer logic in this reasoning but it ignores the main thing – the actual situation, the actual strain of the fighting and the actual state of the men's morale. These men burnt with a passionate and an impatient desire to end the war as soon as possible. Those who want to judge how justified or unjustified the casualties were must remember this."

However, the fact that there was an element of competition between the Allies as to who would be the first to enter Berlin undoubtedly added to the casualty toll, expecially the Russian.

Marshal Zhukov has described how Russian soldiers fell in Berlin on the very eve of victory:

"They died in the laps of the nurses, lay on makeshift stretchers, in courtyards, on staircases, bleeding profusely, losing their breath, whispering their last words. They died silently and suddenly. They died to bring the end of the war and the victory nearer by a few moments. It was not only [military] orders that threw them into that fantastic assault."

Russia had emerged victorious despite unprecedented human and material loss. Although dozens of countries were belligerents, almost three out of every five persons killed in World War Two were Russian. Today it is still difficult to pinpoint Russian civilian losses. However, experts agree that as many as 16 million civilians perished in the war – more than 7 million in prisons and concentration camps, and almost 9 million from hunger, bombing raids, insufferable living conditions, and slave labour. The cost of Russian war damage was said to be $500 billion.

The road to Berlin had indeed been long and sanguinary.

Select Bibliography

Abend, Halett, *Ramparts of the Pacific*, New York, 1942

Alliluyeva, Svetlana, *Twenty Letters to a Friend*, London, 1967

Ambruster, H. W., *Treason's Peace. German Dyes and American Dupes*, New York, 1947

Axell, Albert, *Stalin's War as Seen through the Eyes of his Commanders*, London, 1997

Bartov, Omer, *Hitler's Army: Soldiers, Nazis and War in the Third Reich*, Oxford, 1991

Beevor, Antony, *Stalingrad*, London, 1998

Berezhkov, Valentin, *History in the Making*, Moscow, 1982

Bradley, Omar, *A Soldier's Story*, London, 1965

Bradley, Omar, *A Soldier's Story*, New York, 1951

Bury, Rt. Rev. Herbert, *Russian Life Today*, London, 1915

Butcher, Harry, *My Three Years With Eisenhower*, New York, 1946

Cassidy, H.C., *Moscow Dateline*, Boston, 1943

Churchill, Winston, *The Second World War*, London, 1954

Conquest, Robert, *The Great Terror: Stalin's Purges of the Thirties*, London, 1968

Cooper, R.W., *The Nuremberg Trial*, New York, 1947

Craig, William, *Enemy at the Gates: The Battle for Stalingrad*, New York, 1972

Dirksen, Herbert von, *Moscow, Tokyo, London. Twenty Years of German Foreign Policy*, London, 1951

Dodd, William E., *Diary*, New York, 1941

Dragunsky, D.A., *A Soldier's Life*, Moscow, 1977

Dunn, Walter S., *Hitler's Nemesis: The Red Army*, Westport, Conn., 1994

Ehrenburg, Ilya, *Men, Years – Life: The War 1941–1945*, London, 1964

Eisenhower, Dwight, *Crusade in Europe*, New York, 1948

Erickson, John and Dilks, David (eds.), *Barbarossa, the Axis and the Allies*, Edinburgh, 1994

Erickson, John, *The Road to Berlin: Stalin's War With Germany*, London, 1983

Erickson, John, *The Road to Stalingrad*, London, 1975

Feis, Herbert, *Churchill–Roosevelt–Stalin. The War They Waged and the Peace They Sought*, London, 1957

Fromm, Bella, *Blood and Banquets: A Berlin Social Diary*, New York, 1942

Fuller, J.F.C., *The Second World War 1939–1945*, London, 1948

Gilbert, Martin, *Winston S. Churchill 1941–45*, London, 1986

Select Bibliography

Goebbels, Joseph *The Goebbels Diaries 1942–43*, London, 1948

Guderian, Heinz, *Panzer Leader*, London, 1952

Gunther, John, *Inside Russia Today*, New York, 1958

Hilger, Gustav, and Alfred Meyer, *The Incompatible Allies, German-Soviet Relations 1918–41*, New York, 1953

Hindus, Maurice, *Russia Fights On*, London, 1942

Hodgson, Katharine, *Written With the Bayonet*, Liverpool, 1996

Hull, Cordell, *The Memoirs*, New York, 1948

Ickes, Harold, *The Secret Diary of Harold Ickes*, New York, 1954

Isakov, I.S., *The Red Fleet in the Second World War*, London

Keitel, Wilhelm, *The Memoirs of Field Marshal Keitel*, New York, 1966

Kerr, Walter, *The Secret of Stalingrad*, London, 1979

Kosmodemyanskaya, Lyubov, *The Story of Zoya and Shura*, Moscow, 1953

Kovanov, V.V., *In the Name of Life*, Moscow, 1976

Liddell Hart, B.H., *The German Generals Talk*, New York, 1948

Overy, Richard, *Russia's War*, London, 1998

Overy, Richard, *The Battle of Britain*, New York, 2001

Manstein, Erich von, *Lost Victories*, London, 1959

McCauley, Martin, *The Soviet Union 1917–91*, London, 1993

Pares, Bernard, *A History of Russia*, New York, 1965

Patton, George S., *War As I Knew It*, Boston, 1947

Penguin Hansard, The, No. 6, *The War Moves East*, Middlesex, 1942

Rokossovsky, K.K., *A Soldier's Duty*, Moscow, 1970

Roosevelt, Elliott, *As He Saw It*, New York, 1946

Rzheshevsky, Oleg, *Operation Overlord*, Moscow, 1984

Service, Robert, *The History of Twentieth Century Russia*, London, 1997

Service, Robert, *The Making of Russia, 1991–2001*, London, 2001

Shtmenko, S.M., *The Soviet General Staff at War*, Moscow, 1970

Sharipov, Akram, *General Chernyakhovsky*, Moscow, 1980

Shukman, Harold (ed.), *Stalin's Generals*, London, 1993

Shulman, Milton, *Defeat in the West*, London, 1947

Stettinius, E.R., *Lend-Lease, Weapon for Victory*, New York, 1944

Tippelskirch, Kurt, *History of the Second World War*, New York, 1958

Vasilevsky, A.M., *A Lifelong Cause*, Moscow, 1981

Volkogonov, Dimitri, *Stalin: Triumph and Tragedy*, New York, 1992

Weinert, Erich, *Stalingrad Diary*, London, 1944

Werth, Alexander, *Russia at War 1941–45*, New York, 1964

Yakovlev, Alexander, *The Aim of a Lifetime*, Moscow, 1972

Zhukov, Georgi, *Reminiscences and Reflections*, Moscow, 1985

Notes and Sources

In the preparation of this book, I have drawn heavily on interviews as well as the memoirs of some of the leading persons mentioned in these pages. All of the dialogue in this book is drawn from these interviews and memoirs, and also from official records or other documentary sources. SMR is the abbreviation for *Soviet Military Review*.

Prologue

Eisenhower's and Zhukov's remarks are mentioned in the *New York Times*, 18 July 1957. Ehrenburg is quoted in *Soldiers, Our Way to Victory*, Moscow, 1990. Some of the wartime poetry is translated in Katherine Hodgson's comprehensive *Written With the Bayonet*, Liverpool University Press, 1996. In 1985 Albert Lefebvre, a Frenchman and ex-Maquis, who had been a prisoner at Maulhausen, said he witnessed the icy water-killing of General Karbyshev. (His letter to the *Moscow News*, No. 17. 1985.) For new German war cemeteries on Russian soil, *The Times*, 16 September 2000. Eisenhower on Russian victories, see Zhukov's memoirs, and *Ogonek*, No. 50, 1989. The Field Manual of Russian Army is quoted in *Our Way to Victory*.

1. Barbarossa to Berlin

For Churchill's view of the Eastern Front see his *The Second World War*, London 1949. For a German insight see *The Halder Diaries*, Washington 1950. Pavel Zhilin's remarks are in his *They Sealed Their Own Doom*, Moscow, 1970. For historian Rzheshevsky's comments, see his *Operation Overlord*, Moscow 1984.

2. The Hero Fortress

Heinz Guderian's thoughts just before the assault on the fortress are recorded in Zhilin's *They Sealed Their Own Doom*. T. N. Ankina's *Immortal Garrison, Moscow 1972*, has a full account of the battle. A shorter account of the siege is in "Fortress on the Bug," SMR, June 1976.

Notes and Sources

3. Shopping in Berlin

Alexander Yakovlev, *Notes of an Aircraft Designer*, Moscow, 1958. For General Petrov's impressions of his 1940 visit to Berlin, "Petrov's Special Mission," in *Moscow News*, No. 33, 1986. An interview with Yakovlev, "The Name on the Wings," appeared in *Moscow News*, No. 19, 1986. (The designer, then 80 years old, spoke about aviation in wartime and also the postwar development of new aircraft.)

4. The Night Witch

Author's interviews in 1999. For reminiscences of Russian women who flew combat missions, see "Women's Guards Regiment," SMR, March 1972, and *Moscow News,* No. 26, 1981.

5. Stalin's Son

Author's interview with Yakov's son, Evgeni. See also details about her brother, Yakov, by Svetlana Alliluyeva, in *Twenty Letters to a Friend*, London, 1967. Marshal Zhukov's memoirs contain Stalin's comments on the capture of his son.

6. Zoya's Execution

Pyotr Lidov's "Tanya," in *Moscow-Stalingrad, 1941–42*, Moscow, 1974. An account by Zoya's mother, Lyubov, appears in *Russians Tell Their Story*, London, 1944.

7. The Blockade of Leningrad

Boris Koslov, "A Salute for a Priest," in *Moskovsky Tserkovny Vestnik*, Moscow, May 1990. Hindus' *Russia Fights On*, 1942, has information about the patriotism of the Orthodox Church during the war.

8. The Snipers

For information about Zaitsev, see article, "Soldiers," in *Our Way to Victory*, Moscow, 1990; also "The Duel", SMR, December, 1982. There is some question about whether "Major Konings" actually existed. But there is no doubt that at some point or other Zaitsev pitted his skill against an ace German sniper. Each side adopted counter-measures when menaced by an experienced enemy sniper; and one of them was to bring on a master in the sniper's art. Obviously, when the German side made up its mind to get rid of Zaitsev, it summoned a top practitioner in this art. Russian snipers were so successful on the Leningrad Front that a "conference of snipers" was held by that command in February 1942. It is reported that at the end of that year Russian snipers on this front had killed almost 40,000 enemy officers and men.

Details about Mila Pavlichenko are found in, "The Queen of Fire," in *News From Ukraine*, June, 1980; also, Hubert Griffith, *This is Russia*, London, 1943. On Okhlopkov see, "The Marksman," SMR, June, 1984. "Girl With a Rifle," SMR, April, 1946, describes the life of sniper Nina Lobkovskaya. For details on others snipers, "Hunters from Daghestan," in *Russians Tell Their Story*, London, 1944. Antony Beevor writes of the Zaitsev saga in his book, *Stalingrad*.

254

9. Rammers over Moscow

Colourful details of ramming by Russian pilots appear in Konstantin Simonov, "Letters From the Arctic," *Russians Tell Their Story*; Oleg Argunov, *Air Defense Troops*, Moscow, 1983; and the newspaper, *Izvestia*, 26 October 1986.

10. The Cossacks

For description of a Cossack village, Edgar Snow, *Glory and Bondage*, London, 1945. Maurice Hindus visited Cossack communities before and during the war. His book, *The Cossacks*, gives a short, highly readable account of the Cossacks.

11. The Siberians

Author's interview with Beloborodov. For the general's description of the Battle of Moscow, *They Did Not Pass*, Moscow, 1970. The three most famous Russian marshals of the war, Zhukov, Vasilevsky and Rokossovsky, write glowingly of Beloborodov in their memoirs. For views on the resistance of Japan and the atomic bomb, Admiral William Leahy, *I Was There*; Thomas Finletter, *Saturday Review of Literature*, 5 June 1946; Hanson W. Baldwin, *Great Mistakes of the War*, London, 1949. Also, *Parliamentary Debates*, Fifth Section, Volume 413, House of Commons, London, 1945.

12. A Hundred Jewish Generals

Author's interviews. Criticism of Stalin on minorities is found in Roy Medvedev, *Let History Judge*, New York, 1971.

13. Cabbage Soup in Hell

This as well as dozens of amazing stories like it are told in *Russians Tell Their Story*, London, 1944. Not surprisingly, the Battle of Stalingrad gave rise to many such tales.

14. Endurance

Hindus' *Russia Fights On*, 1942. Also, *Snow's Glory and Bondage*, 1945.

15. The Pilot who Crawled

Author's interview. Boris Polevoi, who wrote the documentary novel, *The Story of a Real Man*, modelled after Alexei Maresyev, said more than a quarter of a century later that he himself could hardly believe the authenticity of Maresyev's story until he first met him in the summer of 1943. It was at a frontline airstrip at a time when the leviathan Battle of the Kursk Salient had reached its climax. The long hard day was almost over. He remembers dozens of Russian pilots returning from combat. One plane, piloted by Meresyev, came in from a combat mission very late at night. Says Polevoi: "I can still see the scene as though it was yesterday: the transparent canopy of the cockpit snapped open and a large blackwood walking stick, with gold monograms all over, made a small parabola and landed on the grass. Then a broad-shouldered, sun-tanned, black-haired man hoisted himself on his strong muscular hands, tumbled over onto the wing and slumped to the ground." Polevoi adds that the full story Maresyev told him, "showed his keen mind, power of observation and big generous heart." (From an article in SMR, May 1966.)

16. The Thirteenth Commandment

Akram Shapirov, *A True Tale of Two Wars*, Moscow, 1981. Gubkin is also mentioned in the book, *General Chernyakhovsky*, published in Moscow, 1980, by the same author. There are also references to Gubkin in Gladkov, *Operation Bagration*, 1984.

17. Tracking the *Tirpitz*

Ivan Isakov, *The Red Fleet in the Second World War*. Also, article, "How they Stopped the *Tirpitz*," *Soviet Weekly*, 20 October 1984.

18. Cemetery under the Barents Sea

Ivan Kolyshkin, *Submarines in Arctic Waters*, Moscow, 1966. Gladkov's *They Led Their Armies to Victory* has more details about Admiral Golovko.

19. Waltzing with the Queen

Article by Konstantin Lyubimov, "Memoirs of the Dervish," in *Soviet Weekly*, 5 September 1991. There are details on this convoy in many memoirs, including Ogden's *My Sea Lady*.

20. "The Wounded Won the War"

V. V. Kovanov, *In the Name of Life*, Moscow, 1976. In his memoirs, Zhukov, mentioning the arrival of the victors in Berlin, says that many of the men had wounds from previous fighting which had not yet healed. But, he says, "The wounded men did not leave the ranks." On the liberation of the Auschwitz concentration camp, see *New Times* (published in Moscow, in Russian and English), No. 17, 1985. Dr. Polyansky's remarks appear in the same issue.

Zhukov has recorded his surprise when, paying a visit to a hospital for wounded German soldiers in Berlin at the end of the war, he found that most of them were "almost children" – between fifteen and seventeen years old.

21. The High Cost of Victory

The author's interviews with Generals Volkogonov and Shavrov. For data in English on Russian losses in the war, see John Erickson's *Barbarossa, the Axis and the Allies*, Edinburgh, 1994, and Martin McCauley's *Stalin and Stalinism*, (Second Edition), London 1995. For Konev's remarks, see Moscow News, Number 15, 1985. Zhukov's comments are contained in his memoir, *Reminiscences and Reflections*.

Index

Index

Index